Should There Be Lesbian and Gay Intellectuals?

In Britain also, some of this is recognizable, but manliness is not quite so important. The man of letters tradition (in fact it should be called the person of letters tradition – the usual term is typically evasive about the input of women) has seemed much easier to justify, mainly because the leisure class, with which it has been intermeshed, has been regarded with less suspicion in Europe than in the United States. Leavisism opposed it in order to establish English as a supposedly serious, academic, masculine discipline. The letters tradition is still very important, within the current cultural ensemble in England – hear it on *Kaleidoscope* on Radio 4, twice a day (confused by demands that it work on market principles).

In Britain and the USA, then, gay studies is not an incidental complication or affront to Englit; it activates a long-standing anxiety. I have kept lesbians rather to one side so far because I've been talking about conventional notions of literature and sexuality, and I think lesbians have figured less in those. It seems to me that differences in the trajectories of lesbians and gay men correspond to the larger constructions of masculinity and femininity. I would expect lesbianism to figure as an anxiety of comparable force, in our cultures, around the roles of women in business, sport, the military, and such like – anything to do with women getting out of the house. But there is lots of exciting work to be done on these topics.

Not everyone, by any means, is happy to see the academy moving in on lesbian and gay literary culture. There are two, divergent reasons for this. Many gay men have found the man of letters tradition rewarding. Richard Dyer has written excellently about this. 'Queerness brought with it artistic sensitivity – it gave you the capacity to appreciate and respond to culture. It was a compensation for having been born or made queer ... It also made you doubly "different" – queer and cultured. And how splendid to be different! Even if you were awful'.[8] Here, style, sensibility and taste are still principal criteria, and academic aspirations towards intellectual rigour seem unsympathetic and inappropriate. This may be less of a problem for lesbians. The conflict finds perhaps its ultimate expression in the essentialism vs constructionism debate. Very many academics are constructionists, whereas I've met scarcely anyone else who is. Of course, I think that's because the constructionist case hasn't been properly put. However, if that is so, it shows the extent of the discursive gap between academic and non-academic gays; we may have to recognize that this may be intrinsic to two entire and scarcely compatible ways of thinking about culture.

The second reason for being uneasy about gaining academic ground is that UK lesbian and gay studies is unthinkable without a *broad left*; and hence is accompanied by a serious suspicion of cultural hierarchy, of the education system as an ideological state apparatus or bank of cultural capital, and hence of Englit. This may be highlighted by contrast with the USA, where there is little suspicion of Englit among its practitioners. Hazel Carby has complained about this in respect of black feminist criticism, which 'for the main part accepts the prevailing paradigms predominant in the academy, as has women's studies and Afro-American studies, and seeks to organize itself as a discipline in the same way'.[9]

UK lesbian and gay studies, then, is situated uncomfortably in relation to the Englit tradition, to US lesbian and gay studies, and to the cultural traditions of others in the lesbian and gay communities. However, I don't regard all this as a reason for stopping. While there is plenty wrong with what we do, it is a mistake to suppose that there is a more authentic site of struggle somewhere else (workerism, that used to be). But we do need to be aware of some of the ways we are situated, and to try to keep in touch with other lesbian and gay cultural traditions (hence my occasional *Gay Times* column, reviewing academic books). It is not a matter of setting the right line, but of negotiating among ourselves, different ways.

Patriarchy and Femininity

Work in our field has tended, far too often, to isolate gay men and lesbians from the ideological framework in which they occur. Studies begin by recognizing that queerness is implicated, ineluctably, with the range of sexual possibilities, especially as the defining other of heterosexuality, but then slide into spotting the gays; the adjacent or enfolding heterosexual system is taken for granted, apparently not in need of explication. However, we should be the first to know that heterosexuality does not go without saying.

Hence my answer to the suddenly topical question: Was Shakespeare gay? He couldn't have been, because they didn't have the idea; *but* by the same token, he couldn't have been straight either. So he belongs as much to us, if you want, as to anyone else. The early-modern organisation of sex and gender boundaries was different from ours. The representations in their texts simply don't align with modern ideas of gayness and straightness. So we find, in practice, that Shakespeare's plays are pervaded with erotic interactions that strike chords for lesbians and gays today. It is not that he was a sexual radical; rather, the ordinary currency of his theatre and society is sexy for us. If we want, we can find ways of expressing ourselves through Shakespeare, as much as any other group. Since 'A' level, as it happens, I have found the farewell with Horatio at the end of *Hamlet* the most moving episode in the plays, though I've never seen this proposed in print (I wrote it for a *Guardian* article, but they cut it!).

It is perhaps obvious that perceptions of lesbians are dependent on perceptions of women. But for gay men also, I believe, there can be no positive prospects while the 'feminine' is despised. A fundamental question, certainly for lesbian and gay activists, is: Does homosexuality really constitute a profound challenge to Western values? Or are lesbians and gay men actually harmless – pretty much like other people except in the odd detail? If the latter, it will just need a bit more tolerance to accommodate us, then everyone can relax and get on with other important matters (such as the environment). But suppose the former is the case – that homosexuality does threaten traditional gender and family identities, and such identities are integral to our present kind

21

of society. Then the tabloids have reason to be hostile.

Homophobia is often discussed as if there is only one kind of gay person. However, male same-sex passion has been tolerated or respected, at diverse times and places, when it is not perceived as effeminate. I'm not sure whether the argument is reversible for lesbians; whether patriarchy may not so much mind women being affectionate and even physical, so long as they don't appear to trespass on the privileges of masculinity. Gay men have taken two routes in response: (a) appearing masculine, and (b) insisting on effeminacy as a challenge to heterosexist norms. Both have been importantly reassessed recently, especially in lesbian theory about butch/femme roles. However, these moves retain the masculine/feminine binary. Of course, men should be feminine and women masculine, and vice versa, if they want; socialised into patriarchal society, we are all trying to make the best of a bad job anyway. What I want to question is the expectation that sexualities must be comprised within and defined through some version of the masculine/feminine binary.

Feminine and masculine are cultural constructs, obviously with the primary function of sustaining the current pattern of heterosexual relations. Of course, very many heterosexuals are not respectively masculine and feminine, or not in certain respects, or not all of the time. As usual, ideological categories fail to contain the confusions that they must release in the attempt to achieve control. That is why we observe heterosexuality plunged into inconsistency and anxiety; it is aggressive because insecure. For homosexuals, the situation is indeed perverse. We are customarily apprehended as some kind of complicated variation on femininity and masculinity. So a model of heterosexuality which is tendentious, inadequate and oppressive in the first place is twisted into bizarre contortions in order to describe us. This is as true of Freud as of the tabloid newspapers. David Halperin and others have credited Havelock Ellis and Freud with a key stage in the development of the possibility of gay identity: separating sexual practices from gender. That sexual object-choice might be wholly independent of such "secondary" characteristics as masculinity or femininity never seems to have entered anyone's head' until Havelock Ellis' *Sexual Inversion* (1897) and Freud's *Three Essays*.[10] But Freud, as much as Ellis, persists in perceiving homosexuality as a variant on an underlying masculine/feminine binary.

Any idea of leaping out of the feminine/masculine binary is, of course, absurdly utopian – it would require a massive ideological shift. Indeed, most of us are socialized into this binary, in one aspect or another; 'If gender is socially constituted', Jonathan Dollimore observes, '*so too is desire. Desire is informed by the same oppressive constructions of gender that we would willingly dispense with*'.[11] I'm not sure about gender-fucking as a strategy in this context. Not only does it retain the binary; arguably it is what lesbians and gay men have been perceived as doing all along (masculine souls in feminine bodies and so on), and it hasn't got us very far. What is clear, I think – and this is the outcome of my argument about situating our sexualities within patriarchy – is that our project cannot be addressed in isolation, especially from that of the Women's Movement. So long as women are regarded as feminine and inferior, lesbians and gay men will be in trouble. Sexual liberation will not occur without women's liberation.

Should there be Lesbian and Gay Intellectuals?

I realise that this is a provocative question. First, who needs intellectuals anyway? – are not abstraction and rationality masculinist? Well, I don't think so; though the official tradition of intellectual thought has been male-dominated. Second, are we not all intellectuals, in the sense of being able to take thought about ourselves and the world? Briefly, yes. But, beyond this, some of us are privileged with time and resources to think and study that exceed those of most working people. I want to use the term 'intellectual' sociologically, to signify those who are paid to occupy roles as cultural producers. Only thus can I get a systematic hold on the responsibilities that might fall upon such a category. For intellectuals are important: they help to maintain or undermine belief in the legitimacy of the prevailing power arrangements. They help to set the boundaries of the thinkable. They confirm or rework the stories through which we tell each other who we are.

Gramsci is a good starting point because he acknowledges that all people are intellectuals and endorses a wisdom in common sense, while specifying as a social category the people who perform the professional function of intellectuals. He distinguishes organic and traditional intellectuals: the former are organic to their class, whereas the latter aspire to an independent stance; they 'put themselves forward as autonomous and independent of the dominant social group'.[12] Both types are of relevance to political struggle: 'One of the most important characteristics of any group that is developing towards dominance is its struggle to assimilate and to conquer "ideologically" the traditional intellectuals, but this assimilation and conquest is made quicker and more efficacious the more the group in question succeeds in simultaneously elaborating its own organic intellectuals'.[13]

Lately, as Foucault has observed, Gramsci's distinction has needed to be reformulated, since the vast majority of intellectuals are no longer leisured gentleman, as the traditional intellectuals mainly were, but are employed — usually to exercise particular skills, often by big business or the state. Before, they spoke as arbiters of truth and justice, as expounders of universal truths; now their effect is exercised through the particular terms and circumstances of their work.[14] This analysis is precisely applicable to Englit, where the Arnoldian-Leavisite claim to speak for Man has been widely refused, especially by feminists, and exposed as little more than a professional routine.

I began this paper intending to argue that people such as ourselves should dedicate ourselves as organic intellectuals of a lesbian and gay movement. 'Ideally', Gramsci says, 'the proletariat should be able to generate its own "organic" intellectuals within the class who remain intellectuals *of* their class'.[15] On reflection I'm not sure how this could work today. Cultural workers may maintain an allegiance to a sexual subculture, as to a class; but it is hard, now, to envisage them becoming effective without some kind of filtering through the kinds of organization that prevail in our kind of economy.

This said, I do want to argue for a priority. The 1980s showed us that there is no security in trying to join the mainstream. While AIDS was thought to affect only gay men, governments did almost nothing about it; but for gay subculture, thousands more would be dying now. Specifically in respect of cultural work, the Section 28 campaign about gay contributions to the arts made me realise this: the votes in the Commons and the Lords at the end were the same as at the beginning. We said: Look, we have made all this art for you. They replied: Yes, we know, that's what poofters are supposed to do, but don't think that means you can get out of your place. Gay men are accepted as purveyors of artistic culture only on condition that we be discreet, thereby acknowledging our own unspeakableness.

Mainstream cultural achievement does not make us respected and liked, it feeds into the pattern through which we may be despised. Contributions to the centre guarantee neither security nor respect. Much more than nine to one, representations in artistic culture assume that lesbians and gays do not exist; if they do, they are usually bad and almost always stereotyped. Even writers, painters and choreographers whom we have reason to think of as gay have very often adopted a heterosexual point of view in their work. It is because they would not have been published, shown or performed otherwise; and/or were persuaded to believe that their work should be 'universal' – that is, heterosexual. Decoding the work of closeted homosexual artists discovers not a ground for congratulation, but a record of oppression and humiliation. The centre takes what it wants, and under pressure will abuse and abandon the subcultures it has plundered. Blacks, it seems to me, also know this. What we celebrated in the Section 28 campaign was not our culture, but our contribution to their culture.

25

Activating Theory: Lesbian, Gay and Bisexual Politics

Lots of us are having a bad time at the moment – worse than many people of my generation expected. Our priority, therefore, needs to be defensive, one of subcultural consolidation. One of my arguments in *Faultlines* (1992) is that an Althusserian understanding of interpellation may be applied to subcultures (thus correcting a leaning towards totalisation in Althusser's formulation). The dominant ideology tends to constitute subjectivities that will find 'natural' its view of the world; well, this happens in subcultures also, but in ways that may validate dissident subjectivities. 'In acquiring one's conception of the world one belongs to a particular grouping which is that of all the social elements which share the same mode of thinking and acting', Gramsci observes.[16] It is through such sharing that one may learn to inhabit plausible oppositional preoccupations and forms – ways of relating to others – and hence develop a plausible oppositional selfhood. By promoting a sufficiently vigorous and comprehensive subculture, we can begin to produce the conditions for a lesbian and gay pride so comprehensive that the solidarity of the demo will last all year round.

This, I believe, is why anxiety about the critique of the individual in constructionism, anti-essentialism is misplaced. Political awareness does not arise out of an individual subjectivity – an essential, individual, self-consciousness of class, race, nation, gender or sexual orientation. Subcultural milieux are where that happens. We don't need essences to get identity; to the contrary, they trap us. Following Teresa de Lauretis, Tania Modleski observes that the 'essence' of woman has always been more of a project than a description of an existent reality. This, she says, suggests 'a way to hold onto the category of woman while recognizing ourselves to be in the *process* (an unending one) of *defining and constructing the category* (which includes very disparate types of people)'.[17] That is the priority I am proposing; a work of collective cultural production. It is up to us to decide who we are.

Within this priority, there may be a role for something like

26

organic intellectuals of the lesbian and gay movement. Their role is to contribute their educational privilege to addressing the issues that confront us. This will be in part a matter of getting Routledge to publish essays so that students and teachers can press for lesbian and gay studies courses. I'm in favour of that. At the same time, though, we need to put a lot of effort into staying in touch; or, rather, getting in touch, with other parts of lesbian and gay subcultures. We should seek ways to break out of professional subcultures and work intellectually (not just live personally) in lesbian and gay institutions. So let's establish queer studies as a base, but one to break out of.

If there is a case for lesbian and gay intellectuals, it is not that we can hide in universities, use long words and become big fish in little ponds, but that we may contribute to the self-understanding and political effectiveness of lesbians and gay men. This will not be a matter of pretending to know best, or of establishing a correct line, but of trying to use our hard-won skills to illuminate histories and problems. As Hazel Carby has shown in respect of the Harlem Renaissance and other black intellectual movements in the early part of the century, it is not easy to steer a line between the presumption of purporting to define and speak for a people, and the irresponsibility of declaring an artistic autonomy that finds its validation, almost inevitably, through dominant institutions.[18] We cannot expect to avoid such awkwardnesses. But there are problems enough for us to address, both in our relations with straight society and among ourselves – misogyny, racism, sadomasochism, self-oppression, class and inter-generational differences, HIV and AIDS.

This said, we need to be strategic. Diana Collecott asks herself: should she, in her professional writing, try to pass? I agree with her reply: 'So long as gays pass as men and lesbians pass as feminists, heterosexism will be normative in education'.[19] Come out – so long as you can afford it. The great divide here today is not to do with gender or sexualities; certainly not with whether we think of ourselves as queer or gay. As in the Literature Teaching Politics movement of the

27

mid 1980s, it is between those with and those without jobs. I raise this not out of sympathy, though I have plenty of that, nor out of guilt, though I may have some of that; but because this divide can be very destructive for us. It is not a good time to be a student: there aren't enough jobs or grants, and some powerful people don't want the likes of us to get them anyway. There have been encouraging academic appointments lately – you have to be about twice as good as the competition to get them. I might just remark, though, that we have hardly begun to tap the potential of the pink economy, and the market sector may present worthwhile opportunities for queer cultural production. One of the lessons of the decline of consensus, I have argued, in *Literature, Politics and Culture in Postwar Britain* (1989) that many people of my generation made a historic mistake when we believed that the state would protect us from capital; the state is the primary institution of capital. It isn't necessarily any cleaner working in a university, and the conditions are rapidly deteriorating. You might actually do better in a queer market. One way or another, there is work to be done, and we may commit outselves to it. I know this sounds pretentious, but it's better than getting sucked into professional Englit.

Notes

[1] C.L. Barber, *Shakespeare's Festive Comedies* (Princeton, NJ: Princeton University Press, 1959), pp244-45.

[2] *Ibid.*, p246.

[3] Charles Kingsley, 'Thoughts on Shelley and Byron', in *Literary and General Essays* (London: Macmillan, 1890), pp43-44, 51. I am grateful to David Alderson for drawing my attention to this essay.

[4] *Ibid.*, p47.

[5] F.R. Leavis, *Revaluation* (London: Chatto, 1936), pp222, 221, 212.

[6] Mark van Doren, 'Walt Whitman, Stranger', in *The Private Reader* (New York: Kraus Reprint, 1968), pp71-72.

[7] *Ibid.*, p73.

[8] Derek Cohen and Richard Dyer, 'The Politics of Gay Culture', in Gay Left Collective, eds, *Homosexuality: Power and Politics* (London: Allison and Busby, 1980), p177.

[9] Hazel V. Carby, *Reconstructing Womanhood: The Emergence of the*

Afro-American Woman Novelist (New York: Oxford University Press, 1987), pp15-16.
[10] David M. Halperin, *One Hundred Years of Homosexuality and Other Essays on Greek Love* (New York: Routledge, 1990), p16. Cf. Jeffrey Weeks, *Coming Out: Homosexual Politics in Britain from the Nineteenth Century to the Present* (London: Quartet, 1977), pp62-66.
[11] Jonathan Dollimore, *Sexual Dissidence: Augustine to Wilde, Freud to Foucault* (Oxford: Clarendon Press, 1991), p325.
[12] Antonio Gramsci, *Selections from the Prison Notebooks*, trans. Quintin Hoare and Geoffrey Nowell Smith (London: Lawrence and Wishart, 1971), p7. See Alan Sinfield, *Literature, Politics and Culture in Post-War Britain* (Oxford: Basil Blackwell, 1989), chapter 12.
[13] Gramsci, *Selections from the Prison Notebooks*, p10.
[14] Michel Foucault, *Power/Knowledge*, trans. Colin Gordon (Brighton: Harvester, 1980), pp126-33.
[15] Gramsci, *Selections from the Prison Notebooks*, p6.
[16] *Ibid.*, p324.
[17] Tania Modleski, *Feminism without Women: Culture and Criticism in a 'Postfeminist' Age* (New York: Routledge, 1991), p20.
[18] Carby, *Reconstructing Womanhood*, pp163-66.
[19] Diana Collecott, 'What Is Not Said: A Study in Textual Inversion', in Joseph Bristow, ed., *Sexual Sameness: Textual Differences in Lesbian and Gay Writing* (London: Routledge, 1992), p92.

Queer Theory and the War of the Sexes

MARY McINTOSH

Queer theory, unlike lesbian or gay male theory, is not gender specific. In fact, like the term 'homosexual', queer foregrounds same-sex desire without designating which sex is desiring. As a feminist, I am aware of the problems that congregate at this site.
– Sue-Ellen Case[1]

Feminism is a form of politics deeply rooted in humanism. Its project is liberatory, its subjects women. To be a feminist necessarily involves a belief that women and men are intrinsically free and equal and that women's oppression lies in the denial of the development of our full capacities.[2] This is why the question of defining women, in terms other than those of biological reductionism, has been so important. And this is why differences between women – along lines of race, class, sexuality and so on – have been so divisive. For in recent years, liberatory projects have lent themselves to identity politics, privileging the lived experience of oppression, so that feminism is only for women, anti-racism only for black people, and so on. In a context of humanism, the way to avoid the divisiveness of identity politics is through theorizing the various oppressions and their interrelationships at a structural level. But this has proved a particularly difficult task where the groups concerned have a biological as well as a social definition. The difficulties, and especially the need to break with commonsense biological reductionism, have led to forms of theory that appear abstract, tortuous and only available to an intellectual élite. With the eclipse of Marxism and rise of Thatcherite individualism, too, structural theories and coherent political strategies have been less popular than identity politics and tactical alliances.

Queer politics, on the other hand, is rooted (albeit rather shallowly) in a queer theory that is deconstructive of categories and subjectivities. Queer theory has no time for disputes about whether bisexuals are really gay or transsexuals really women; it has no time for hierarchies of oppression or for all the divisiveness of identity politics that beset the movement in the 1980s. Kobena Mercer has spoken of the need to get away from binary thinking: 'binary thinking ends up with the static concept of identity rather than the more volatile concept of identification'.[3] Certainly the binary thinking involved in the terms of sex and gender has plagued feminist theory; feminism rejects gender divisions, yet much of its theory is concerned with drawing attention to gender and its inequalities and oppressions. The queer project is different. As a leaflet circulated in London in 1991 put it:

> Queer means to fuck with.gender. There are straight queers, bi queers, tranny queers, lez queers, fag queers, SM queers, fisting queers in every single street in this apathetic country of ours.[4]

Queer is a form of resistance, a refusal of labels, pathologies and moralities. It is defined more by what it is against than what it is for. Its slogan is not 'get out of my face' (let alone 'gay is good'), but rather, 'in your face'.

Perhaps the most sustained and interesting work of queer theory is Jonathan Dollimore's exploration of sexual dissidence, which he sees as a major form of resistance to 'those conceptions of self, desire and transgression which figure in the language, ideologies, and cultures of domination'.[5] He contrasts 'humanist transgression', which rejects existing categories in a quest for authenticity, with 'transgressive reinscription' 'which finds expression through the inversion and perversion of just those pre-existing categories and structures which its humanistic counterpart seeks to transcend, to be liberated from'.[6] From this

31

anti-humanist perspective, Dollimore explores the examples of cross-dressing in early modern England and the putative 'gay sensibility' of writers like Jean Genet and Joe Orton. Queer politics today is perhaps a rather self-conscious attempt to take up this strategy of resistance, to embrace the otherness of 'queer' as straights have defined it. As such it has been criticized by those in the gay movement who would promote positive images. But, as Dollimore says:

> Humanistic transgression in the name of authenticity has never been able to comprehend this other kind of transgression, that performed in the name of inversion, perversion, and rein- scription.[7]

The question is: can queer thinking, rooted in resistance rather than identity, transcend the binary divisions between women and men in the gay movement? Can we – and should we? – move beyond socially given identities towards politically formulated identifications?

The War of the Sexes in Gay Politics

The question of whether lesbians and gay men can work together has surfaced and resurfaced repeatedly since at least 1972, when most of the women left the Gay Liberation Front in London, precipitating its demise. The issues then were complex ones. The women were swept up in a feminism that was even more radical and challenging than GLF; to them, the men in GLF were committed only to a 1960s type of 'lifestyle politics' that did not try to transform the structures of oppression but was happy to use the exploitative 'straight' gay ghetto as its base. They were uncomfortable about the implications of the 'gender fuck' drag actions of the radical queens, which seemed either to celebrate the stereotyped, brassièred, sexy-for-men femininity that feminists were challenging, or else to parody the dowdiness and sexlessness of ordinary women or nuns. They found the gay men were every bit as sexist and complacent about male privilege as straight men – and that they dominated GLF meetings.

In the decades since GLF, the issues have changed, but the fundamental problem of working together has remained the same. Women have been critical of men's involvement in cottaging, casual sex, pornography and SM; men have found women's emphasis on 'vanilla sex' and relationships to be moralistic and repressive. Men have resented women for being relatively sheltered from the scourge of AIDS; some women have been heavily engaged in AIDS activism and campaigns around the laws that penalize men, but have found men to be uninterested in issues around breast and cervical cancer screening, artificial insemination or lesbian custody. Women have seen men as misogynist; men have seen women as castrating. Men have dominated the gay press and it is men's 'pink pound' that has shaped the culture of the gay community; on the other hand, women have all the cultural credit of feminism behind them, institutionalized in equal opportunities policies, women's studies courses, journals, conferences and a long and respected history. At the end of the day, lesbians and gay men ask ourselves, what on earth do we have in common? Unlike heterosexuals, we do not even fancy each other and can hardly begin to understand each other's sexual desires.

Divergences in Lesbian and Gay Male Theory

Such have been the frictions within the movement, the overt problems in working together politically. The question of what we have in common may be posed at the analytical level too, and the answer is far from straightforward. Annabel Faraday has pointed out that the common term 'homosexual' can be deceptive. She put it like this:

> What is *not* recognized is that while both lesbians and gay men are not 'heterosexual', heterosexuality itself is a power relationship of men over women; what gay men and lesbians are rejecting are necessarily polar experiences.[8]

In the decade or so prior to the advent of queer theory, the dominant approach among lesbian and gay theorists was that of social constructionism, the idea that sexualities are not given in nature and biology but are mediated by history and culture.[9] Social constructionist theories of sexual orientation and identity have their origin in two very different observations. The first is that historical and anthropological evidence shows that the socially recognized categories of sexual orientation vary from one culture and one period to another. While there may well be homosexual *behaviour* in all societies, it is commonly not recognized as a penchant of particular individuals, so that *the* lesbian or *the* homosexual does not exist as a deviant type or as an alternative identity. This means that no one is a heterosexual or a homosexual independently of culture. The second observation is that, even within a culture such as ours where these categories are well entrenched, patterns of sexual behaviour are not neatly polarized into the categories 'heterosexual' and 'homosexual'. This means that relatively few people actually are behaviourally heterosexual or homosexual in the way that the culture supposes. Many fall in between, or move to and fro during their lifetime, yet the bisexual is scarcely recognized as a social type.

Though social constructionism can be applied to both women's and men's sexuality, lesbian and gay male theorists have tended to use it rather differently. Among lesbian theorists, the starting point has usually been the asymmetry of heterosexuality mentioned by Faraday. Adrienne Rich, in 'Compulsory Heterosexuality and Lesbian Existence',[10] locates this asymmetry in the fact that the search for love and tenderness in both sexes originally leads towards women and that heterosexuality is a result not of women's preference but of social institutions of 'compulsory heterosexuality' imposed by men. So, for her, heterosexuality is socially constructed and it might be possible to read her as saying that lesbian relationships are the natural ones for women. She certainly sees what she calls 'lesbian existence' as being present in all periods of history and in all societies. But for Rich, what is present is not emotional-erotic bonding between pairs of women but a 'lesbian continuum' of woman-identified experience – ranging from genital sexual activity with another woman to 'dying at ninety touched and handled by women'.[11] Rich is torn between seeing these forms of lesbian existence as ways of resisting compulsory heterosexuality and seeing compulsory heterosexuality as a set of 'societal forces that wrench women's emotional and erotic energies away from themselves and other women and from women-identified values'.[12] So she is torn between a view of both the heterosexual and lesbian existence as socially constructed within patriarchal societies and a view of lesbian existence as primordial and pre-given and heterosexuality only as socially imposed. In this sense, hers is not an elaborated theoretical analysis but a polemical statement whose main impact is to identify the lesbian and the feminist – to reduce lesbianism to 'nascent' feminism, or to reduce feminism to lesbianism, according to your perspective. Such a definition of the lesbian is clearly one that precludes any equation with the male homosexual. Rich recognizes that lesbians have often shared a social life and common cause with homosexual men, but she attributes this to their 'lack of a coherent female community'[13] and says that she perceives 'the lesbian experience as being, like motherhood, a profoundly *female* experience' in the sense that, for women, the erotic is not genitally focussed and pervades female comradeship, rather than being confined to physical sexuality. The problem is, however, that Rich has accomplished this radical separation of male and female homosexuality by definitional fiat: by counting many relationships that do not involve genital sexuality as lesbian, she is able to demonstrate that the lesbian experience is not narrowly sexual like male homosexuality.

The other problem with Adrienne Rich's influential essay is that her polemic applies to all times and all places, or at least to all of patriarchy. Indeed, part of her project is to criticize the 'neglect of lesbian existence in a wide range of writings, including feminist scholarship' – and including work on historical periods when there was no lesbian subculture as we know it today. Rich, like a number of other radical feminist writers,[14] draws on examples from many different societies with the intention of demonstrating similarities and continuities. If we want to explore the social construction of lesbianism as a form of sexuality and sexual identity – which in the usual uses of the term it is – we need to examine its historical variability and not to define it so broadly that it is found to be universal. On the other hand, it is not very helpful either to redefine lesbianism so that it only equates with a modern radical feminist conception that it is 'a blow against the patriarchy', as Celia Kitzinger has sought to do.[15] Kitzinger seems to deny any continuity with women who have defined their lesbianism as sick, or as an individually chosen lifestyle. The same sort of thinking has persuaded some who are involved in running archives of lesbian material to exclude, as 'negative images', items that are racist or male-identified.

'When we rewrite, indeed, recreate, our lost past, do we too readily drop those parts of our past that seem unattractive to us?', Martha Vicinus has pertinently inquired.[16] In an extremely interesting essay, she has posed the question: 'Whom should we include and why in the history of the modern lesbian?' She sees that history as rooted in two very different types of female desire, producing, on the one hand, women who passed as men and as 'female husbands', who if discovered were accused of homosexual *acts* and, on the other hand, women who entered long-term romantic friendships, which were thought of in terms of *relationships* rather than sex acts. In addition, she suggests, there have been the lovers of 'passing' or 'crossdressing' women, the equivalents, perhaps, of the modern 'femme', and – much neglected – the intermittent lover of women, who might nowadays adopt a bisexual identity.

Women who dressed as men are hardly the creditable foremothers that radical feminists would care to acknowledge. It is hard now to know what their motives may have been but they were undoubtedly varied and complex. Writing of the early modern period in the Netherlands, Rudolf Dekker and Lotte van de Pol have suggested:

Lower-class women had a means of dealing with sexual feelings for another woman via the tradition of cross-dressing. Once transformed into a man, one's sexual feelings for another woman

36

fell into place. The fact that some women who fell in love with other women transformed themselves into men and even officially married the objects of their affections should therefore not be seen as an unnecessarily risky sort of deception, but rather as the logical consequence of, on the one hand, the absence of a social role for lesbians and the existence of, on the other hand, a tradition of women in men's clothing. In many of the life histories … the confusion of gender identity caused by feelings of love for another woman is evident.[17]

Behind this 'lesbian' motivation, then, there was a tradition of cross-dressing, from a variety of motives: to follow a husband abroad, to sea, to the East Indies, to fight in a war, to have greater opportunities for earning a living or greater social freedom in general, to facilitate a criminal career.[18] It is impossible to disentangle sexuality from gender at this period. But whatever their motivation, these women did not challenge male prerogatives and the heterosexual paradigm; they sought individual solutions within the existing framework. It was for this reason that, as the modern lesbian role emerged in 1929, Radclyffe Hall, the model of the new mannish lesbian, was outraged by 'Colonel Victor Barker', a woman who lived as a man and married an apparently unwitting bride.[19]

There has been a good deal of feminist interest in the exploration of romantic friendships and love between women in the period before the emergence of a socially recognized, and stigmatized, lesbian identity, starting at the end of the nineteenth century. There is evidence of such intense friendships from the seventeenth century onwards,[20] and they appear to have flourished among women of the British and American bourgeoisie from the mid-eighteenth to the mid-nineteenth century.[21] From a modern perspective, it is hard to read some of the letters that they wrote to each other except as expressions of lesbian love in the way that we experience it today:

Dear darling Sarah! How I love you & how happy I have been! You are the joy of my life … I want you to tell me in your next

letter, to assure me, that I am your dearest ... I do not doubt you
and I am not jealous but I long to hear you say it once more ...
Goodbye my dearest dearest lover – ever your own Angelina.

Or:

I wanted so to put my arms round my girl of all the girls in the
world and tell her ... I love her as wives do love their husbands,
as *friends* who have taken each other for life – and believe in her
as I believe in my God ... If I didn't love you do you suppose I'd
care about anything or have ridiculous notions and panics and
behave like an old fool who ought to know better. I'm going to
hang on to your skirts ... You can't get away from [my] love.[22]

Yet these relationships were in no way secretive or frowned
upon and were not seen as incompatible with marriage and
motherhood. Indeed, Carroll Smith-Rosenberg argues that
they were part and parcel of a female world of ritual
surrounding marriage, childbirth, family visiting, the training
of daughters, mutual aid. She sees them as the product of '[a]
different type of emotional landscape [which] existed in the
nineteenth century',[23] one characterized by a high degree of
social segregation between the lives of men and the lives of
women. They were normal and socially learned relationships
in a society that allowed people – or women, at least – a good
deal of freedom in exploring a wide latitude of emotions and
sexual feelings and did not confine them to a heterosexual
normality or a pathologized homosexuality.

Clearly, then, a quite considerable change has taken place.
Faraday has explored the gradual growth of discussions about
lesbians in early twentieth century England, finding that
many of these revolved around girls' schools and that the
campaign for co-education often whipped up anxieties about
spinster teachers seducing young girls in the sexually
over-heated atmosphere of the single-sex school.[24] A concern
about possible bad influences on ordinary impressionable
women and girls seem to characterize many of these early
discussions. Girls' schools, and indeed women's education in
general, were a very appropriate target for such concerns in
the period after the First World War, when women's

fulfillment through marriage and motherhood was being celebrated. For, as Vicinus has shown, during a brief period around the turn of the century, teaching had provided 'a happy resolution of a single woman's desire for a satisfying public and personal life'.[25] The community of women and long-lasting and deep, sometimes passionate, friendships all became questionable once the asexuality of single women came under doubt. And the kind of personal life that homoerotic friendships between schoolgirl and teacher or between two teachers represented was the antithesis of the life of sacrifice and suppression of self for women in the nuclear family.[26] This women's world became stigmatized as, at best, barren and, at worst, a hotbed of perverse passions.

Lillian Faderman attributes a similar change in the United States to the rise of anti-feminism. She writes:

> Love between women – relationships which were *emotionally* in no way different from the romantic friendships of earlier eras – became evil or morbid.[27]

Such relationships became sexualized, whether they were or not, and women could no longer love other women in innocence; they either had to turn to men or else see themselves as lesbian, which meant 'twisted' and perverted.

Faderman sees all this as part of the tightening grip of patriarchy.[28] Along with that she sees lesbian-feminism as an attempt to recapture the space for love between women, with 'lesbian' defined in terms more similar to those of Rich, as putting women first in their lives, rather than in erotic terms. Politically, this implies a rejection of what lesbians have actually been during the twentieth century and a wish to return to romantic friendship, albeit with the realistic possibility of living and working together which our forebears lacked.[29] This involves a notion that romantic love for other women, not necessarily sexualized or with the sexual merging with the rest of the relationship, is in some way intrinsic to women and only suppressed by patriarchy. Smith-Rosenberg's comment that nineteenth-century romantic love was a product of *its* period seems particularly apposite here.

For the difference between Faderman and Smith-Rosenberg is the difference between essentialism and a strong form of social constructionism. Faderman believes in a natural form of love between women which becomes distorted by patriarchal ideas about genital sexuality and suppressed in the patriarchal interests of dividing women from each other and tying them individually to men. Smith-Rosenberg believes in the historical specificity not only of socially acceptable forms of expression of sexual and emotional feelings, but also of the development of those feelings themselves. For her it was a sexually segregated society that drew women towards each other in that way.

Whatever the divergences between them, lesbian theorists have always put gender and its asymmetries at centre stage. For gay male theorists, gender has lurked in the wings, and when it has appeared it has usually been in the guise of 'manliness' and 'effeminacy' – a component of the individual's psychic profile – rather than in the more elaborated form of family patterns and power relations.

Rather than developing, along the lines of Smith-Rosenberg's suggestive remarks, an analysis of the reasons why people might have wished to enter various kinds of relationship at different periods of history, gay male theorists have tended to concentrate upon the way in which social definitions of relationships and sexual activities are constructed at different periods. In particular, in recent years, they have followed Michel Foucault in his concern with the growth of sexual discourses, working it seems with the assumption that discourses construct identities, so that no separate consideration of experiences or motivation is necessary.

Foucault gives a perceptive summary of the historical construction of the male homosexual:

> As defined by the ancient civil or canonical codes, sodomy was a category of forbidden acts; their perpetrator was nothing more than the juridical subject to them. The nineteenth-century homosexual became a personage, a past, a case history, and a childhood, in addition to being a type of life, a life form, and a morphology, with an indiscreet anatomy and possibly a

40

mysterious physiology. Nothing that went into his total composition was unaffected by his sexuality ... It was consubstantial with him, less as a habitual sin than as a singular nature ... Homosexuality appeared as one of the forms of sexuality when it was transposed from the practice of sodomy onto a kind of interior androgyny, a hermaphrodism of the soul.[30]

Several interesting aspects of this have been developed. The most obvious is the way in which the shift from homosexual activity to homosexuality as a condition introduces the possibility of a homosexual identity. The change is a dramatic one over a relatively brief period of scarcely a century; and at the end of it there is a species, not perhaps as monolithic as 'man' or 'woman', but almost as much naturalized as were the 'racial' types.

In an early article published in 1968, I placed this change – evidenced by the emergence in London of a male transvestite-homosexual subculture – at the end of the seventeenth century.[31] Since that time, there has been a great deal of historical scholarship. On the one hand, something of a dispute has developed between those who agree with this dating, in particular Alan Bray, in *Homosexuality in Renaissance England*,[32] and those who place the shift much later, towards the end of the nineteenth century, like Jeffrey Weeks[33] and Foucault himself. In part, this is a disagreement about the interpretation of the eighteenth-century evidence, with Bray seeing the London 'molly houses' as part of a well-developed homosexual subculture with its own way of life and Weeks seeing it as an 'embryonic' subculture, 'emergent rather than ... developed'. In part, though, these writers are looking at different features of the shift, Bray seeing something akin to modern homosexuality once there is a homosexual subculture and Weeks emphasizing the developments of widely available public discourses around the homosexual. On the other hand, other historians have argued that there was no real shift at all. Foremost among these is Randolph Trumbach,[34] who has said there is evidence pointing to the existence of sodomitical subcultures from the twelfth century onwards. Trumbach has recently come to the view that, despite this, there was a 'profound shift' from an older pattern in which sodomy was part of a diversified debauchery of men who might indulge themselves (actively) with women as well as boys to a modern pattern in which masculinity became associated with exclusive heterosexuality, so that to be attracted to one's own sex was to be effeminate and passive.[35] I might add that, despite what Foucault correctly identifies as the 'interior androgyny' of the homosexual as represented in modern discourses, the separation of 'the homosexual' from 'the transvestite' was also a significant change, and this did not occur until the late nineteenth century.

It now seems to be agreed that a major shift has taken place, though there may be disputes and room for further development in understanding its form and timing. It is the development of a particular – stigmatized – form of institutionalized homosexuality, this specific shift is peculiar to Western societies. Other societies have had other forms, sometimes involving less stigma, such as the temporary relations between older men and adolescent boys acknowledged in ancient Greece, or such as men who are treated socially as women like the *berdache* among some native North American peoples. But nowhere before has it taken the form that we know today.

The second aspect of the quotation from Foucault that is interesting is the way in which his sexuality dominates every aspect of the homosexual's identity. This is part of Foucault's general account of the rise of sex as central in the organization of identity in Western society. 'Sex becomes a means of access both to the life of the body and the life of the species'. So if this is explicit in discourses around the homosexual, it is implicit in those around the heterosexual man. 'The homosexual', of course, is a much more homogeneous species than 'the heterosexual'; divisions of class, status and even age are accorded less significance. Nevertheless, proven and undoubted heterosexuality is in some sense at the basis of a man's identity as a man.

This leads to the final aspect, Foucault's 'interior androgyny' of the homosexual, the other side of which is the way in which full manliness is incompatible with homosexuality. The earliest definitions of the homosexual saw him as effeminate or as an 'intersex'. Trumbach sees this as 'the most salient characteristic of the homosexual role from about 1700 to the present day'.[36] As a homosexual subculture spread and expanded in the first decades of this century, the assumption of effeminacy remained. To the outside world, and often to himself, the homosexual was an invert. In camp culture, language and humour, he was a 'queen', often with a feminine pronoun and exaggeratedly feminine mannerisms. His sexuality was inverted in its meaning, in the sense that he adopted the feminine role: he wanted to be desired and courted as a woman is – by a man. Quentin Crisp captured this when he wrote in 1968: 'they set out to win the love of a "real" man. If they succeed, they fail. A man who "goes with" other men is not what they would call a real man'.[37] Thus was homosexuality uncomfortably accommodated to a rigid binary definition of gender in which heterosexual orientation always corresponded to gender, at the expense if necessary, of its correspondence to biological sex. A man who loved men became a woman in a man's body, since loving women was part and parcel of being a man. Psychiatric opinion sought to cope with this by distinguishing 'active' from 'passive' homosexuals, the passive and feminine being the 'true' homosexual, the active one merely seeking a substitute for a woman, often, as among seamen and prisoners, in a situation where women were unavailable.

On this basis, John Marshall has argued that the concept of homosexuality as the distinguishing characteristic of a particular type of person did not emerged in the late nineteenth century, as writers like Weeks and Foucault have suggested.[37] For what was called homosexual then was completely suffused with heterosexual assumptions. It was not until much later that the possibility of a 'straight-looking gay', a homosexual who was 'queer' only in his sexual orientation and might be a good citizen with a successful manly career began to be canvassed, especially by the homophile movement of the 1950s and 1960s. For Marshall, the term 'homosexual' should be distinguished from 'gender-invert' and the concept only recognized as existing when same-sex sexual orientation is not seen as having any implications for gender role in general. He believes that such changes as the relaxation of legal sanctions in England and Wales in 1967 and the rise of the gay liberation movement in the 1970s made it possible for homosexuals to be freed from the (worse) stigma of gender inversion, though he admits that the current cult or machismo among homosexuals is evidence of 'the extent to which definitions of male homosexuality continue to be pervaded by the tyranny of gender divisions'.[39]

Indeed, the hope that sexual orientation can be cut free from all other aspects of gender is perhaps a naïve one, given the centrality of sexuality in current gender definitions and given that sexual orientation is now firmly a feature of individual identity rather than of particular acts or episodes. The male gay subculture is suffused with elements of the dominant culture, and especially with gender difference and male domination.[40] For a long time it has reproduced stereotypes of femininity, only to ridicule them in self-mocking camp humour. More recently, in its 'macho man' phase, it has reproduced stereotypes of masculinity – manual workers, sportsmen, the armed services – with much less humour. But as a deviant culture it also resists the dominant culture that it confronts. The essential irony of camp undermines the 'straight' world view by highlighting it in such a way that its taken-for-granted character is questioned. If men use feminine pronouns and epithets among themselves, they are playing with them, releasing them from their 'natural' use, problematizing them. The practice and defence of casual sexual encounters, as well as more enduring pairings, challenges the dominant heterosexual ideal of sex as an expression of a love relationship (though it also mirrors the heterosexual assumption that men are 'naturally' promiscuous and only forced into monogamy by women). And more recently, in the wake of the Gay Liberation Movement, there have been more conscious attempts to subvert gender – for instance, by the 'gender fuck' of political cross-dressing – rather than just seeking to evade it or accommodate to it. But, as Gregg Blatchford comments:

> although the language, casual sexual patterns, the styles of clothing and camp itself can be seen as a real struggle to try to work out solutions to the oppressive situations in which homosexual men find themselves, the solutions cannot represent a very significant threat to the dominant culture.[41]

Foucault's 'hermaphrodism of the soul', it seems, has not been transcended and, indeed, cannot be as long as the world is divided by definitions of gender that are loaded with sexuality.

Foucault is not at all concerned with questions of explanation, and what he says is, therefore, at this level, purely descriptive. As Sonja Ruehl has put it:

> the history of sexuality in [Foucault's] sense, is the history of discourses about sexuality – a history which seems to be only traceable though internal links between discourses. So, critics ask, what is the relation of such discourses to 'real life' supposed to be?[42]

So other writers have tried to explore the reasons for the development of the conception of homosexuality as the organizing characteristic of a particular sort of person. For instance, in his early work, Weeks attributed it to an increased control over sexual expression associated with economic changes at the end of the nineteenth century:

> the gradual exclusion of women from the primary workforce ... the creation of a mass, propertyless working class, whose labour power was reproduced and serviced in the bosom of the family, had profound and still unexplored effects on the socially ascribed gender roles of men and women. What is apparent is that, as social roles became more clearly defined, and as sexuality was more closely harnessed ideologically to the reproduction of the population, so the social condemnation of male homosexuality increased.[43]

45

But this explains the imperatives of control without saying anything about why individuals might have wanted to embrace or resist a homosexual identity. John D'Emilio has argued that capitalism produced for the first time the conditions where sexuality could be released from the 'imperative' to procreate. The same conditions that allowed heterosexuality to develop as a means of establishing intimacy and a whole sphere of personal life also allowed 'some men and women to organize a personal life around their erotic/emotional attachment to their own sex'.[44] It is quite possible that both Weeks and D'Emilio are right, since 'the creation of a specialized, despised and punished role of homosexual keeps the bulk of society pure'[45] and more fully committed to heterosexuality. But this still does not explain why men might have wanted to take up the opportunity of a homosexual lifestyle.

Beyond the Divide?

This exploration of the separate development of lesbian and gay male history reveals that each of them could have learned a great deal from one other. One of the most striking things about them is the abject acceptance of gender stereotypes on both sides. In lesbian history the *status quo ante* is often assumed to be romantic friendships between women, not involving genital sexuality; in the case of men it is usually sodomy and other 'abominations', conceived as without a desiring subject. Yet it seems probable that women who engaged in sexual relations were not a complete figment of male pornographic imagination, as Faderman seems to suggest. And it is certain that men were once able to form closer, more intimate friendships and to sleep in the same bed without being subjected to the taint of homosexuality. It is hard to believe that at roughly the same period women-loving women became translated from the sphere of the whole personality to that of the specifically sexual while men were translated from the specifically sexual to the whole personality. There must have been some connection between

46

the two, and also some greater similarity between the two transformations than either side has acknowledged. Yet the history of male homosexuality has assumed a parallel completely modelled on its version of the male transition and the history of lesbianism has assumed no connection at all.

Another major divergence is over the kind of social constructionism espoused in the two traditions. A thoroughgoing rejection of essentialism marks much of the male homosexual history. In the case of the interactionists, this stems from a principled anti-positivism, in the case of the Foucauldians, from a principled anti-humanism. Among the radical-feminist historians of lesbianism, the rejection of essentialism has come from a very different source: not so much from a principled anti-essentialism as from a critique of the naturalizing labels that men have put upon women.[46] This means that 'queer theory' has an odd relationship to pre-existing lesbian and gay male theory. For queer theory, being *de*constructionist, has much in common with the more radical forms of social constructionism represented in the male gay tradition. Indeed, queer theory may be said to be a development of that tradition, which has simply laid claim to a more all-encompassing status.

If so, this is horribly reminiscent of what feminists have often found about 'male-stream thought'. But I have argued that lesbian theory ought in any case to have learnt something from gay male theory. It should have learnt something of the importance of the sexual and of sexual transgression in the making of the lesbian. This is not to say that women's sexuality or women's transgression has been the same as men's – it has in fact been specifically womanly and has had to contest gender boundaries from the other side – but that an important element in the construction of the lesbian has been sexual and has been transgressive.[47] On the other side, queer theory should not forget that the heterosexuality in terms of which we are defined as other is a highly gendered one, so that our otherness and the forms and meanings of our dissidence are also gendered.

Lesbian and gay theorists are among the first and the

foremost critics of those feminist theories that see a deep gender chasm at the psychic, cultural and structural levels and a complete congruence, or mutual determination, between those three levels. If gender is a neatly wrapped parcel in which sexual orientation is tied up with gender identity, then it leaves us out of the account altogether. So, for instance, film theory that sees subjectivity as constructed through cinematic representation may leave no space for indeterminacy between levels. And insofar as it relies on psychoanlalytic theory, there is a danger that 'it *presumes* heterosexuality to such a degree that it often seems to *demand* it', as Bad Object-Choices put it.[48] Juliet Mitchell sought to defend psychoanalysis as 'not a recommendation *for* a patriarchal society, but an analysis *of* one'.[49] The problem is, as Cora Kaplan has pointed out, that 'Freudian theory ... emphasises, perhaps too heavily, the unalterable distance between gender positions so that they remain ... stuck at distant poles.'[50] If this is true of psychoanlysis, it is equally true of much other feminist theory, though it can be argued that the concept of gender offers more ways out than the concept of sexual difference.[51]

But the fact that some feminist theory may have been too determinist and failed to take account of the actual heterogeneity of identities does not mean that we can ignore the whole issue of gender, as Simon Watney has proposed.[52] This position was notoriously taken to its logical extreme by Monique Wittig when she declared that 'Lesbians are not women,' on the grounds that ' "woman" has meaning only in heterosexual systems of thought and heterosexual economic systems.'[53] This challenging proposition is, of course, both true and not true in terms of our identity. It is usually false as a statement of how we are socially defined by others. Its value as a political position depends very much on the alignments that are available at any particular conjuncture. But Wittig espoused a 'materialist lesbianism', recognizing a need for an economic and political transformation of the relations between women and men, as well as a change in language. So when she said 'If we as lesbians and gay men continue to speak of ourselves and to conceive of ourselves as women and as men, we are instrumental in maintaining heterosexuality,'[54] she was speaking of a prefigurative 'transformation of the key concepts', rather than clinging to an infantile belief in the omnipotence of thought. Her words, intended to shock us out of complacent binary thinking, have been taken too literally – not least by herself. We should not be misled into pursuing a political strategy that might be called 'androgyny in one ghetto', unless we do it in ways that actively challenge the social reality of gender divisions both within and beyond the queer ghetto.

Queer theory and queer politics, I conclude, are important for feminists. They do not replace feminism, which remains as a humanist and liberatory project with its own more structural theories. But, on the one side, queer theory provides a critique of the heterosexual assumptions of some feminist theory and, on the other, feminists must agitate for an awareness of gender in queer thinking.

Notes

[1] Sue-Ellen Case, 'Tracking the Vampire', *Differences* 3:2 (1991), p2.

[2] Ernesto Laclau and Chantal Mouffe have argued that we can regard feminism as being simply a product of an historically specific discourse, democratic humanism, rather than having any extra-discursive foundation, and that this does not in any way detract from its importance: see *Hegemony and Socialist Strategy: Towards a Radical Democratic Politics* (London: Verson, 1985), p151. See also Kate Nash, 'The Feminist Production of Knowledge: Is Deconstruction a Practice for Women?', *Feminist Review* (forthcoming). But it would be difficult to maintain a sense of feminist outrage against oppression and inequality if you saw democratic humanism as merely one discourse among many, especially as the usual practice of discourse analysis has implicitly or explicitly equated deconstruction with discrediting.

[3] Kobena Mercer, in the discussion following his paper, 'Skin Head Sex Thing: Racial Differences and Homoerotic Imagery', in Bad Object Choices, eds, *How Do I Look? Queer Film and Video* (Seattle: Bay Press, 1991), p216.

[4] Quoted in Cherry Smyth, *Lesbians Talk Queer Notions* (London: Scarlet Press, 1991), p17.

[5] Jonathan Dollimore, *Sexual Dissidence: Augustine to Wilde, Freud to Foucault* (Oxford: Clarendon Press, 1991), p21.

[6] *Ibid.*, p285.

[7] *Ibid.*

[8] Annabel Faraday, 'Liberating Lesbian Research', in Ken Plummer, ed., *The Making of the Modern Homosexual* (London: Hutchinson, 1981), pp112-29.

[9] For a good introduction to social constructionism, see Carole S. Vance, 'Social Construction Theory: Problems in the History of Sexuality', in Dennis Altman et al, eds, *Which Homosexuality?* (London: GMP, 1989), pp13-34. See also Edward Stein, ed., *Forms of Desire: Sexual Orientation and the Social Constructionist Debate* (New York: Garland, 1990).

[10] Adrienne Rich, 'Compulsory Heterosexuality and Lesbian Existence', first published as a pamphlet by Onlywomen Press, London, in 1979, reprinted in Ann Snitow, Christine Stansell, and Sharon Thompson, eds, *Desire: The Politics of Sexuality* (London: Virago Press, 1984), pp212-41.

[11] *Ibid.*, pp227-28.

[12] *Ibid.*, p217.

[13] *Ibid.*, p228.

[14] See, for instance, Kathleen Barry, *Female Sexual Slavery* (Englewood Cliffs, NJ: Prentice-Hall, 1979); Susan Brownmiller, *Against our Will: Men, Women, and Rape* (Harmondsworth: Penguin Books, 1976); and Susan Griffin, *Pornography and Silence: Culture's Revenge against Nature* (London: Women's Press, 1981).

[15] Celia Kitzinger, *The Social Construction of Lesbianism* (London: Sage, 1987).

[16] Martha Vicinus, ' "They Wonder to Which Sex I Belong": Roots of the Modern Lesbian Identity', in Altman et al, eds, *Which Homosexuality?*, pp171-98.

[17] Rudolph M. Dekker and Lotte C. van de Pol, *The Tradition of Transvestism in Early Modern Europe* (London: Macmillan, 1989), p58.

[18] *Ibid.*, chapter 3.

[19] Julie Wheelwright, *Amazons and Military Maids: Women Who Dressed as Men in the Pursuit of Life, Liberty and Happiness* (London: Pandora, 1989), p3.

[20] Carroll Smith-Rosenberg, 'The Female World of Love and Ritual: Relations between Women in Nineteenth-Century America', *Signs 1:1* (1975), pp1-29. Elaine Hobby has argued that some of the seventeenth-century English material suggests a lesbian identity and even a network of lesbians: 'Seventeenth-Century English Lesbianism: First Steps', in *Homosexuality, Which Homosexuality?*, Conference Proceedings, 1 (1987), pp44-55.

[21] Lillian Faderman, *Surpassing the Love of Men: Romantic Friendship and Love between Women from the Renaissance to the Present* (London: Junction Books, 1985).

[22] Quoted in Smith-Rosenberg, 'The Female World of Love and Ritual', pp4-5, 7.

[23] *Ibid.*, p28.

[24] Faraday, *Social Definitions of Lesbians in Britain, 1914-1939: 'Subject to Query'*, PhD dissertation, University of Essex, 1985.

[25] Vicinus, *Independent Women: Work and Community for Single Women, 1850-1920* (London: Virago, 1985), p210.

[26] *Ibid.*, p208.

[27] Faderman, *op. cit.*, p411.

[28] Sheila Jeffreys has given a similar, though less nuanced, account in which she lays great stress on the role of Havelock Ellis, sexology, and the sexual reform movement as articulators of patriarchal ideology: see *The Spinster and Her Enemies: Feminism and Sexuality, 1880-1930* (London: Pandora, 1985), and *Anticlimax: A Feminist Perspective on the Sexual Revolution* (London: Women's Press, 1990).

[29] In an interesting discussion of a female couple who *were* able to live and work together from 1870 to 1913 (namely, Edith Cooper and Katharine Bradley, who jointly produced poetry under the pseudonym 'Michael Field'), Chris White disputes Faderman's view that these women were not conscious of any erotic element in their relationship. She thus takes issue with Faderman's analogy between romantic friendship and modern lesbian-feminism: see ' "Poets and lovers evermore": The Poetry and Journals of Michael Field', in Joseph Bristow, ed., *Sexual Sameness: Textual Differences in Lesbian and Gay Writing* (London: Routledge, 1992), pp26-43. See also Lesbian History Group, *Not a Passing Phase: Reclaiming Lesbians in History, 1840-1945* (London: Women's Press, 1989).

[30] Michel Foucault, *The History of Sexuality: Volume One: An Introduction*, trans. Robert Hurley (Harmondsworth: Penguin Books, 1978), p43.

[31] Mary McIntosh, 'The Homosexual Role', *Social Problems*, 16:2 (1968), pp182-92, reprinted in Plummer, ed., *The Making of the Modern Homosexual*, pp30-44, and in Stein, ed., *Forms of Desire*, pp25-42.

[32] Alan Bray, *Homosexuality in Renaissance England* (London: Gay Men's Press, 1982).

[33] Jeffrey Weeks, *Sex, Politics, and Society: The Regulation of Sexuality since 1800* (London: Longman, 1981), chapter 6.

[34] Randolph Trumbach, 'London's Sodomites: Homosexual Behaviour and Western Culture in the Eighteenth Century', *Journal of Social History*, 11 (1977), pp9-11.

[35] Trumbach, 'Sodomitical Subcultures, Sodomitical Roles, and the Gender Revolution of the Eighteenth Century: The Recent Historiography', in Robert P. MacCubbin, ed., *'Tis Nature's Fault: Unauthorized Sexuality during the Enlightenment* (Cambridge: Cambridge University Press, 1987), pp109-21.

[36] Trumbach, 'Gender and the Homosexual Role in Modern Western Culture: The Eighteenth and Nineteenth Centuries Compared', in Altman

et al, eds, *Which Homosexuality?*, pp149-69.

[37] Quentin Crisp, *The Naked Civil Servant* (London: Michael Joseph, 1968), p62.

[38] John Marshall, 'Pansies, Perverts, and Macho Men: Changing Conceptions of Male Homosexuality', in Plummer, ed., *The Making of the Modern Homosexual*, pp133-54.

[39] *Ibid.*, p154.

[40] Gregg Blatchford, 'Male Dominance and the Gay World', in Plummer, ed., *The Making of the Modern Homosexual*, pp184-210.

[41] *Ibid.*, p209.

[42] Sonja Ruehl, 'Sexual Theory and Practice: Another Double Standard', in Sue Cartledge and Joanna Ryan, eds, *Sex and Love: New Thoughts on Old Contradictions* (London: Women's Press, 1983), pp222.

[43] Weeks, *Coming Out: Homosexual Politics in Britain from the Nineteenth Century to the Present Day* (London: Quarter, 1977), pp5-6.

[44] John D'Emilio, 'Capitalism and Gay Identity, in Snitow et al, eds, *Desire*, p145.

[45] McIntosh, 'The Homosexual Role', in Plummer, ed., *The Making of the Modern Homosexual*, p32.

[46] Ruehl has noted that in Faderman's approach there is a 'latent essentialism in its treatment of *men's* sexuality ... so that although the rigidity of defining women in terms of sexuality is broken down, this is at the expense of a very rigid division along gender lines': 'Sexual Theory and Practice', p218. The same can be said about the world of Jeffreys, for whom the 'enforcement of heterosexuality' appears as a male strategy for dominating women': see *The Spinster and Her Enemies*, pp2-3.

[47] See, for example, Anna Marie Smith, 'Resisting the Erasure of Lesbian Sexuality', in Plummer, ed., *Modern Homosexualities: Fragments of Lesbian and Gay Experience* (London: Routledge, 1992), pp200-13.

[48] Bad Object Choices, eds, *How Do I Look?*, p20. See also Mandy Merck, 'Difference and Its Discontents', *Screen*, 28:1 (1987), pp1-9.

[49] Juliet Mitchell, *Psychoanalysis and Feminism* (London: Allen Lane, 1974), pxv.

[50] Cora Kaplan, 'Radical Feminism and Literature: Rethinking Millett's *Sexual Politics*' in *Sea Changes: Culture and Feminism* (London: Verso, 1986), pp15-30.

[51] Joan W. Scott, 'Gender: A Useful Category for Historical Anlysis', *American Historical Review*, 91 (1986), pp1065-75.

[52] In 'The Banality of Gender', *Oxford Literary Review*, Sexual Difference issue, 18 (1986), pp13-21, Simon Watney knocks down a travesty of what gender theory has been.

[53] Monique Wittig, *The Straight Mind and Other Essays* (Hemel Hempstead: Harvester Wheatsheaf, 1992), p32.

[54] *Ibid.*, p30.

Psychoanalysis and Lesbian Desire: The Trouble with Female Homosexuals

MERL STORR

In a much-quoted and rather bizarre passage of 'On Narcissism' Freud writes:

> With the onset of puberty, the maturing of the female sexual organs ... seems to bring about an intensification of the original narcissism ... Women, especially if they grow up with good looks, develop a certain self-contentment ... Strictly speaking, it is only themselves that such women love ... The importance of this type of woman for the erotic life of mankind is to be rated very high. Such women have the greatest fascination for men ... For it seems very evident that another person's narcissism has a great attraction for those who have renounced part of their own narcissism and are in search of object-love. The charm of a child lies to a great extent in his narcissism, his self-contentment and inaccessibility, just as does the charm of certain animals which seem not to concern themselves about us, such as cats and large beasts of prey. Indeed, even great criminals and humorists, as they are represented in literature, compel our interest by the narcissistic consistency with which they manage to keep away from their ego anything which would diminish it.[1]

Femininity is embodied for Freud in this figure of the narcissistic woman which he calls 'the type of female most

53

frequently met with, which is probably the purest and truest one'.[2]

The narcissistic woman is the point of convergence of many currents within Freudian psychoanalytic thought; Sarah Kofman, in particular, posits the narcissistic woman as a troublespot in Freudian theory, a fascinating and uncanny figure who represents for man the 'paradise lost' of pre-Oedipal primary narcissism.[3]

In this paper, I want to focus on the role of feminine narcissism in Freud's and Lacan's theories of sexual object-choice. I shall demonstrate that the two types of object-choice posited by psychoanalytic theory are mapped onto the concepts of 'masculine' and 'feminine' in such a way that femininity is always constituted as the object for a masculine subject – is always, that is, definitionally heterosexual. My argument will focus on the predicament of lesbian[4] desire both in Freudian theory and in Lacan's re-reading of Freud, and on how that desire confounds the binary structure within which Freudian concepts of femininity – and especially the concept of the 'female homosexual', as it is deployed in Freudian psychopathology – seek to contain it.

Freud's Problem of Object-Choice

This passage from 'On Narcissism' occurs on the course of Freud's discussion of the two types of sexual object-choice, which he calls the 'narcissistic' and the 'anaclitic' types:

The first auto-erotic sexual satisfactions are experienced in connexion with the vital functions which serve the purpose of self-preservation. The sexual instincts are at the outset attached to the satisfaction of the ego-instincts; only later do they become independent of these, and even then we have an indication of that original attachment in the fact that the persons who are concerned with a child's feeding, care, and protection become his earliest sexual objects: that is to say, in the first instance his mother or a substitute for her. Side by side, however, with this type and source of object-choice, psychoanalytic research has

54

revealed a second type, which we were not prepared for finding. We have discovered, especially clearly in people whose libidinal development has suffered some disturbance, such as perverts and homosexuals, that in their later choice of love-objects they have taken as a model not their mother but their own selves. They are plainly seeking *themselves* as a love object which must be termed 'narcissistic' ... We say that a human being has originally two sexual objects – himself and the women who nurses him.[5]

Despite his emphasis that the two types of object-choice are not mutually exclusive and are both equally open to any individual,[6] Freud goes on immediately from this passage to characterise anaclitic object-choice as masculine: 'A comparison of the male and female sexes then shows that there are fundamental differences between them in respect of their type of object-choice. Complete object-love of the attachment type is, properly speaking, characteristic of the male'.[7] In other words, men, unless 'their libidinal development suffers some disturbance', will take the women who nurse them as models for their love-objects, whereas 'perverts and homosexuals' will become locked in the narcissism which we have seen to characterise femininity, and make their object-choice accordingly. In fact, the narcissistic type of object-choice which characterises femininity barely qualifies as a type of object-choice at all: feminine narcissism is 'unfavourable to the development of a true object-choice',[8] and the narcissistic woman does not seek a love-object of her own, but wishes rather for someone of whose masculine-anaclitic object-choice she will be the sexual object. Object-love as such outside motherhood, is only open to women who 'feel[s] masculine and develop[s] some way along masculine lines'.[9] This is of course an elegant version of the classic heterosexual division of labour between active-masculine (reaching out in search of the object) and passive-feminine (awaiting the seeker's attentions).

The distinction between anaclitic and narcissistic object-choice thus conflates sexual object-choice with sexual difference: in both cases there are only two positions available, masculine or feminine. Moreover, this conflation designates all sexual object-choices as heterosexual; the male homosexual who chooses other men does so because of his 'feminine' narcissism, not because of the promptings of any same-sex masculine desire. Freud's assertion that 'both kinds of object-choice are open to each individual'[10] is by no means, therefore, a permission of the free play of erotism. Far from it. As Judith Butler points out, 'for Freud *bisexuality is the coincidence of two heterosexual desires within a single psyche*'.[11]

But what about women who choose each other? Is same-sex object-choice between women anaclitic or narcissistic, masculine or feminine? What place can be given to such object-choice within the binary structure of Freudian sexual difference? What follows will show how the distinction between narcissism and anaclisis generates the peculiar hybrid 'female homosexual', half heterosexual woman and half homosexual man; and how the lesbian, on the contrary, in being neither, is the snag that undoes the psychoanalytic concepts of both.

Narcissistic Object-Choice: The Lesbian as Heterosexual Woman

In drawing his distinction between anaclitic and narcissistic object-choice, Freud makes a clear alignment between homosexuality and femininity. The narcissistic object-choice of the homosexual, whose disturbed libidinal development drives him to seek himself as love-object, converges with the dispositional narcissism of the woman who wishes only to be the object of another's love. In this framework of desire, if the male homosexual is placed as feminine, the female homosexual is doubly so: she both seeks her own likeness as object of desire – which is what homosexuals and other perverts do – and simultaneously positions herself as that object of desire – which is what normal women do. She thus succeeds twice over in the narcissistic quest of loving herself. Female homosexuality is, in this sense, not a failure of Freudian femininity but, on the contrary, an excess of it;

falling, like its heterosexual counterpart, on the 'feminine' side of the anaclitic/narcissistic divide, female homosexuality, it seems, differs from female heterosexuality only in degree. The female homosexual is just too much of a woman.

Once it is carried over into Lacan's re-reading of Freud, the contradictions involved in the narcissistic/anaclitic divide become clearer. 'On Narcissism' presents the (only) two possible kinds of sexual object-choice as a choice between the two original objects of libidinal investment, oneself and the woman who nurses one. To choose oneself is to make the feminine choice; to choose one's mother or mother-substitute is to make the masculine choice. Lacan endorses this distinction,[12] and clarifies its status: the equivalence of the terms narcissistic, specular and imaginary for Lacan[13] highlights the premise that both types of object-choice are imaginary[14] in that they originate in primary narcissism, one being constituted through a libidinal investment in one's own image, the other through an investment in the image of the one who attends to the satisfaction of the ego-drives. Lacan then makes a distinction between love and *Verliebtheit* who leaves little doubt that the 'correct' kind of object-choice in Lacanian theory is an anaclitic and heterosexual one. *Verliebtheit*, imaginary love, is merely an entrapment, a narcissistic and potentially self-destructive absorption in the image of the other, whereas *love* is an exchange between subjects made in the context of the symbolic order:

> Love, now no longer conceived of as a passion but as an active gift, is always directed, beyond imaginary captivation, towards the being of the loved object, towards his particularity ... [L]ove, to the extent that it is one of the three lines of division in which the subject is engaged when he realises himself symbolically in speech, homes in on the being of the other. Without speech, in as much as it affirms being, all there is is *Verliebtheit*, imaginary fascination, but there is no love.[15]

Love as an exchange between subjects in the symbolic is exemplified in the past of heterosexual marital fidelity, and is moreover in active conflict with *Verliebtheit*:

The love which constitutes the bond of marriage, the love which properly speaking is sacred, flows from the woman towards ... *all men*. Similarly, through the women, it is *all women* which the fidelity of the husband is directed towards ... It's the universal man, the universal woman, the symbol, the embodiment of the partner of the human couple ... But there is a conflict between this symbolic pact and the imaginary relations which proliferate spontaneously within every libidinal relation, all the more so when what intervenes belongs to the order of *Verliebtheit*.[16]

The homosexual, on the other hand, is condemned by his narcissistic desire never to go beyond the order of *Verliebtheit*: his desire will lose itself in endless self-reflection, will never be capable of exchange with another subject:

The requirement of this style of desire [i.e. homosexuality] can only be satisfied in an inexhaustible captation of the desire of the other ... An incessant see-saw of the lark-mirror which, at each moment, makes a complete turn on itself – the subject exhausts himself in pursuing the desire of the other, which he will never be able to grasp as his own desire, because his own desire is the desire of the other. It is himself whom he pursues ... The intersubjective relation which subtends perverse desire is only sustained by the annihilation either of the desire of the other, or of the desire of the subject ... The other subject is reduced to being only the instrument of the first ... Perverse desire finds its support in the ideal of the inanimate object.[17]

Here, as one might expect, *Verliebtheit* and homosexuality fall on the side of narcissism and hence of femininity: like the woman, the homosexual attempts to position himself as *object* of the desire of the other – in ignorance or disavowal of the fact that the desire of the other is his own desire ('man's desire is the desire of the other', according to Lacanian formula)[18] – hence the endless spiralling of his desire which chases its own tail and which will never achieve the symbolic anchoring of love.

To achieve that symbolic anchoring, the homosexual would have to go beyond his (*sic*) attachment to his own image and enter the circuit of heterosexual/symbolic exchange (with which his imaginary love(s) would henceforth be in conflict). But the symbolic part of heterosexuality does not require that the woman give up *her* narcissism. As for Freud, feminine heterosexual 'object'-love for Lacan seeks a man for whom she can be the object, in that 'the woman is introduced into the symbolic pact of marriage as the object of exchange between ... fundamentally androcentric lineages'.[19] In fact, far from requiring the woman to 'go beyond' her narcissism, the symbolic 'goes beyond' *her*, and her 'choice' of the universal man as her love-object is in reality little more than an effect of her place in the symbolic:

> [T]he symbolic order literally subdues her, transcends her. The *all men* of Proudhon is here the universal man, who is both the most concrete and the most transcendent man, and that's the impasse into which the woman is pushed by her specific function in the symbolic order ... In other words, in the primitive form of marriage, if a woman isn't given, or doesn't give herself, to a god, to something transcendent, the fundamental relation suffers every form of imaginary degradation.[20]

In other words again, the woman who embraces a man thereby embraces the symbolic order, and positions herself as object for both. When she narcissistically places herself as object of desire, the woman, unlike the male homosexual, is making no mistake; the conflict between the imaginary and the symbolic arises for her not because of any inherent contradiction between her positions *in* the imaginary and the symbolic, but merely because the 'concrete' man cannot, just in himself, fulfil the transcendent function of the symbolic ('... because we aren't, and haven't been for a long time, cut out to embody gods').[21]

All of this is of course predicated on the mirror stage[22] which gives to the formula 'man's desire is the desire of the other' its structure.[23] In making the alienating distinction between itself and its mirror image, the mirror-stage child also introduces a distinction between itself as unified 'one' and the mother with whom it has hitherto enjoyed a more or less unbroken union. Thus the unifying/alienating effect of the mirror stage releases two original figures which can occupy the place of the 'other': the image of oneself, and the image of one's mother as distinct from oneself. Either of the two figures can come to occupy that place in the formula that 'man's desire is the desire of the other', and the pre-symbolic or mirror-stage child has no need of a definite decision or choice in favour of one of the other. But as soon as the subject passes through the castration complex to enter the symbolic and thereby becomes 'sexed', he or she must choose according to the familiar Freudian pattern. Masculine desire chooses anaclitically, that is, chooses the image of the mother to fill the place of the 'other', and strives for the desire of the (m)other through 'having' what she lacks – namely, the phallus; feminine desire chooses narcissistically, that is, chooses its own image as the 'other', and positions itself in the heterosexual relation as 'being' the phallus, the object (or signifier) to be exchanged in the marital pact as described above.[24]

The distinction holds good in the case of the male homosexual: in choosing his own image, he makes the feminine choice of 'being' the phallus; hence his desire's dependence on 'the ideal of the inanimate object', for, in 'being' the phallus for himself, he repeatedly reduces himself (and/or his sexual partner) to an object by trying to make exchange with himself of what he (and his partner) already has (have). For Lacan, female homosexuality is likewise characterised by an emphasis on 'being' the phallus, that is, as an excessive distortion of feminine heterosexuality:

> Paradoxical as this formulation might seem, I would say that it is in order to be the phallus, that is to say, the signifier of the desire of the Other, that the woman will reject an essential part of her femininity ... It is for what she is not that she expects to be desired as well as loved ... [T]he man manages to satisfy his demand for love in his relationship to the woman to the extent that the signifier of the phallus constitutes her precisely as giving in love what she does not have.[25] In that such a love prides itself more than any other on being the love which gives what it does not have, so it is precisely in this that the homosexual woman

excels in relation to what is lacking to her.[26]

Both the heterosexual and the homosexual woman excel in giving what they do not have; the difference being that the homosexual woman, whose refusal to accept castration leaves her suspended in the belief that sexed male subjects (and according to Lacan, she might paradoxically consider herself to be one such) could *really* 'have' the phallus, 'has' correspondingly less than her heterosexual counterpart not to give.[27]

Thus both Freudian and Lacanian theory posit feminine homosexuality as an extreme or excessive version of feminine heterosexuality, both being forms of narcissistic desire as it falls within the terms of the masculine-anaclitic/feminine-narcissistic distinction. However the distinction between the anaclitic and the narcissistic type of object-choice is maintined on the condition that one's primary object-choice is based on the sexual(ised) *difference* between the image of oneself as ideal or model (the narcissistic choice) and the image of one's mother as model (the anaclitic choice). What both Freud and Lacan conveniently forget of course is that, for a woman, the sexual object which resembles herself will *also* resemble her mother, according to the binary terms of the system of sexual difference. The female sexual object who is the image of both myself and my mother confounds the Freudian structure of 'female homosexuality' – heterosexuality by any other name – and reveals lesbian desire as simultaneously a narcissistic relation and an anaclitic object-choice; as in fact a desire which renders the distinction between those terms – and hence the very definition of either – meaningless.

For example, in his 1915 paper 'A Case of Paranoia Running Counter to the Psychoanalytic Theory of the Disease', Freud describes the origins of a paranoid woman patient's delusions as follows:

We can see by what means the girl freed herself from her homosexual dependence on her mother. It was by means of a small piece of regression: instead of choosing her mother as a love-object, she identified herself with her – she herself *became* her mother. The possibility of this regression points to the

61

narcissistic origin of her homosexual object-choice and thus to the paranoic disposition in her.[28]

This 'girl' (actually a thirty-year-old woman) suffered delusions of being watched which, according to Freud, arose from her narcissistic identification with her own mother while lovemaking (at the 'primal scene'). Thus her paranoid delusions resulted directly from her 'homosexual' object-choice, which Freud regarded as narcissistic even when its explicit object was her own mother. Freud sees the woman's symptoms as arising from an inner struggle between her heterosexual impulses towards her male suitor and her so-called homosexual attachment to her mother. But one might well consider that the real struggle in this case is between the woman's unruly desire and Freud's determination that it be made to fit within the binary structure of the narcissistic/anaclitic divide – that the woman should conform to the model of narcissistic femininity, the importance of which for the erotic life of mankind is rated so very highly.

Anaclitic Object-Choice: The Lesbian as Homosexual Man

I have been arguing so far that Freudian and Lacanian theory attempts to keep same-sex desire between women within the narcissistic/anaclitic divide by characterising it as 'female homosexuality', and that, by insisting that a woman's desire for another woman is a narcissistic desire for and in the image of herself, the theory places any such desire on the side of heterosexual femininity. There is, however, an alternative account of 'female homosexuality' in Freudian theory running alongside the narcissistic one, which shifts the emphasis from 'female' to 'homosexual' and represents lesbian desire not as an excess of femininity, but as a transgressive masculinity – the masculinity of the homosexual man.

In his paper 'Some Neurotic Mechanisms in Jealousy, Paranoia and Homosexuality', Freud argues that male homosexuality is the result both of narcissistic object-choice (as already discussed) *and* of the boy's over-strong anaclitic attachment to his mother which, alongside his narcissism, leads him later to identify with her and to look for men or boys for whom he can care as his mother once cared for him. He writes:

> Observation has directed my attention to several cases in which during early childhood impulses of jealousy, derived from the mother-complex and of very great intensity, arose [in a boy] against rivals, usually older brothers. This jealousy led to an exceedingly hostile and aggressive attitude towards these brothers which might sometimes reach the pitch of actual death-wishes, but which could not maintain themselves in the face of the subject's further development. Under the influence of upbringing – and certainly not uninfluenced also by their own continuing powerlessness – these impulses yielded to repression and underwent a transformation, so that the rivals of the earlier period became the first homosexual love-objects.[29]

This account by Freud of a 'new mechanism leading to homosexual object-choice'[30] – intended not to replace but to supplement his previous accounts of male homosexuality as narcissistic – thus posits homosexuality in boys as the outcome of sibling rivalry over the mother, that is, as the outcome of early anaclitic attachment to her.

In an early paper called 'Motifs du crime paranoïaque', originally published in 1933, Lacan labels this mechanism of homosexuality the 'fraternal complex', and he uses it as the key for understanding the notorious and macabre case of the Papin sisters. Earlier that year these two sisters, employed as maids in the same household, had jointly killed their mistress and her daughter in a horrific double murder, and had then retired together to the same bed. During their trial it was claimed that the sisters were suffering from a 'folie à deux', a double madness, and furthermore that their relationship was an incestuously and pathologically 'homosexual' one.[31] According to Lacan, this 'fraternal complex' lay at the root of both the Papins' homosexuality and their severe paranoic illness. He thus 'analyses' the Papin sisters – neither of whom, incidentally, was ever a patient of his – as if they were homosexual men whose jealous anaclitic attachment to their mother had driven them into each other's arms. In equating the Papins with homosexual men in this way, Lacan does not undermine the parallel equation of 'female homosexuality' with an excess of femininity. Quite the contrary. As we have already seem, male homosexual object-choice is characteristically narcissistic, and this is so even in cases where the original impetus has been an over-strong mother fixation:

> [The progression of the fraternal complex] is made however according to the law of least resistance by an effective fixation still very close to the solipsistic ego, a fixation which deserves to be called narcissistic and in which the object chosen is that which most resembles the subject: such is the reason for its homosexual character.[32]

Moreover, the *jealousy* at work in the fraternal complex is, in Lacanian theory, endemic to the orthodox narcissistic feminity which 'gives what it does not have'. It is of female homosexuality in particular that Lacan writes:

> Far from its being the case that the passivity of the act corresponds to this desire, feminine sexuality appears as the effect of a *jouissance* wrapped in its own contiguity (for which all circumcision might represent the symbolic rupture) to be *realised in the envy* of desire, which castration releases in the male by giving him its signifier in the phallus.[33]

Female homosexuals who 'appeal to their quality of being men'[34] in articulating their homosexuality do so out of Lacanian penis envy, 'phallus envy' or envy for the position of subject of desire which their status as women in the symbolic order seeks to deny them. Men and female homosexuals are seen by Lacan as 'the holders of desire and the claimants of sex ... [who] work against each other as rivals':[35] this rivalry over who gets to hold the 'masculine' position of subject of desire derives from, is indeed merely a sophisticated version of, the rivalry over who gets to satisfy the anaclitic attachment to the mother as it is played out in the fraternal complex. Girls can take part in the competition as much as boys can, but it's a competition run on boys' terms, and the girls will lose.

Anaclitic love in girls became quite a problem for Freud himself. The question of how and why girls should renounce their attachment to their mothers and become heterosexually attached to their fathers is the impetus behind his paper of 1931, 'Female Sexuality', in which, nearly twenty years after 'On Narcissism', he famously writes that 'Our insight into this early, pre-Oedipus, phase in girls comes to us as a surprise, like the discovery, in another field, of the Minoan-Mycenaean civilisation behind the civilisation of Greece'.[36] It does not, however, take him so much by surprise as to render him unable to assimilate it into the thesis of 'On Narcissism' that anaclisis is masculine. The girl's pre-Oedipal attachment to her mother is the focus of 'active and in every sense masculine trends',[37] which she renounces when she 'represses her previous masculinity', makes her 'transition to the father-object,[39] and only then finds that 'the path to the development of femininity now lies open'.[40] In other words, anaclisis is *always* masculine, even though Freud in this later paper now believes that it is the primary form of object-love for both boys and girls. Consequently there is little if any distinction to be made between the male homosexuality which is based on rivalry over the mother and any other kind of homosexuality – including 'female' homosexuality – based on anaclitic attachment, regardless of the very important point that, according to Freud's own hypothesis, such attachments make boys choose their own sex *in place of* their mother's, whereas girls will choose their own sex *because it is the same as* their mother's. Thus even when recognising the possibility of a female same-sex desire which is not the passive and self-contented narcissism of heterosexual femininity, both Freud and Lacan still seem unable to conceive of such desire except in heterosexual terms: if not narcissistic then anaclitic, if not heterosexually feminine then heterosexually masculine, *all* desire must be one or the other and there must always be a difference – precisely a *sexual* difference – between the two.

My argument may have appeared somewhat paradoxical, in that I have been maintaining that, on the one hand, 'female homosexuality' in Freudian and Lacanian theory is feminine-narcissistic while, on the other hand, it is also sometimes masculine-anaclitic. The point I am trying to make, however, is not just that psychoanalytic theory is wrong in trying to define same-sex desire between women as either one or the other – although, as I hope I have shown, that is certainly the case; I want to argue more importantly that Freudian psychoanalysis is wrong in trying to define same-sex desire between women in terms of the anaclitic/narcissistic divide at all. Lesbian desire is a desire that defies the binary structure of 'female homosexuality', which as we have seen is based on polarised heterosexual concepts of masculinity and feminity. Being both narcissistic *and* anaclitic, and yet at the same time not really either, lesbian desire reveals the Freudian theory of sexual object-choice as a rather precarious heterosexual scaffolding.

The collapse of that scaffolding might open the way for precisely that free play of erotism that Freudian 'bisexuality' denies. Indeed the effects of any such collapse of the binary structure by which both identity and desire are regulated – anaclitic versus narcissistic, heterosexual versus homosexual, masculine versus feminine – might prove so radical as to be literally unimaginable for us who still live within a system where heterosexuality remains compulsory even for those designated homosexual. Despite Freud's and Lacan's various attempts to paper over the cracks in the system with their theories of object-choice and their constructions of 'female homosexuality', same-sex desire – particularly same-sex desire between women – cannot be made to fit within this or any other binary heterosexual structure. For Freudian psychoanalytic theory, any lesbian desire on the loose is a very alarming prospect indeed.

Notes

[1] Sigmund Freud, 'On Narcissism: An Introduction', trans James Strachey, in *Pelican Freud Library Vol. 11* (Harmondsworth: Penguin, 1984), pp59-97, pp82-3.

[2] *Ibid.*, p82.

[3] Sarah Kofman, *The Enigma of Woman: Woman in Freud's Writings*, trans. Catherine Porter (Ithaca: Cornell University Press, 1985), pp50-65.

[4] The term 'lesbian' is a problematic one, both politically and theoretically. Desire for other women may be experienced by women who do not identify as lesbian, and women who *do* so identify may experience desire for persons (or objects) who are not female. For the purposes of this paper, I use the term 'lesbian desire' simply to designate same-sex desire between women, and the term 'lesbian' to designate subjects who experience such desire. However, as Valerie Traub puts it: '[I]n its singularity and self-identity, "lesbian" is a politically necessary but conceptually inadequate demarcation: ... less a person than an activity, less an activity than a modality of pleasure, a position taken in relation to desire. Its problematic ontological status suggests that it is better used as an adjective (e.g. "lesbian" desire) than as a noun signifying a discrete order of being ... "[L]esbian" is a point of reference around which erotic difference can and must rally politically, but upon which it should never stand for long': Valerie Traub, 'The Ambiguities of "Lesbian" Viewing Pleasure: The (Dis)articulations of *Black Widow*', in Julia Epstein and Kristina Straub, eds, *Body Guards: The Cultural Politics of Gender Ambiguity* (New York, Routledge, 1991), p324. Thus although I use the noun 'lesbian' as a term to be set *against* Freudian psychopathology's 'female homosexual' – my argument in this paper being that 'female homosexuality' is in fact a purely heterosexual construct – I do not intend thereby to set up 'lesbian' as any kind of stable, closed or 'authentic' ontological category, or to make any definitional claim about the forms that 'lesbian desire' might take: I use these terms as a political tool or point of reference merely. While I am aware of the difficulties of this position, I am also aware that exploring those difficulties fully would mean writing another paper altogether.

[5] Sigmund Freud, 'On Narcissim', pp80-81.

[6] *Ibid.*, p81.

[7] *Ibid.*, p82.

[8] *Ibid.*

[9] *Ibid.*, p83.

[10] *Ibid.*, p81.

[11] Judith Butler, *Gender Trouble: Feminism and the subversion of identity* (New York, Routledge, 1990), p61; her emphasis.

[12] Jacques Lacan, *The Seminar of Jacques Lacan Book 1: Freud's papers on technique, 1953-4*, trans. John Forrester (Cambridge: Cambridge University Press, 1988), see pp131-2.

[13] *Ibid.*, p188.
[14] *Ibid.*, p132. The term 'imaginary' is a technical term in Lacanian theory which denotes the realm of narcissism and identification, where ego-formation and object relations occur; it is placed against the 'symbolic order' which is the realm of language and of exchange between speaking subjects. Readers unfamiliar with Lacanian theory are referred to Elizabeth Grosz's excellent *Jacques Lacan: A Feminist Introduction* (London: Routledge, 1990), pp24-49, for an explication of these and other terms.
[15] *Ibid.*, pp276-7.
[16] Lacan, *The Seminar of Jacques Lacan Book 2: The Ego in Freud's Theory and in the Technique of Psychoanalysis, 1954-5*, trans. Sylvana Tomaselli (Cambridge: Cambridge University Press, 1988), pp260-61.
[17] Lacan, *Seminar Book 1*, pp221-22.
[18] *Ibid.*, p77.
[19] Lacan, *Seminar Book 2*, p262.
[20] *Ibid.*
[21] *Ibid.*, pp262-63.
[22] See Lacan, 'The Mirror Stage as Formative of the Function of the I as Revealed in Psychoanalytic Experience', in *Ecrits: a Selection* trans. Alan Sheridan (London: Tavistock/Routledge, 1989), pp1-7.
[23] The mirror stage is essentially the phenomenon of the infant's seeing its own image in a mirror and recognising it as such, which according to Lacan generally occurs between the ages of six and eighteen months. The child recognises the figure in the mirror as being 'me'; and yet at the same time the figure in the mirror displays a bodily coherence and unity which the child itself has not experienced. Hence the mirror-stage child both identifies with, and is alienated by, its mirror image: Lacan takes this unifying/alienating relation to be foundational of subjectivity as such. The mirror stage comes to an end when the child passes through the castration complex – the complex through which the child attains both subjectivity and sexual identity – and enters the symbolic order. Again, for a full explication of the mirror stage and the castration complex, see Grosz, *Jacques Lacan*, pp31-47.
[24] See Lacan, 'The meaning of the phallus', trans. Jacqueline Rose, in Juliet Mitchell and Jacqueline Rose, eds, *Feminine Sexuality: Jacques Lacan and the Ecole Freudienne* (London: Macmillan, 1982), pp74-85.
[25] *Ibid.*, p84.
[26] Lacan, 'Guiding Remarks for a Congress on Feminine Sexuality', trans. Rose, in Mitchell and Rose, eds, *Feminine Sexuality*, p96.
[27] *Ibid.*, pp96-7.
[28] Freud, 'A Case of Paranoia Running Counter to the Psychoanalytic Theory of the Disease', trans. Strachey, in *Pelican Freud Library Vol 10* (Harmondsworth: Penguin, 1979), p155.
[29] Freud, 'Some Neurotic Mechanisms in Jealousy, Paranoia and Homosexuality', trans. Strachey, in *Pelican Freud Library Vol 10* (Harmondsworth: Penguin, 1979), pp195-208, pp206-7; parentheses in the

original translation.

[30] *Ibid.*, p206.

[31] See Lacan, 'Motifs du crime paranoïaque', in *Minotaure*, no 3-4 (1933), pp25-8. The case is given an extensive and detailed Lacanian reading in Francis Dupré's *La 'Solution' du passage à l'acte: le double crime des soeurs Papin* (Toulouse: Editions Erès, 1984). I am grateful to Nicole Ward Jouve for drawing my attention to this case and to the literature surrounding it.

[32] Lacan, 'Motifs du crime paranoïaque', p28; my translation.

[33] Lacan, 'Guiding Remarks for a Congress on Feminine Sexuality', p97.

[34] *Ibid.*

[35] *Ibid.*

[36] Freud, 'Female Sexuality', trans. Strachey, in *Pelican Freud Library Vol 7* (Harmondsworth: Penguin, 1977), p372.

[37] *Ibid.*, p388.

[38] *Ibid.*, p387.

[39] *Ibid.*

[40] *Ibid.*

Death Desire and Identity: The Political Unconscious of 'New Queer Cinema'

JOSÉ ARROYO

I came out in the late 1970s. I remember singing 'Glad to be Gay' at a demo, participating in discussions about the 'inviolability of desire' and feeling terrorized and ashamed the first time I saw gay men on screen. The film was *Cruising* (1980), directed by William Friedkin. The mingling of terror and shame, greatly familiar by then, was doubly and differently inflected by the context of viewing and the film itself. I felt afraid first because I was not sure my fake I.D. would get me in to see the film and later because the film represented homosexuality as an all too brief and sordid lifetime sentence – gay desire meant alienation, drugs, night, violence and led to death. I felt ashamed because I had to cross a gay picket line in order to get into the theatre and because the film, homophobic to the hilt, still turned me on.

The favourite slogan at the last demo I went to was 'We're here, we're queer, get used to it'. Discussions with gay male friends will as often as not centre on safe sex, AIDS, who one's in love with, and which common acquaintance has recently died. These are new times indeed. The old combination of desire and death, now in the pandemic linked by disease, have new and multiple ramifications. Homophobia, institutional and internalized, is still a major danger – so great that

70

even *Newsweek* noticed, making 'Gays Under Threat' its 14 September 1992 cover story. However, these days other dangers could just as easily, albeit invisibly, come from your lover or your own body. The old romantic notion of dying for love or even dying of love seems less melodramatic today.

I offer this preamble as personal parameters of a social context in which an increasing range of filmic representations by gay men seem to have found a market. These movies are sometimes screened at a local Odeon, more often at a local art house, and almost always at the lesbian and gay film festivals that seem to be sprouting all over North America (less so in Western Europe). Some of these recent movies (*Poison* [Todd Haynes, USA, 1990], *No Skin of My Ass* [Bruce La Bruce, Canada, 1990], *The Living End* [Greg Araki, USA, 1992], *The Hours and Times* [Christopher Munch, USA 1991], *The Making of 'Monsters'* [John Greyson, Canada, 1991] and a few others) have been lumped together as 'New Queer Cinema'. According to Ruby Rich:

> the new queer films and videos aren't all the same, and don't share a single aesthetic vocabulary or strategy or concern. Yet they are nonetheless united by a common style. Call it 'Homo Pomo': there are traces in all of them of appropriation and pastiche, irony, as well as a reworking of history with social constructionism very much in mind. Definitively breaking with older humanist approaches and the films and tapes that accompanied identity politics, these works are irreverent, energetic, alternatively minimalist and excessive. Above all, they're full of pleasure.[1]

In what follows I will be looking at two recent hit films by gay men which represent gay male desire and which, arguably, primarily address a gay male audience (the largest possible art-house audience is the contender). Which films are queer and which are not is hotly debated. There is, however, relative agreement on *My Own Private Idaho* (Gus Van Sant, USA, 1991) and *Edward II* (Derek Jarman, UK, 1991). My intent is not to measure how new, how queer or how cinematic these films are. I will instead try to tease out

71

their commonalities, compare what gay identities they construct and how they represent them, and explore the extent to which these films depict, displace or elide the context of the pandemic. I will then conclude with some thoughts on the degree to which other 'New Queer' films share such traits and the significance of such similarities.

Love and Death and the Whole Damp Thing

My Own Private Idaho is the most financially successful of the bunch. Part of the reason is surely that, unlike the others, it has two stars. The image of Keanu Reeves and River Phoenix on a motorcycle now adorns gay bars from Montreal to Madrid. And I am sure this is only because more revealing images from the movie, such as Keanu and River on the covers of gay porn magazines or their threesome with Udo Kier, are difficult to acquire. Two movie stars in a gay movie is the fulfilment of a desire long denied. It means not having to make creative leaps in the imagination like with Wayne and Clift in *Red River* (1948), Newman and Redford in *Butch Cassidy and the Sundance Kid* (1969) and, more recently on television, Kirk and Spock, *Starsky and Hutch, Simon and Simon* and other buddy fictions. The number of gay art videos and 'slash videos' (gay and straight)[2] which re-edit these texts to make the relationships explicitly gay testify to the power of such a fantasy. *Idaho* fulfils this fantasy even as it problematises it.

Idaho is not *about* AIDS in a conventional sense. The pandemic is not even mentioned in the film. However, in this section of the essay I would like to demonstrate, via textual analysis, that the pandemic is both *Idaho*'s absent cause and an important interpretative context.[3] I will describe the sexual differentiation between Scott (mostly hetero) and Mike (mainly homo), the way they are represented, the imagery associated with them, their role in the narrative, the different desires they are attributed and the different socio-political possibilities to which the film gives them access. I hope it will become evident that all of these factors are not only informed by the pandemic but in fact help *Idaho* convey the way gay men's relations to their bodies, their sexuality, and their social positioning have been changed by it.

In *Idaho* River Phoenix is Mike Waters, a narcoleptic teenage hustler. Keanu Reeves plays Scott Graves, the Mayor's son and a hustler by choice. They travel through vast, unpopulated highways in the American Northwest's interior to ply their trade in the sprawling yet urban centres, primarily Seattle and Portland. The film is set in autumn in the weeks surrounding Scott's twenty-first birthday, when he will inherit his fortune.

Mike and Scott function in the narrative as each other's double and opposite. Mike was conceived in incest. Scott was born into a nuclear family. At one point in the film Mike tells Scott, 'You have it made. If I had a normal family and a good upbringing then I would have been a well-adjusted person'. Their class is inscribed in their very bodies. Scott is robust, clean shaven and has good colouring. He either wears a suit or street clothes that connote alternative chic. Mike has a slouch. His skin pale and pimply, his face stubbly, Mike sniffles and coughs his way from trick to trick.

We are never shown Scott prey to the elements and he is always in control of every situation. Mike, on the other hand, shivers while he waits for his tricks. We see him sometimes sleeping under a makeshift tent of plastic and rocks on a rooftop, sometimes so sick he has to crawl to get under his sleeping-bag on the street. The elements and the environment have as much of a material effect on his body as his tricks.

Mike is totally helpless. In moments of stress, he falls asleep, and even the little control that he has over how he is going to be exploited is taken away from him. The character of Scott is based on Prince Hal, and he is sometimes given Shakespeare's words. Mike, by contrast, is down-and-out sub-prole, cast out not only of America but sometimes, through his narcolepsy, out of this world. The mise-en-scene sometimes presents him via the iconography of Christian martyrs – his pose for the cover of the porn magazine

73

G-String, reclining against a wooden pole, echoes images of St. Sebastian. In several scenes, when he is in a narcoleptic state, Mike sprawls over Scott's lap like Christ over Mary Magdalene's.

The differences between Scott and Mike are the very motor of *Idaho*'s narrative. These are most clearly illustrated by each one's quest throughout the film. Scott's trajectory is an Oedipal one. He became a hustler to get away from the reach of his father's power and to hurt and humiliate him. In one scene we are shown the facade of a big bourgeois home, the window framing a silhouette of a couple fighting. Mike is going into his trance. Scott is holding him as he does so often in the film and, in a quasi-theatrical aside, he tells us:

> I grew up in a neighbourhood like this one ... [My father] has more fucking righteous gall than all the property he lords over and those he also created like me his son. But I almost get sick thinking that I am a son to him. You know you have to be as good as him. To keep up, you have to carry as big a weight. You have to throw the weight as far or make as much money or be as heartless. My Dad doesn't know I'm just a kid. Thinks I'm a threat.

Scott's aim is that when he attains his majority, he will transform himself into a dutiful son so completely that his father will be astounded and love him the more. 'I will change', he says via bits of Shakespeare, 'when everyone expects it the least'.[4] Until then, he has adopted Bob (based on Falstaff) as his new father. His biological Dad and his adopted one are, like Mike and Scott, each others' doubles and opposites. The Mayor is from the top social echelon, rich and respectable. Bob is a social outcast, poor and an object of derision. Both are crippled – the Mayor physically (he is in a wheelchair and wears a heartpacer) and Bob by his physical deterioration, his social context, and his addiction. But both rule their own roosts – the Mayor the city; Bob the gang of juvenile delinquents. Scott's biological Dad has considered him a threat and kept him at arm's length. His adopted Dad has loved him carnally ('Yeah we had a thing once. He was in love with me', Scott tells Mike). Scott's rejection will be the cause of both their deaths. And their deaths will make a 'man' of him.

Scott learns of his father's death just after he has fallen in love with a girl in Italy while helping Mike find his mother. Bob dies just after Scott turns his back on him in public in favour of the power and social position his wealth affords him. The last image we see of Scott in the film is at his biological father's funeral. There is a preacher, a sermon, and a very well-dressed crowd. His girlfriend, dressed in black, is sitting down, knitting by his side. His mother is at his other side. Bob is also being buried in the same cemetery. His funeral train is riotously anarchic. His mourners scream, dance and simulate sex on his coffin. The film alternates from one ceremony to the other. One burial is carnivalesque, the other is a dirge. The alternations are motivated mainly by Mike and Scott looking at each other. But each remains on his own side. The deaths of Scott's two fathers pave the way for his entry into socially accepted heterosexual union and the upper strata of capitalism. Scott can now be as good, carry as big a weight, throw that weight around, make as much money and be as heartless.

The struggle of Scott for socio-sexual identity within the patriarchy is in counterpoint to Mike's quest for his mother. Whereas Scott quests after power and ego, Mike's quest for his mother is in actuality a desire for the home, safety and security he felt as a child and which is now lost. The contrast between Scott and Mike also illustrates the importance of sexual difference to narrative structuring for it plays a role even in this film. It is not that Scott is depicted as masculine and Mike as feminine. Mike is visibly male and through neither dress nor gesture is he depicted as feminine. Yet whereas Scott is exclusively characterized by traits socially attributed to men (power, control, strength, rationality), Mike is characterized by many traits socially attributed to women (powerlessness, dependence, frailty, physical weakness, fantasy). In *Idaho* Scott drives the motorcycle and Mike rides pillion literally and metaphorically.

75

Instead of gender it is sexual preference that demarcates sexual difference in *Idaho*. In the sequence where they're modelling on the cover of porn magazines, Scott addresses the audience directly and tells us that he only had sex with men for money because as soon as one gives it away for free, one grows wings, becomes a fairy. He then solicits Mike's agreement but Mike remains evasive. Later, in the campfire scene over half-way through the film, Scott repeats the same sentiments but this time Scott disagrees. 'Well, I don't know. I can love somebody even if I wasn't paid for it. I love you and you don't pay me'. This is perhaps the climax of the film. It is the only, brief, moment where Mike connects emotionally and sexually.

The function of Scott in the film is to be an object of desire for, and to help illuminate the character and situation of, Mike. But Mike's desire for Scott is only momentarily fulfilled. This is illustrated by the rural scenes in Italy. The setting is an old house in a pastoral setting – a visual echo of the prairie house that symbolizes Mike's dream of safety and security. And it is here that Scott falls in love with a young woman and Mike loses the only person in his present life we are shown him caring about. Mike is conscious of his loss. He finds Scott's girlfriend crying and tells her 'I understand'. 'Do you?' she asks. 'Yes', he replies, 'I know how you feel'. This heterosexual union which results in loss for a homosexual is significantly framed by short sequences before and after showing Mike lying down on the street with hustlers (before) and once again having to sell his body (after) in Rome. Scott is Mike's lack socially as well as sexually.

Scott's heterosexuality is one more thing that oppresses Mike. But the film does not depict homosexuality per se as a positive value. The film represents homosexuality as a fluid spectrum with a concomitant variety of possible identities. Some of the men who have sex with men in the movie are not primarily homosexual, others are but remain married. Moreover, not all men who have sex with men are good. In one scene a group of hustlers exchange horror stories – we hear of several bad tricks and one rape with a wine bottle.

76

Some of Mike's tricks are physically repulsive while others are slightly pathetic (Hans, the Dutch Boy Fetishist).

In 'Capitalism and Gay Identity', John D'Emilio makes a distinction between homosexual behaviour and gay identity, the latter 'the result of capitalist development that has spanned many generations'.[5] D'Emilio disproves the myth of the 'eternal homosexual' and convincingly argues that the 'homosexual' is a modern creation, one not composed of a set percentage of the population for all time. 'There are', he claims, 'more of us than one hundred years ago, more of us than forty years ago ... Capitalism has created the material conditions for homosexual desire to express itself as a central component of some individuals' lives'.[6] *Idaho* bypasses 1970s Gay Lib identity politics. In depicting various kinds of homosexual desires and in giving expression to multiple homosexual identities, the film supports D'Emilio's contention that terms such as 'homosexual' are historically specific. *Idaho* suggests that terms like 'homosexual', 'gay' and 'desire' are sites of struggle (and thus in flux).

The homosexuality that *Idaho* values the most is Mike's. And Mike is not looking for sex but for love. Sex is what he exchanges for money. It is often meaningless, sometimes frightening. The film depicts him having an orgasm once. And whereas in such different movies as *To Catch a Thief* and *Fireworks* it is represented by fireworks – light, bright, evanescent explosives shooting up. In *Idaho* it is represented by the dream house, the symbol of his safety and security, crashing down into the ground and destroying itself. What the film valorizes, partly by its place and significance in the narrative, is Mike's baring his heart and offering his love to Scott. In *Idaho*, sex without love might be necessary but also nightmarish in these new times.

Mike is the protagonist of the film. It is his quest that *Idaho* is about. The film begins and ends with him. It is his character, his development and his fate that we are told about and it is he who the film constructs as the focus of audience identification. We never get to see inside Scott's mind except through his mouth. The flashbacks, the trances, and the

symbolic tableaus are sparked by Mike's states of consciousness. Some stylistic devices, like the fastly edited still
photographs to depict lovemaking and the tableau in which
the cover-boys of the porn magazines came to life and talk, are
shared by Scott and Mike. But it is with the objectives of
depicting the latter's state of mind that the film puts in place
the rest; the time lapse photography to signify him going or
coming out of a trance; the jerky, faded hand-held super eight
footage to signify childhood memories; the tableau of the little
house on the prairie so pastel-pretty it looks unreal. All these
devices, along with the gritty on-location photography of the
street scenes, give the film a look and tone of poetically
bittersweet grunge, a new style of romantic realism.

The scenes on the highway have a particular significance.
First of all, they begin and end the film. Secondly, the
landscape, almost pastel greens, yellows and blues, put in
place a colour scheme and iconography that are halfway
between the film's 'realistic' sequences and the trance scenes.
The highway in American culture is a symbol for freedom,
space, and opportunity. Indeed for some it signifies America
itself. At the beginning of the film, Mike tells us that he
always knows where he is by how the road looks and that this
one looks like a fucked-up face saying 'Have a nice day'. Then
he goes into a trance. We are shown the time lapse
photography of the landscape, his mother appears holding and
comforting him, and we get a shot of salmon going upstream.

The last scene is an echoed response to the first scene's call.
It begins with the salmon still going upstream; Mike appears
on the highway again. 'I'm a connoisseur of roads. Been
tasting roads my whole life. This road will probably never
end. It probably goes all around the world'. Mike then suffers
an attack and falls on the ground. The camera pulls back,
seemingly engulfing and diminishing his person. As he begins
to go into his trance, we hear him utter something that sounds
like 'mother'. A truck appears. A mournful version of 'America
the Beautiful' begins playing on the soundtrack, and two men
steal his boots. Another vehicle appears, a man puts him in it,
we get a dream image of the house that symbolize's Mike's

home, his shelter from the horrors of the world, and the film ironically ends with the title, 'Have a Nice Day'.

Mike does not fulfil his quest. He does not find his mother. Whereas the message in *The Wizard of Oz* was that there was no place like home, *Idaho* questions whether there ever was such a place. The ending gives the impression that new times in America mean an uphill struggle characterized by isolation, alienation, exclusion and exploitation; that as far back as Prince Hal, those who have got shall get and those who have not will lose. And though for many the uphill struggle, like for the salmon, ends with reproduction and death, Mike's sexuality condemns him to dying in struggle. New times for sexual outlaws in America are a painful fulfilment of the death instinct.

Though the only overt reference to AIDS in the entire film is a scene in which Mike digs into his pocket and comes up with a pack of stuff that includes a condom, the context of the pandemic permeates *Idaho*. It is easy to read Mike's narcolepsy as a displacement of AIDS. Mike's shivering, his lack of energy, his pallor, and his thinness contribute to the symptomatology. Mike moves in a world undergoing a seasonal death – it is autumn, cold, damp, empty and the days get shorter quickly. Orgasm is a shattering experience for Mike. He longs for a time when he was safe, loved and when it was safe to love. Now he is not only outcast for his sexuality but his illness makes him even more vulnerable to those who would hurt him for his sexual preference. Yet, Mike can still love without getting paid for it. And it is that possibility of love that makes, for Mike as for so many of us in the pandemic, the fucking that one gets worth the fucking that one gets.

Queer Edward II

Edward II lived in the early fourteenth century but *Edward II* is as much about the present as *Idaho*. In fact, the two films have a lot more in common than that the sexual orientation of their directors, main characters or (at least one) intended audience. That *Idaho* and *Edward* both draw on Elizabethan plays (albeit to different extents – *Edward* is an adaptation of Christopher Marlowe's play whereas *Idaho* only borrows selectively from William Shakespeare's *Henry IV*) is a relatively minor connection. More important is the way both films depict the context of the pandemic through their use of style, their romanticism, their representation of sexuality and time, and their dystopic viewpoint.

The film's plot is relatively straightforward. Edward (Steven Waddington) is named King upon his father's death. His first act is to write his exiled lover Gaveston (Andrew Tiernan) and command him to return and share his kingdom. Gaveston does so and misuses the King's favour as means of seeking vengeance on those responsible for his previous misfortune. The King's favour and Gaveston's own actions alienate Church and Nobility and Edward is forced to exile him. Queen Isabella (Tilda Swinton), who hungers for Edward's love, decides that she doesn't stand a chance until Gaveston is totally out of the way. She forms an alliance with Mortimer (Nigel Terry) to recall Gaveston so that he may be murdered. The result of this is a civil war which pits the King against his Lords and Bishops (led by Mortimer and Isabella, now a couple). The King loses and is executed (or is he?) by having a red-hot iron rod shoved up his arse.

Edward exemplified Ruby Rich's contention that New Queer Cinema is alternatively minimalist and excessive. Perhaps because of its television funding, the film is shot on an intimate scale: the film's framing predominantly ranges from close-up to medium long-shot. The camera barely moves. Most of the film is set in interiors and those are often bare. Setting is often suggested by a few selected props or costumes. Overhead lighting predominates but is often supplemented by one other source, strikingly visible in its dominance.

The film is excessive in various ways. First are its outsized characters and emotions. The old cliché used to advertise the sword and sandal spectacles of the Fifties, 'An epic story of sweeping emotion,' fits *Edward* well. However, in the Fifties 'epic' lengthy attempts were often made to depict an external reality by panoramically photographing thousands of costumed extras in a historical setting. Many of these films' scope was limited to the lenses they were shot with. *Edward* abdicates representation of external reality. The film is epic because, through its minimalist devices, it successfully conveys the sweeping scope of its subject matter: high-born people (King, Bishops, Nobles) fight for big stakes (a King's power) and the conflict is the setting for Big Emotions (Love, Desire and Hate, also the title of Jackie Collins' novel) which dramatize Big Themes (Good, Evil, Damnation, Redemption, Justice, Destiny). Edward is at the centre of the maelstrom.

The film may also be considered excessive in its use of props and costumes. Thus, for example, when the Queen and Mortimer play chess, they do so with gigantic peppermills. The costumes and accessories are also extravagant or caricatured, an array of gay male camp iconography: uniforms, elegant evening dress, designer accoutrements, leopard-skin coats, Levis and leather. These props and costumes (along with the dominant source of lighting), which would be a little *de trop* under any circumstance, seems more so against the stark setting.

Edward's excesses amount to more than a mere exercise in style. In the dedicatory page in *Queer Edward II*, the published script of *Edward II*, Derek Jarman asserts that, 'It is difficult enough to be queer, but to be queer in the cinema is almost impossible. Heterosexuals have fucked up the screen so completely that there's hardly room for us to kiss there'.[7] There is arguably even less room for us to feel. Most discourses on homosexuality have focused on the sexual element. The emotive has necessarily been repressed: in life for obvious reasons; in art because depicting feeling is not the usual route to representing the inhuman, the monstrous. This absence might be a reason why, in recent history at least, opera, genres like melodrama, and women stars who express feelings passionately have been so popular with gay men. For many of us, the excessive has often been only the mere grounds of possibility. Just as our sexuality is often regarded as transgressing the bounds of the socially acceptable, it has historically been forms that threaten to transgress the bounds of the aesthetically acceptable that seem to give us greater access to identification, that sometimes offer hints that 'we' (at least one other person like me and I) exist. Also, it has traditionally been mostly through that which is seen as excessive (any number of examples from Oscar Wilde to the films of Kenneth Anger) that we have been able to represent ourselves to ourselves at all.

The use of props and costumes in *Edward* are a visual means of camping around. Richard Dyer has written that 'to have a good camp together gives you a tremendous sense of identification and belonging. It is just about the only style, language and culture that is distinctively and unambiguously gay male'.[8] The excesses of prop and costume not only help communicate setting and character but signal a sensibility. In *Edward*, camp constitutes a form of address, a means of letting gays in the audience know that it is a gay film. Excess is one element of *Edward*'s style (indeed of Jarman's entire oeuvre) via which room is wrested from the history of cinema for us to kiss and feel. *Edward* goes even further by inverting at least some aspects of the dominant cinema's historical coding of sexual preference, a source of great pleasure to at least this gay spectator.

Heterosexuality is vilified in *Edward* in much the same way homosexuality has been throughout much of the cinema's history. This is done through attribution of certain characteristics and through visual coding.[9] Of the prominent heterosexual male characters in *Edward*, Kent, is like the old homo we were often invited to pity, Mortimer the fag we were often invited to fear. Kent looks like everyone else (one of the things that make homosexuals so dangerous), but reveals himself by his actions: well intentioned but ineffectual, cowardly, indecisive, easily swayed. Mortimer is like the old figure of the ruthless and decadent fag who still crops up in the occasional Chuck Norris movie. He is equally at home in uniforms and leopard-print house-coats. He kills and lets himself be whipped with as much ease and equal pleasure. His decadence is signified as much by his social position as by his sexual practices: Mortimer drinks cocktails and plays chess with the Queen; he is promiscuous, enjoys multiple partners and is a kinky masochist.

Isabella reminded me of the various representations of lesbians we used to see.[10] She is as coolly elegant as Candice Bergen in *The Group* (Sidney Lumet, USA, 1965), though from an even higher social stratum. Sexually manipulative, she can make men's lives even more miserable than Lauren Bacall did Kirk Douglas' in *Young Man with a Horn* (Michael Curtiz, USA, 1950). Heartless, she remains as unruffled by torture as the lesbian Nazi in *Rome, Open City* (Roberto Rossellini, Italy, 1945). Predatory, she stalks her quarry as calculatingly as Coral Brown in *The Killing of Sister George* (Robert Aldrich, UK/USA, 1968). Her neck bites are gruesome and just as fatal as any lesbian vampire. And like so many lesbians in the cinema, Isabella might have been different had she received that one good fuck. ('New queer cinema' has been criticized for the absence of women. But really, they're there – as mothers, bitches or background, just like in the dominant cinema.)

Edward's desire for Gaveston propels the narrative. Mortimer and Isabella are the blocks to its fulfilment. Edward's desire is so great it is tragic. Several times in the film, the King is asked 'Why shouldst thou love him whom the worlds hates so?' 'Because' answers Edward, 'he loves me more than all the world'. Another recurring line is 'Was ever a King as overruled as I?' These two lines, almost functioning as leitmotifs throughout the film, posit and respond to the King's dilemma. Edward loves him whom the world hates so because the despised Gaveston loves him best. But this is interpreted, in the words of Mortimer, as making him 'brain sick' and thus vulnerable to overrule. Edward's love is pure and selfless because the only gain he can hope from it is its return. It is tragic because it will be the cause of his ruin if not his death. It is romantic because as he tells Gaveston, 'Knowest thou not who I am? Thy friend, thy self, another Gaveston.' The film represents love in the romantic tradition, as a mystical merging of matching parts in which the incomplete self is lost in order to transcend to a more perfect union. And as in the romantic tradition, gambling one's life is but a small price for so sublime a prize.

Edward is willing to die for his love because without it he feels dead anyway. This is underlined by the mise-en-scene. When with Gaveston and unthreatened, Edward looks divinely fulfilled. He is dressed in gold, sky blue and, most often, white. The two, be it in bed or the throne room, are often bathed in a bright clean light which makes Edward's reddish-blonde hair shine like a halo. At the scene of their parting, ethereally lit, they dance together as Annie (*Diva*) Lennox achingly sings sublime Cole Porter which conveys what Marlowe would not let him utter: 'Every time we say goodbye, I die a little'. While there is still hope of Gaveston we are shown the King as a lesser being: he is often depicted in darkness, raging, dirty, sometimes with blood in his hands. With no hope of Gaveston, the King is literally underground, in the depths of a dungeon. And he is lit in earth tones, brown, amber, yellow. Sometimes there are dispersed, undulating rays cast over his body which have a slight blurring effect, as if he were underwater. The King is often shown lying down, shivering, defeated.

Heterosexuals are the source of all evil in *Edward*. But this does not result in a reified positive image of homosexuals. Gaveston, for example, I find a horror. The film makes it clear that he loves the King. But we are also told that the King's favour is also food for Gaveston's pride, his hunger for power and his vengefulness. 'I must have wanton poets, pleasant wits/musicians that with a touching of a string/may draw the pliant King which way I please', he says. Andrew Tiernan plays Gaveston like a malevolent satyr (he sometimes imitates poses that resemble photographs of Nijinsky in *Aprés-midi d'une faune*). Swinging naked in Edward's throne, he cackles with pleasure at the havoc he's causing. He tries to seduce Isabella to demonstrate his new power and is gleeful at her humiliation. In a frightening scene, after his thugs have undressed and beaten up the Bishop of Winchester, Gaveston forces his false teeth from him, blessed him with them and pushes him to the ground. Gaveston is no 'positive image' of a gay man.

Edward, like *Idaho*, depicts various homosexual men. Near the film's beginning we are shown Gaveston and Spencer with two sailors with whom they have presumably just had sex. Upon receiving Edward's summons to join him in England, he dismisses them by saying, 'there are places for men like you'. Gaveston obviously does not see himself as one of them. The film indicates that the class divide is not manifested merely in terms of access to goods. It also offers different possibilities of being in the world. But Edward and Gaveston overestimate the powers of class to shield their sexual orientation. They are unable to imagine the reverse – that socially transgressive sexual practices can be the excuse for stripping away class privilege. The reason that the nobles turn on Edward is not because he is sleeping with Gaveston but because he is publicly elevating him. Edward and Gaveston could have had homosexual sex in private. It is for publicly expressing their love and their sexual longing that they get punished. They die for flaunting it.

Edward demonstrates how gay men can be different depending on personal qualities (the differences between the King and Gaveston for example) and how men can be gay differently (depending upon class or other factors). Yet, though the film depicts various types of homosexuals, unlike *Idaho* it assumes only one paradigm of homosexuality – the 1970s Gay Lib one.[11] In its ideal form this can be characterized in the following terms: binarisms – only the two poles of the Kinsey scale are recognized, one is either heterosexual or homosexual; essence – the myth of the 'eternal homosexual' D'Emilio denounces; ontology – homosexuals are the same as heterosexuals except they happen to love members of the same sex.

My deliberate reductiveness is evidenced by the film. Edward has a son so he must have closed his eyes and thought of the succession. But until she forms her alliance with Mortimer, Isabella is explicitly sexually frustrated ('Oh, how a

Activating Theory: Lesbian, Gay and Bisexual Politics

kiss revives poor Isabella'). The film also tells us that homosexuals have been around forever. As Kent says of Edward:

> Let him without controlment have his will.
> The mightiest Kings have had their minions,
> Great Alexander loved Hephestion,
> The conquering Hercules for Hylas wept,
> And for Patroclus stern Achilles drooped;
> And not King only, but the wisest men;
> The Roman Tully loved Octavius,
> Grave Socrates, Wild Alcibiades.

Gayness in *Edward* is also depicted by the usual characteristics: Edward, for example, is beautiful, sensitive, he loves the arts, he works out. Yet in *Edward* heterosexuals and homosexuals are not the same. As I demonstrated earlier the film attributed all the negative qualities generally associated with homosexuality to its heterosexual characters (while retaining the more positive ones). Thus, even though sexual orientation is distinctly differentiated within the diegesis, a possible extra-diegetic reading is an even stronger argument for gays being just like straights. But this line of reasoning can only be taken up to a certain point.

In *Edward* gayness is depicted as a political identity. The film illustrates Simon Watney's assertion that 'What the term "gay" does insist upon is a political and legal *unity of interest* between subjects variously categorized as perverse/sick/mad/queer/contagious and so on'.[12] Edward is in danger of losing his throne because he flaunts his sexual orientation. In the film heterosexuals attribute a whole litany of pejorative characteristics to gays with which to better remove them from the public sphere. They are 'brain sick', 'girl-boy' and 'God, himself is up in arms [against them]'. Edward's self-identification as part of another community is a means to combat this oppression. A shared sexual orientation with his jailor may prevent his death. While a shared experience of oppression is an impetus for members of this community to join Edward in struggle.

86

Death, Desire and Identity

Death overhangs *Edward* as much as it did *Idaho*. Many members of the audience would be familiar with the story of Edward's demise before seeing the movie. The film itself begins with the death of Edward's father. It also actively foreshadows Edward's death. The jailor is shown heating the iron, sometimes a shadow of him holding the smoking iron is reflected on the wall of Edward's cell where it connotes a caress of a huge, orgasmic penis. Brutal killings, Gaveston's, Mortimer's, Spencer's and a host of lesser characters, are explicitly depicted throughout. Yet *Edward*'s makers are hesitant to let Edward die. His murder is shown as a red-drenched premonition. But the audience is left wondering whether it is fulfilled. The scene is followed by his jailor dramatically extinguishing the hot rod by throwing it in the sewer and then kissing Edward. But the film does not end here. On the one hand, to have given *Edward* a happy ending, contravening Marlowe's play and what we know of historical circumstances, would perhaps have come across as just plain false. On the other hand, perhaps ending the film with a scene in which a gay man dies because he's had a penile object inserted in his rectum would butress the prejudice that gay sex equals death and provide fuel for homophobes. In any case, the film then backtracks.

In the next scene, the last one, we get mournful music, chiaroscuro lighting, and the camera pans left over an army of activists ('Gay Desire is Not a Crime', says the T-shirt of one of them), their placards on the floor, heads bowed as Edward's voice tells us, 'I know not, but of this I am assured,/That death ends all, and I can die but once'. We then hear a flutter of strings, the screen fades to black and Edward's voice continues, 'Come death, and with thy fingers close my eyes,/Or if I live let me forget myself.'

The film is ambivalent about hope. It is almost as if there is a wish for hope in the face of hopelessness. Two aspects of the film illustrate this. One is the gay activists. There is no question that the film valorizes their community, their struggle and the way that they fight back. At the end they are shown heads bowed, music mournful, with talk of death via voiceover. But this can be read as a moment of mourning for what has been lost rather than as a defeat. Certainly, they are unified and, even at the end of the film, in much better circumstances than, as we will see, Isabella and Mortimer whom in *Edward* represent the repressive state apparatus.

The role of Edward's son in the narrative can also be read as a wish for hope. He is the new generation. He travels freely between the gay camp and the straight camp bearing witness to all the atrocities, vulnerable to some, implicated in others. He watches in horror as his mother kills Kent with her own teeth, is terrified for his own future ('What safety may I look for?') but nevertheless dips a finger in his own uncle's blood for a taste. Yet, if we read the young prince as the future, then the future is gay. In a key sequence in the last scene of the film, between the King and his jailor kissing and the mourning militants, we are shown a shot of the young Prince (now crowned) sitting on the throne in vestments of state. This is followed by a medium close-up of the new King dancing to his walkman, wearing lipstick and huge earrings. The camera then pulls back and we see that he is dancing with his mother's shoes over a cage in which Isabella and Mortimer crouch, defeated, dishevelled and smeared in white make-up to connote the living dead. The new King is dancing on the cage of the vanquished previous regime to the tune of Tchaikovsky's 'Dance of the Sugar Plum Fairy'. This is the return of the repressed with a vengeance. Yet what could have been a triumphal final message is mitigated by the sequence of the mourning militants which end the film.

Edward's attempts at utopia are also tempered by its representation of time. In *Imagined Communities*, Benedict Anderson writes about how time in the Middle Ages was depicted as 'a simultaneity of past and future in an instantaneous present'.[13] *Edward* achieves a similar effect through narrative structure and mise-en-scene. In some respects, the narrative is quite traditional: original equilibrium is disturbed, events happen through cause and effect, new problems are resolved until the climax and a return to a new equilibrium; the original death and new reign at the beginning is replaced by at least a perceived death and another new reign at the end. However, the film is structured around flashbacks. It actually begins with Edward in his dungeon awaiting death and then flashes back to his being named King and calling for Gaveston. Throughout the rest of the film we will return to Edward in his dungeon. The information we get there will sometimes refer specifically to his present in the dungeon, sometimes it will convey information that helps tell the story of his past and sometimes it will be a flash-forward premonition. In other words the story is clearly told, giving the impression of chronological development as in Marlowe's play but in fact the plot takes us through different time schemes. The story's illusion of diachrony is achieved through synchronic plotting of space and time.

Time is also mixed through the mise-en-scene's use of anachronism. The film retains Marlowe's speech and is set in the fourteenth century but characters often wear contemporary clothing and have access to modern appliances. Likewise, the medieval power struggles in Marlowe's text becomes affirmative collective actions à la OutRage but fought with shotguns as well as demonstrations and media coverage.

The mixture of times in *Edward* contributes to a sense of hopelessness. In the Middle Ages the simultaneity of past and future in an instantaneous present was read through a belief in destiny and divinity. Such a hermeneutic is no longer available to us because the beliefs in which it was rooted now enjoy little currency. But if men and women are to make history, even under conditions not of their choosing, then it is necessary to imagine a distinct and different future in which changes can be made. Time is represented in *Edward* as if Walter Benjamin's Angel of History were periodically to take a peek at the future and find it so much worse that he'd speed back to the past only to get caught in the storm once more and be propelled through an already experienced present/future over and over again. The storm is no longer called progress and the disasters at his feet are known. He would, to use Benjamin's words, still 'like to stay, awaken the dead, and make whole what has been smashed,'[14] but no longer sees the point. If the future is no different from the past, if homosexuals are condemned to chronic oppression, why Act Up?

The film is its own answer to this question. For the very attempt to represent a gay dystopia, as well as the way it is represented, are themselves utopian gestures. Fredric Jameson has written that 'interpretation is not an isolated act, but takes place within a Homeric battlefield'.[15] The same necessarily applies to representation. *Edward* can be situated in the middle of the battlefield using its style and even its romanticism as weapons with which to win particular meanings from histories of visual vocabularies predisposed against them so as to be able to give a different view, tell a new story, even if it is via an old one.

Mourning and Militancy

The world we live in, and the way we live in it, has changed to such an extent that we are often told we live in a new era. Some call it Postmodernity, others Late Capitalism, or Post-Fordist society or New Times. The variety of terms, each categorising entire bodies of literature, indicate divergent views over how the world has changed and what it is now like. But I think many would agree that Western capitalist societies are increasingly characterized by fragmentation, diversity and difference. Postmodernism is seen by many to be the dominant aesthetic mode of this new epoch. Jameson calls it the cultural logic of late capitalism.[16] To demonstrate that recent films made by gay men utilize irony and pastiche, represent fragmented subjectivities, depict a compression of time with sometimes dehistoric results, and that they are dystopic, is another way of arguing that gay men also live in this new world. Such attributes describe any number of non-gay postmodern works equally well. This new world, however, is experienced differently by gay men in various ways.

Speaking of New Times, a debate generated by the former

Communist Party of Great Britain and *Marxism Today*, Stuart Hall and Martin Jacques write that 'The argument here is not that we have suddenly moved from one world to another ... Rather, it is suggested that, in the last decade or so, we have witnessed a qualitative change, which has shifted the centre of gravity of the society and the culture markedly and decisively in a new direction'.[17] What also happened in the last decade or so, however, was the appearance of what turned out to be a pandemic. AIDS resulted in an epochal change for gay men, one that was socially experienced precisely as if we had suddenly moved from one world to another. These changes affected all aspects of our lives, for many of us markedly changing the way we live them. On this issue, Douglas Crimp is worth quoting at length:

> we are blamed, belittled, excluded, derided. We are discriminated against, lose our housing and jobs, and are denied medical and life insurance. Every public agency whose job it is to combat the epidemic has been slow to act, failed entirely, or been deliberately counterproductive. We have therefore had to provide our own centers for support, care, and education and even to fund and conduct our own treatment research. We have had to rebuild our devastated community and culture, reconstruct our sexual relationships, reinvent our sexual pleasure. Despite great achievements in so short a time and under such adversity, the dominant media still pictures us only as wasting deathbed victims; we have therefore had to wage a war of representation, too.[18]

Crimp is speaking of people who are seropositive. But I think many of his observations are applicable to gay men in general. The fact that HIV may take years to manifest itself and that the pandemic has hit gay communities with devastating force means that, though everyone is a possible seropositive, gay men's lived relation to this possibility is much more immanent. This understanding that we are at special risk has affected the construction of our communities, our views of society, sexuality, bodies, relationships, time, history and culture. Though there are obvious continuities (we were belittled and oppressed before the pandemic; many of us

91

carry our pre-pandemic past as a component of our present subjectivity), AIDS has affected what amounts to an epistemic shift in gay culture. We know different things about ourselves and we know ourselves differently (and part of this change is a questioning of who is 'we' and what is the self). AIDS is why there is New Queer Cinema and it is what New Queer Cinema is about.

AIDS has resulted in an unprecedented degree of organization of gay men at all levels. Organizing around health issues has developed personal skills as well as infrastructure which can then be put to various uses. The context of the pandemic has created a demand for representation, both political and artistic at a time when representation in the media increasingly becomes a precondition for political representation. Broadcasting and journalism are still largely closed off to us and video doesn't enjoy the same prestige as film and subsequently garners less attention. But films get broadcast and talked about on TV and in newspapers. The context of AIDS has provided gay men's cinema with various types of subject matter, demanded of it new forms of expression, created new channels for its distribution, and helped to create a market for it.

The effects of this socio-political context is evident in New Queer Cinema. I think it no accident that the moniker mostly refers to films made by gay men from either North America or England. The pandemic has affected Britain, Canada and the United States differently. Because all of those countries have a different socio-political make-up, gay men in each of them have experienced the pandemic differently (class, 'race', ethnicity, geography and other factors of course contribute to different relations to the pandemic within each country). But, while acknowledging cultural specificity (so obvious in *Edward* and *Idaho*), I think we must also recognize a shared Anglo-North American gay culture. As *Edward* and *Idaho* attest, gay cultural production travels across these three countries with relative ease.[19]

It is significant that a Spanish film such as *Las cosas del querer* (Jaime Chavarri, 1989) that was exhibited in North

America contemporaneously with *Swoon* is not deemed New
and Queer. It too exhibits traces of appropriation, irony and
pastiche. It too goes back to the past and tries for some Social
Constructionism via attempting to recreate/imagine a history
of gay people in Franco's Spain. Heterosexuality in *Las Cosas*
is also a block to the fulfillment of the gay man's desire (he's in
love with a straight man). Finally, the story is also dystopic –
the gay man is exiled from Spain because of his sexuality.
However, the narrative is quite traditional and a culture of
AIDS is also absent from the film. These factors are not
unrelated.

I tried to demonstrate earlier that *Idaho* and *Edward*, along
with important differences, share equally important similarities: a purposeful stylishness; an evocation of imagined
histories via a representation of time in which past, present
and future co-mingle; a privileging of romantic homosexual
desire; heterosexuality as a symbolic blockage to homosexual
coupling; and narrative in which death and decay figure
prominently. Many of these characteristics are evident to
different extents in films as varied as *Swoon, Poison, Looking
for Langston, The Making of Monsters* and *The Living End*.
The political unconscious of all of these films (or the conscious
in the case of *The Living End* and others), are attempts to
grapple with the ways in which the pandemic has changed our
lives. Their style and narrative structure, however different,
are attempts to represent them.

All of these films are purposefully stylish because they are
struggling to represent a new context against the legacies of
both dominant cinema and, as we can see in *Swoon, Looking
for Langston* (Isaac Julien, UK, 1989), *Poison* and *Tongues
Untied* (Marlon Riggs, USA, 1989), a previous history of gay
representation (though they borrow as much as they reject).
They try to place gays in history because imagining gays in
history is to a certain extent a way of legitimising present
existence and, more importantly, a way of imagining a future.
They represent a view of time which reflects a changed sense
of mortality. Gay desire leads to death in most of these films.
But the films' romanticism creates dead queer movies very

different from *Cruising*. Characters in New Queer Cinema do not die of a kinky fuck, they die for love. The films are often dystopic because they are made in a context in which death, directly or indirectly, has touched us all.

New Queer Cinema, then, may be read as works of mourning. But in a context in which, as David Harvey has argued, 'images are increasingly important to identity ... [and] image makers and the media assume a more powerful role in the shaping of political identities'[20], they must also be read as militant gestures, a particular form of ACTing-UP, and thus utopian. Films like *Idaho* and *Edward* are not only attempts to represent a new historical context for gay men. Their very existence constitute an effort to change it.

Notes

I would like to thank Joseph Bristow, Kirsten McAllister, Martin Stollery and Carl Stychin for their feedback while writing this essay.

[1] Ruby Rich, 'New Queer Cinema', *Sight and Sound* 2:5 (1992), p32.

[2] See, for example, Constance Penley's 'Feminism, Psychoanalysis, and the Study of Popular Culture', in Lawrence Grossberg, Cary Nelson and Paul Treichler, eds, *Cultural Studies* (New York: Routledge, 1992), pp479–493.

[3] According to Fredric Jameson, 'the whole paradox of what we have here called the subtext may be summed up in this, that the literary work or cultural object, as though for the first time, brings into being that very situation to which it is also, at one and the same time, a reaction. It articulates its own situation and textualizes it, thereby encouraging and perpetuating the illusion that the situation itself did not exist before it, that there is nothing but a text, that there never was any extra- or con-textual reality before the text itself generated it in the form of a mirage'. See *The Political Unconscious: Narrative as a Socially Symbolic Act* (Ithaca, NY: Cornell University Press, 1981), pp81–82. See also Jameson's discussion of Althusser's notion of History as absent cause, Necessity and the Real in the same volume: pp74–102.

[4] *Idaho* borrows several plot elements (Scott and Mike scaring their own colleagues and then stealing their bounty, for example) and several bits of dialogue from Shakespeare's *King Henry the Fourth – Part One*. This speech is adapted from Prince Hal's soliloquy at the end of Scene II in Act V when Prince Hal says,

And nothing pleaseth but rare accidents.

So, when this loose behaviour I throw off
And pay the debt I never promised,
By how much better than my word I am,
By so much shall I falsify men's hopes;
And, like bright metal on a sullen ground,
My reformation, glitt'ring o'er my fault,
Shall show more goodly and attract more eyes
Than that which hath no foil to set it off.
I'll so offend to make offence a skill,
Redeeming time when men think least I will.

See *William Shakespeare: The Complete Works*, ed. by Peter Alexander (London: Collins, 1951), p483.

[5] John D'Emilio, 'Capitalism and Gay Identity', in Ann Snitow, Christine Stansell and Sharon Thompson, eds, *Powers of Desire: The Politics of Sexuality* (New York: Monthly Review Press, 1983), p109.

[6] *Ibid.*, p109.

[7] Derek Jarman, *Queer Edward II* (London: BFI Publishing, 1991), frontispiece.

[8] Richard Dyer, 'It's Being So Camp As To Keep Us Going', *Only Entertainment* (London: Routledge, 1992), p135.

[9] See, for example, Vito Russo's *The Celluloid Closet: Homosexuality in the Movies* (New York: Harper and Row, 1981).

[10] According to Andrea Weiss, many of these representations still offered pleasures to at least some lesbian spectators because, among other reasons, they were open to various readings and 'audiences bring their own personal experiences and social histories to the viewing of films, and these obviously differ widely among lesbians.' See *Vampires and Violets: Lesbians in the Cinema* (London: Jonathan Cape, 1992), p66.

[11] Derek Jarman's work brings up interesting questions in relation to New Queer Cinema which I do not deal with in this piece but which may be worth pointing out. First, since there seems to be so much stylistic and thematic continuity in his oeuvre, what (aside from AIDS) makes *Edward II*, as opposed to his other movies, a New Queer film? The second issue which I find very interesting is that of generational difference. Jarman, as we can see from his autobiographies, was very much influenced by the Gay Lib Movement: see particularly *At Your Own Risk: A Saint's Testament* (London: Vintage, 1992). One can argue, though perhaps in an overly narrow auteris sense, that this informs his representation of identity in *Edward*. In any case it's substantially different than the way it is represented by Todd Haynes or Tom Kalin, filmmakers of a different generation whose identities as gay men were shaped in the pandemic.

[12] Cited in Joseph Bristow, 'Being Gay: Politics, Identity, Pleasure', *New Formations* 9 (1989), p61.

[13] Benedict Anderson, *Imagined Communities: Reflections on the Origin and Spread of Nationalism* (London: Verso, 1988), p30.

[14] Walter Benjamin 'Theses on the Philosophy of History', *Illuminations*, ed, Hannah Arendt, trans. Harry Zohn (New York: Schocken Books), p257.

[15] Fredric Jameson, *The Political Unconscious*, p13.

[16] As we can see from the title of his book, *Postmodernism or the Cultural Logic of Late Capitalism* (Durham: Duke University Press, 1991).

[17] Stuart Hall and Martin Jacques, 'Introduction', in Stuart Hall and Martin Jacques, eds, *New Times: The Changing Face of Politics in the 1990s* (London: Lawrence and Wishart, 1989), p12.

[18] Douglas Crimp, 'Mourning and Militancy', *October* 51 (1989), pp15–16.

[19] I would assume one could say the same about other English-speaking industrialized countries such as Australia and New Zealand. But as I am not too familiar with gay cultures in these countries, this must remain an assumption.

[20] David Harvey, *The Condition of Postmodernity* (London: Basil Blackwell, 1989), p289.

'Queer Nigger': Theorizing 'White' Activism

HELEN (CHARLES)

I have noticed that when language is spoken, as opposed to read, the full stop and the comma can be accommodated fairly adequately by pausing. To ensure that the audience understands that the speaker understands the inadequacies of present-day language – both written and spoken – it has been necessary either to eliminate all traces of quotations marks around words, thereby risking the confusion of the listener, or to wiggle intermittently both forefingers in the air, well above the head, so that there is no mistaking the fact that the word or phrase being said is either laced with irony or has not had sufficient new language to explain its multiple meanings, its history, its future possible death.

Since it takes a written form, this chapter avoids much of the possible confusion. All you have to do is be aware of the punctuation. In this chapter, the word 'queer', since it has an illustrative role, will sometimes be surrounded by quotation marks. On some occasions, it bears a capital Q, while on others, it remains, so to speak, unclothed. This multiple identity foreshadows the linguistic testing-ground. Queer is a word that has not been fully appropriated and used in the lesbian and gay community, even if it has been around for ages. The word 'negro' was around for a while too, and if I were to use it here it would also have to be equipped with 'decorative' quotations marks since it is no longer part of our everyday language. This before and after construction sets up the parameters of some aspects of cultural identity, and in the middle a process of deconstruction can occur, until it breathes its last contemporary breath.

To go back to the word 'negro': we know that it is no longer used. The word 'coloured', on the other hand, is having a hard time dying, particularly in the suburbs. In the Harlem Renaissance of the 1930s, Langston Hughes, Zora Neale Hurston, and others on the scene were described as 'New Negroes' and were part of a literary movement called the 'Nigerati'. It is the tongue-in-cheek reclamation of language (re)construction that for some makes the right statement at the time. This modification, with its pejorative roots, carries inspiration but also bitter cynicism.

The word 'nigger' has long been used in African-American language, and is not frowned upon in the way that it would be in Britain. In the 1960s school playground, it was still possible to receive the pejorative name-tags 'queer' and 'nigger'. They are both still alive and kicking. I wonder how many American bands with names like Niggers With Attitude it will take before younger British generations see a non-controversial side to this appellation. I wonder how 'Queer' is going down in the suburbs of small British towns. Queer culture is urban and metropolitan, not universal. Speaking to the old and new middle classes, the old and new perverts, is 'Queer' speaking to potential 'new niggers'?

This essay was a first to me, in terms of exposure, articulation politics, academic ponderings on a public platform, and being able to sit together with another black woman at a virtually all-white conference. The pressures on black women academics are such that we are often in isolation from one another: a handful of 'minoritized' people, dispersed throughout this country, making communication *between* us problematic to say the least.

I was offered the opportunity to say something about 'identity' at this conference. Did this mean that I was to switch to token status? The likelihood was probable, so how do I position myself? Would the dual presence of Inge

Blackman and myself make any impact on the audience – and, if so, would it be political or aesthetic?[1] Is our non-singular black visibility odd in any way? Is it queer?

I chose to speak on queerness because it's topical. And in doing so, I place myself in the fashion-statement hierarchy. What I am really doing, though, is trying to discover whether queer is something I understand from several different and interchangeable angles – woman or black woman, feminist or black feminist or womanist, zami or lesbian or khush or dyke or lezzie, black or mixed-race or of colour, working-class or middle-class, differently abled or partially (dis)abled, activist or theorist. Hopefully, you will begin to see, if you don't see already, the multiple position that some of us are in. It's a wonderful position at times, and can be very useful when you find yourself (as you do) in such diverse situations, places or company. But people who are seen by the dominant culture as 'other' or 'different' (and that goes for the dominant cultures *within* subcultures too) do not necessarily see themselves as such. Some of us simply see anybody who isn't *us* as someone 'other'. Nice and simple.

Being white seems to be nice and simple too. For example, 'whiteness' is still not being widely seen in this country, northern Europe, or North America as an ethnicity, as a colour, as pertaining to anything to do with 'race'. Why? Is it simply because there are so many white people in comparison to the so-called 'non-whites' that there exists widespread occlusion within the 'white' community? I have often wondered whether white people *know* that they are white. I know that Richard Dyer does.[2] And if they do, is it only when their notion of the 'other' as 'non-white' is placed before them? Is it only when the binary opposition of white and 'black' or 'Asian' is within their field of vision? And can they only speak for themselves from the borrowed position of who they construe as 'other'?

From the small amount of literature that I have been able to read, together with the couple of conferences I've attended and the conversations I've held, I have not been able to come any closer to a clear definition of what Queer is or what it

99

attempts to be. Instead, I have found that, like the early attempts at defining postmodernism and global feminism, what surfaces in the process of analysis is the sense that an eclectic 'anything goes' understanding is required to be posited.

So what I'm offering to you is a shopping list of questions and conjectures, which by its very nature itemizes purchases of theory-based packages – if, that is, they are in stock. And if they are not, it leaves me wondering whether they are needed in the first place. Are they luxuries to be avoided in these times of economic chaos? Or are they essential in order to get through these times of sexual chaos?

The AIDS epidemic has released another sexual aesthetic. I think it's debatable whether it's an aesthetic that is 'new and different'. It has triggered a no-time-to-waste, fast pace, no-nonsense activism from which I think Queer is a direct descendant. Queer posture is transgressive, rude-positive, non-accommodationist, risky. It reminds me of my sex-life, and of a recent article by Pat Califia where she says: 'Sex has always been a high-risk activity'.[3] Risk, then, appears to be one of the non-optional ingredients of Queer. An awareness of it as it crosses and pans in and out of daily existence. A criticism of it when it takes over the body that was not in the too distant past attached to words like 'struggle' and 'subordination' and 'empowering'. Now these words can be replaced by borrowing words from other cultures, like 'nation', or by using popular expletives, like 'fuck', all of which nestle under the protective umbrella of 'queer'. Will it soon be risqué to say 'I'm a Queer feminist'? Will Queer manifest itself as an inadequate term in isolation? Will it begin to gather appendages, like Jewish middle-class rad-fem queer?

Choosing to be outside the so-called dominant sexual culture always involves a sense of risk: exposure, ridicule, queerbashing, and so on. The choice already incorporates and has developed aspects of strategies that Queer Nation and OutRage employ – simply by refusing to live by the rules of mainstream society. And lots of so-called straight people do this too. There are always hierarchies, ones which are constructed by people more privileged than others. To *know* that privileged queers will be able to understand, support, and back up newcomers to the queer movement without using patronizing language and behaviour is a little difficult if you have had some experience of this before. Prior knowledge of these things puts you in a strong position because you can make better decisions for yourself, and your choice is still with you. If you find that your voice is not being listened to at meetings, you either fight (which automatically puts you on a lower rung) or you go away, never to return again.

The way I see the direction of Queer is that it is not only aimed at mainstream gay and lesbian peoples. It has 'perversion' as a reverse-discourse strategy sitting next to it, and this title is being used to attract *anybody*. Queer sex could be inter-racial straight SM or celibacy with an 8'' dildo. Queer theory could be a straight white woman talking about gay men's camp or a black straight man talking about lesbian desire. If this is going to break down the barriers of racism, sexism and homophobia, fine. If it is merely glossing over difference(s) and inequality, not fine.

Recently, I've been getting the feeling that the new brand of sexuality status as QUEER has been offered to me in various guises: at recent seminars and conferences, the word has slipped in and out of conversations at coffee time as the sign of the times. The speaker either questions that status or simply assumes or knows that the listener will take on board the arrival of a new striving-to-be-dominant ideology. No questions asked, for fear that what's 'in your face' will show up a lack of the 'get with it' mentality or expose a sense of uncertainty about the term which might indicate a refusal to accept it. But what may be happening, as with all new definitions, is that some people like to know a bit more about the product before buying it. And some people, even if a little unconvinced, will think 'what the hell, I'll try it and see'. But what happens when you get the product home, open it, sample it in your own surroundings? What happens to the definition of 'queer' when you're washing up or having a wank? When you're aware of a misplacement or displacement in your colour, gender, identity? Do they get subsumed, as Gloria Anzaldúa says, into a homogeneous category, where class and other things that make up a cultural identity are ignored?'⁴ Gloria Anzaldúa also has concerns about defining herself as queer, although she accepts the term. Her point is that she is Chicana first and foremost, then come the rest of the titles in her identity. But her concerns move outwards from her Chicana identity towards the realm of those writers who would call themselves Queer. She asks: 'Can a straight woman or man write a lesbian story?'⁵ Obviously, that's entirely possible. Some of you may remember when a book written by a man (Toby Forward) was almost published under an Asian female pseudonym by Virago Press. So these things are always possible. But the signals I seem to be getting from the wider context of Queer culture suggest that in the 1990s it would be cool to do such things. It would be transgressive enough for 'Toby Forward' to achieve a Queer culture membership card. You wouldn't have to be ethnic-specific or gender-specific anymore. Will that phase out overt or covert racism? Sexism? Will it?

When I read Cherry Smyth's *Lesbians Talk Queer Notions* I was eager to see what all the hype about Queer was from a lesbian point of view. It was to introduce me, in edible portions, to what queer meant to over twenty-five people, the majority of whom were women. I went straight to the section entitled 'What's in a Name', which said:

> Each time the word 'queer' is used it defines a strategy, an attitude, a reference to other identities and a new self-understanding. (And queer can be qualified as 'more queer', 'queerer' or 'queerest' as the naming develops into a more complex process of identification.)⁶

The sentence in parentheses was what interested me. A visible hierarchy of queer positions. The foregone conclusion that comparatives ('queerer') and superlatives ('queerest') would be the given order of an enhanced queer identity. And that queer identity, of course, *had* to be part of a complex process. Getting identities together is pretty complex already

(I speak for myself), and although I'm not unhappy with the fragmented possibilities of my own cultural identity, I wonder at the thought that maybe the next thing on the agenda will be the suggestion that 'Nigger' should be transported from the British playground and placed into a reverse-discourse theory and practice. What would be the superlative of 'Nigger'? Would it have a capital 'N'? Would an indefinite article be needed, or could it exist naked, in the way that 'queer' is portrayed in Cherry Smyth's book?

Does queer go up in a puff of smoke only to materialize when its bottle is rubbed in the right direction? Ultimately, is Queer something we feel we have to pin down, utilize, define, in order for it to be comfortably accepted by a majority? (And I'm not talking about the dominant culture here.) And, if so, is it necessary to do it at breakneck speed?

I hoped Cherry Smyth's book would help me write this essay. And it did, in so far as my feeling easier about the knowledge that Queer did not pertain to any single philosophy or discourse. It meant that I could say I was still uncertain but less unclear about the Queer movement, and that I still had some worries about its activism being dominated by that strange category of people who are 'white, male, and middle-class'. I am hoping that it is well-known in the 'community' that 'queer' and 'dyke' are working-class words taken up by the middle classes. That from the mid-nineteenth century there was a rush towards defining, categorizing, and inventing new words and phrases. That nineteenth-century sexologists wanted to coin everything in sight – sadomasochism, homosexual, invert. That one of the meanings of the word 'gay' defined prostitutes and sex workers as 'loose women'. Nineteenth-century sexual diseases triggered a heightened awareness of sexuality. It is no longer taboo to create and realize fantasy, but there still exists the risk factor.

AIDS and HIV came at a time when most of us would not remember syphilis. But we have the memory of sexual disease through cultural traditions – 'sin', for example. In different cultural legacies that have been passed down to us, there is a fear without knowing why. AIDS has reactivated those fears. But this time, for most of us – and, I think, particularly for older lesbians and gay men – the 'struggle' (these words never die out, do they?) is in the 'Now'. And sometimes it is frightening to be in the *know*.

With AIDS and HIV at the forefront of consciousness – or, hopefully, at least somewhere on the back burner – there appears to be a rush towards defining the sexual self in a way that tries to cancel out any notion of 'otherness' within now-queer, new-queer communities. The word 'Queer' has implications for welcoming and establishing people new to the lesbian and gay scene and those seasoned queers who have been 'with it' for a long time.

It seems to me that Queer cannot be entirely pinned down – yet. It seems that is the make-up of its structure – if it has one. For there is only 'transgression', fast becoming a nebulous term, as a point on which to focus. The fact of queer identity is confined by a breaking of the limits. It's what actually attempts to break limits, it's what is disturbed. It's what will manifest itself uncomfortably within the arena of transgression as transgression loses its fashionable status. For transgression's sake, it must soon be introduced as the *ultimate* transgression. Ultra-transgression? Like guerrilla warfare, Queer's sexuality (as a homogeneous or heterogeneous display) uses the method of re-exploiting its own packaging. Through clothes, hairstyles and what is generally called 'gender-fucking', the new image of 'get used to it' sexualities sets out to make it as uncomfortable as possible for the straight mind in *every* part of each community. There is, of course, a parallel here with the 'get used to it' Black Power movement of the 1960s.

The spate of Reclaim the Night Marches comes to mind at this juncture. When white feminists took to the streets in the 1970s, there was the same 'in your face, get used to it' attitude. Okay. But there was also something that some white feminists hadn't thought of: some streets were black neighbourhoods where, at the time, it was the walking-down-the-street-rights of black boys and men, in particular, that were being infringed. Exclusion politics are subtle but rife within the British women's movement. Are exclusion politics also to be an unexpressed factor of the Queer movement? White gay men orientated this queer thing. Are white women being tagged along?

I keep getting information that Queer is theory *and* activist-bsaed. Does this mean that, perhaps for the first time, theory and activism have found a meaningful relationship with each other? If it is, do you still have to view each 'partner' as a separate, individual entity:

theory = 'New Queer Cinema'; the writings of Eve Kosofsky Sedgwick or Judith Butler;[7]
activism = 'Queer as Fuck' T-shirts *not* underneath a jumper.

If queer was a book, it would not start with the words of experience politics – i.e. 'I grew up in …'. There is a strong sense that, psychologically, queer is not trying to justify itself. And I would agree with this method in principle. But I *do* want it to justify having black lesbians and gay men, and white women in it.

This brings me to blackness as a masking ethnicity. Are black lesbians and gay men becoming accommodationist while being co-opted into Queer? I did that when I joined a white women's consciousness-raising group in 1977. Once bitten, twice pissed off.

Queer activism might die because of its limited diverse numbers, not to say the dominant forces of straight society. It might die also because of greater popularity in the kind of Queerism that is not pounding the streets or mailing letters to the homophobic media. Queer looks like it's in for aestheticizing itself into avant-garde filmic representations. Maybe that is the best place for it. Direct action will continue as it always did, and supporting campaigns like Black Lesbians and Gays Against Media Homophobia will be just as important whether you define yourself· as Queer or not. Although Queer's militancy is strategy-orientated, the striving-to-be-eclectic composition of queers is failing to list its ingredients on its product. And when the sell-by date arrives, it will inevitably be too late.

Jonathan Dollimore said at a conference held at the ICA in London (October 1992) that 'Queer is the ruination of identity'. In this single sentence, you have the constructs of any new or revamped movement. There is the problem of juggling the stability that is required in identity-formation with the unstable passage of desire.

Now think of Queer without its quotation marks. Linguistically, it becomes the norm – subsumed into the ease of a dominant language but without the polemic of the 'Queer Nigger' that might come next.

I'm thinking of Gloria Anzaldúa's words again. She quotes from Dianna Williamson's commentary on ' "To(o) Queer the Writer": "Where are our alliances, in our culture or in our crotch?".' And I would like to ask: Can our alliances be in each other's differences *and* in our dicks, dildos, arses, tits and clits?

Notes

I would like to thank, as always, Tina Papoulias for being a true source of inspiration. Also, thanks to Cherry Smyth for writing back.

[1] Inge Blackman, 'Queer as Fuck: But What the Fuck is Queer?', paper delivered at Activating Theory: Lesbian Gay Bisexual Politics, University of York, October 1992.
[2] Richard Dyer. 'White', *Screen* 29:4 (1988), 44–65.
[3] Pat Califia, 'Slipping', in Dennis Cooper, ed., *Discontents: New Queer Writers* (New York: Amethyst Press, 1992), p95.
[4] Gloria Anzaldúa, 'To(o) Queer the Writer – Loca, escritora y chicana', in Betsy Warland, ed., *Inversions: Writings by Dykes, Queers, and Lesbians* (London: Open Letters, 1992), p250.
[5] *Ibid.*, p256.
[6] Cherry Smyth, *Lesbians Talk Queer Notions* (London: Scarlet Press, 1992), p20.
[7] See Eve Kosofsky Sedgwick, *Epistemology of the Closet* (Hemel Hempstead: Harvester-Wheatsheaf, 1991), and Judith Butler, *Gender Trouble: Feminism and the Subversion of Identity* (New York: Routledge, 1990).
[8] Anzaldúa, 'To(o) Queer the Writer – Loca, escritora y chicana', in Warland, ed., *Inversions*, p252. Anzaldúa notes that Williamson's (apparently unpublished) commentary to her essay is dated April 1991.

Is Transgression Transgressive?

ELIZABETH WILSON

In a 1990 paper on postmodernism, given at the Socialist Scholars' Conference in Sydney, Mervyn Hartwig, Ann Junor and Rachel Sharp[1] castigated the whole postmodern enterprise as either fascistic in itself or as leading to fascism. At the time, this argument seemed over-simplified. The oversimplification had partly to do with the rigid way in which the battlelines were drawn at that time in the Australian academic community between the supporters (from, as they saw it, a radical perspective) and the opponents of postmodernism. Postmodernism, of course, as a philosophical or critical body of thought has had a high profile and it could be argued that it suggests all things to all people. One of the reasons I have found it difficult to reject out of hand, despite its often reactionary political implications, is the way in which it can articulate a transgressive aesthetic, a bohemian sensibility in its artistic and literary manifestations. It is rather odd that it hasn't been much discussed within the lesbian and gay community (so far as I know), but perhaps the term 'queer' operates in rather the same manner as postmodern.

I still feel that it is simplistic to dismiss every manifestation of postmodernism fascist out of hand. Yet I have to admit that, since 1990, the threat of overt fascism and neo-Nazism in a postmodern world, or at least a postmodern Europe, has become more evident and more threatening. In this context, one of Walter Benjamin's most famous pronouncements seems more relevant than ever. Benjamin wrote:

> Mankind's ... self-alienation has reached such a degree that it can experience its own destruction as an aesthetic pleasure of the first order. This is the situation of politics which Fascism is rendering aesthetic. Communism responds by politicising art.[2]

Yet I have always found this aphorism problematic, too. Nevertheless, it raises questions that are important for us because, apart from anything else, lesbian and gay politics, long before it called itself queer, incorporated an aesthetic of performance and display, and one which, appropriately enough, centrally emphasises the body. The way in which lesbians and gay men dress is often itself a political statement: sexuality inscribed on the body. Lesbians and gay men frequently use dress as did the well-established bohemian and political tradition of counter-cultural dress, and I think that it can be taken as a mode whereby politics is aestheticised – that is, given an aesthetic expression. This does not make it fascistic. And anyway, isn't this also a way of politicising fashion, which is a form of art (among other things)? So maybe we should begin to question whether Benjamin's antithesis *is* such an antithesis after all. Benjamin, however, was writing at a period when the Communist movement was alive and kicking. Things must look different, and even more alarming, when one half of the equation has simply disappeared down the plughole of history – today there is no Communism (in the broadest sense of a left, radical movement) to politicise art. Radicalism is everywhere in disarray – although lesbian and gay politics has, in a peculiar way, bucked this trend.

In a recent television appearance, the Scottish comedian Billy Connolly admitted that he was no longer a socialist, that he had had to recognise that people had rejected socialism world wide and that, therefore, it must have been wrong. I believe the truth to be much more complicated than that, and see no reason to reject the ideals for which socialism stood – and stands: justice, equality, diversity and the right to militancy.

The term trangression, which has become so popular, cannot be understood, however, without acknowledging the importance of the current lack of a leftwing referent. Lesbian and gay politics, like other politics, has had half its continuum cut away from it, and transgression is what we are left with in this lopsided political world. We are then close to the position again addressed by Walter Benjamin when he quotes Flaubert as having said: 'Of all of politics I understand only one thing: the revolt.'[3] The concepts of transgression, dissidence, subversion, and resistance – which have become familiar in radical discourse since the mid 1980s – are oppositional, negative. They are the politics of being *against*, they are the politics of rebellion. Yet since they are cast in the terms set by that which is being rebelled against, they are the politics, ultimately, of weakness.

For what, after all, *is* transgression? Transgression has a slightly Sadeian ring, almost as if a notion of blasphemy were lurking somewhere about. In secular terms, what is implied is a flouting of the rules, or a rule, behaviour antagonistic to what is established, the opposite, a radical challenge to what is prescribed. Yet, just as the only true blasphemer is the individual who really believes in God, so transgression depends on, and may even reinforce, conventional understandings of what it is that is to be transgressed.

A rather different view is expressed by Deborah Cameron and Elizabeth Frazer, in an article against pornography.[4] These authors emphasise the importance of Sade as a product of the Enlightenment. He transferred to the arena of transgressive sexuality the Enlightenment compulsion towards mastery and transcendence. In this interpretation, transgression not only becomes extremely powerful, but comes almost to be characteristic of the whole of Enlightenment thought, leading inevitably to scenarios of sexual violence. A critique, or even rejection, of the Enlightenment is quite usual in postmodernist writings, but I would question the implied assumption made by Cameron and Frazer that transgressive equates with mastery and control.

Foucault, in 'A Preface to Transgression' (1963),[5] defined transgression rather differently: as the crossing of a boundary

– a going further – but argued that this then set up a new boundary which was in its turn to be transgressed. What you then have is a transgressive spiral which at least in theory is interminable. From that point of view, transgression can define no final goal, and there can never be any final mastery; it is rather a process of continuously shifting boundaries, the boundaries of acceptable behaviour, the boundaries of what may be shown in terms of sexually explicit representations for example. As Jeffrey Weeks has said, transgression may be the cutting edge, but it is continually cutting itself away, undermining itself. What Foucault plays down, although it is implicit in his description, is the desire to shock, which has always been seen as central to a deliberately transgressive act.

Now the desire to shock is *not* a feature of every challenge to the status quo. On the contrary, a demand, say, such as the demand for universal suffrage involved an invocation to bourgeois notions of justice and equality. What was intended to appear shocking in the propaganda of the women's suffrage movement was the fact that women didn't have the vote, that women were equated, for example, with lunatics and criminals. The liberal notions of justice and so on were not flouted but *reaffirmed* and confirmed by the demand for the vote. The demand for the vote was a demand for *inclusion*, not an affirmation of difference or a rejection of society's dominant values. By contrast, the shock of transgression occurs because all that the bourgeoisie or the ruling class or straight society or whatever you wanted to call it holds dear is turned upside down and subjected to an onslaught of ridicule and impiety.

It may be, therefore, that transgression expresses best or is most suited to a minoritarian form of politics. In throwing down the gauntlet of transgression we – whoever the 'we' is at any given moment – are saying: we expose your hypocrisy; we do not want to be like you. It defines a difference, and a separation. Yet what exactly is implied if we reject inclusionary politics? Are we merely reaffirming the boundaries of our own ghetto, paradoxically while attempting to cross, to transgress them?

Because of the fluctuating and often repressive history of

the sexual impulse in Western societies (although not in those societies alone) the transgressive shock seems to be especially suited to sexual politics. Here is a whole huge area in which mainstream society is brilliantly shockable – still – uptight, confused, caught up in a host of contradictory anxieties and paranoid fantasies about what might happen if anything is allowed to change. And the term transgression in a sexual context implies not only shock but – perhaps most strongly – forbidden pleasures. So the transgressor, getting under the skin of mainstream society, claims not only to expose the falsity of the society that is shocked, but also claims access to some kind of intensity of experience from which the mainstream of society is cut off.

I suppose, therefore, it would be possible to argue that the transgressive impulse is ultimately élitist in so far as once a transgression becomes merely a widespread habit it has lost it magical aura of initiation and privileged experience. Adultery, for example, no longer counts in any sense as a transgression. Nor perhaps does drug use. One result, and perhaps the most usual, is the inevitable inflation of transgression – the search for ever more shocking extremes of behaviour. Another is that the transgressive spiral tends to become simply cyclical and circular, going neither up nor down but simply biting your own tail, or to put it more elegantly, disappearing up your own orifice. And, starting in a defiance of the status quo, there is no reason why it should not become increasingly self-referential.

In this context, I should like to be a little critical of the idea of bisexuality as the latest in a whole series of new oppressions which are added on to the ever lengthening list. In principle, to raise issues of racism, sexism and so on within the general context of radical politics was intended to transform that radicalism, and insofar as that has been achieved, that is good. In practice, it has too often amounted to little more than an 'add-on' approach to oppression, and as often as not has led to an attack less on the main oppressor than on the group nearest to you. Feminists did, of course, rightly target men as oppressors, but the men who ended up as the immediate objects of attack were men within the Left, trades unionists, and so on, who in the general order of things were really not the main oppressors, on a collective scale at least – however unpleasant their behaviour as individuals might at times be. While feminists attacked 'left men', the white, male ruling class went unscathed.

Similarly, when racism came onto the agenda, who were the main objects of attack? Not the National Front, not white men, not the Tory Party or even the Labour Party: it was white feminists or white working-class people who bore the brunt of an understandable anger, which was nevertheless misdirected at those (in the case of feminists, at least) who were most easily guilt-tripped, again leaving the most racist practices and institutions pretty much unscathed. While I am sure it was valuable, if painful, for me to have my unintentional racism challenged, and to be made to face the extent to which, as a white woman, I benefit from the systems of racism, and while in the long run it has added a richness of diversity to the women's movement, fragmentation and sectarianism have also been the result.

Another reason I am less and less certain of the value of this approach is that oppressions of class, disability, 'race' and sexual orientation are not exactly alike, as this add-on model implies (even if unintentionally). If bisexuality is, as I believe (taking a 'weak' psychoanalytic model here) a potentiality, initially at least, in all human beings, it is not constructed and does not function in exactly the same way a 'race' or disability – although all are socially constructed at some level. In what sense can bisexuality operate as an effective political identity in the way that, say, 'Irishness' may do? Also, the demand for the recognition of bisexuality challenges the foundations of the lesbian and gay movement, which for better or worse, is predicated on the assumption that the lesbian/gay identity is at least relatively fixed. We might argue for or believe in the possibility, or indeed the existence in many cases, of more fluid sexualities. Yet we must also recognise the problems this poses for political activism, and the bisexual movement in its demand for recognition primarily from the lesbian and gay

112

movement has been insensitive to these difficulties.

In addition, bisexuality has come forward at a particular moment in time, and we must understand it in that context. It is explicitly posed as transgressive, as an extract from an article in the US magazine *Outlook* demonstrates:

> When I strap on a dildo and fuck my male partner, we are engaging in 'heterosexual' behaviour, but I can tell you that it feels altogether *queer*, and I'm sure my grandmother and Jesse Helms would say the same.[6]

For this couple, ironically, *heterosexuality* has become the transgressive act against the stifling norms of political correctness, radical feminist separatism and binary oppositions. Yet, no matter how queer these two subjectively feel (and that's fine), unless they dress in a very extreme way or proclaim their sexual behaviour in some other fashion, so far as the world is concerned they are still a heterosexual couple – it's just that they are a *kinky* heterosexual couple. And we have to question whether sexual experiment on its own is necessarily political or subversive at all. As Inge Blackman said (in a discussion of this paper), it's happening all over the suburbs all the time. We aren't exactly seeing a social revolution as a result.

This illustrates a more general weakness and a political inadequacy in the way in which 'transgression' has operated or may operate, or rather can't operate: it can't deal with the systematic or structural nature of oppressive institutions. On the contrary, it reaffirms and may even reinforce them. An act of defiance may be personally liberating and may indeed make an important ideological statement, but whether it can do anything more seems uncertain. Like those other words I mentioned – dissidence, subversion, resistance – it is a word of weakness. We can rage against the fading of the light, we can shake our fist at society or piss on it, but that is all.

There is another disturbing aspect of the discourse around transgression. Like another contested term, queer, transgression sometimes operates as a rebellion against our own history – or at least against a part of the political history of lesbianism:

113

the feminist part. For some lesbians and gay men feminism, seems to have become the wicked stepmother, originator of the hated political correctness against which it's become so important to rebel. In this, significantly, what has been occluded is socialist feminism, which opposed the political thought police of separatist feminism, and which was always in favour of working politically with men (and indeed of sleeping with them). Transgression may also be a rebellion without content – since it is the fact of the rebellion that becomes the point and not what is being rebelled against or affirmed in contrast. The loss of a political alternative leaves us, like Flaubert, with only negation.

This is really the Camille Paglia case. A surprising number of intelligent individuals seem not to notice what she is actually saying because the way in which she says it is indeed transgressive. And yet the mixture of biological essentialism plus cocktail of death, sex and operatic romanticism adds up to something very close to a certain kind of fascism.[7] It's all too easy to sling terms like fascism around. Yet let's be quite clear – fascism had a very transgressive aspect to it. It wasn't just all about Kinder, Kirche and Küche with a bit of Jew-baiting thrown in: it was seriously queer. It could never have had the mass appeal it did had it not plugged into more than people's desire for authority: the emphasis on physical beauty, the covert homoeroticism, the chiarascuro, the intensity, the paganism and the dark romanticism speak of transgression as much as of conformity; which is why Syberberg's *Hitler: Ein Film Aus Deutschland* has such a disturbing and ambiguous effect on audiences today.

Transgression is nevertheless a shifting and ambiguous concept. It could therefore be seen as a very postmodern concept, emphasising the single, fragmented act of defiance, unencumbered by any overarching theory or coherent world view. It is also consistently used in discussions of film, texts and other aesthetic productions. Is it not then that aestheticisation of politics that Benjamin deplored?

But now we come to the other side. While it is important to remember what we have lost in terms of socialist and Marxist thought, wasn't there always something unsatisfactory about the way in which, for the most part, the Marxist tradition conceived of art? I'm not just talking about socialist realism, but about a wider set of assumptions about the purpose of art, its positive, affirmative role and also its agitational, educational role. How often in the 1970s did I have to sit through films such as *Red Detachment of Women, The Salt of the Earth* and so on – a terrible worthiness against which is to be set issues of pleasure, consumption and the liberating potential of fantasy. As Benjamin saw it, if you go too far down the road of viewing everything in aesthetic terms you lose all moral sense. Indeed, it has been suggested that philosophers such as Richard Rorty *have* gone down that road.[8]

Yet we still need to ask: *why* is it that some forms of political protest appear more effective when couched in aesthetic terms? Why are there periods, like now, or the early to mid-1960s, when politics seems to have to be expressed in aesthetic terms? Why have there always been bohemians, punks, a tradition of protest that precisely has never fitted into established political categories? I cannot claim to have answers to these questions. But they prevent me from taking any sort of absolute view, or from rejecting transgression out of hand. And I believe that these aesthetic forms of protest are valuable, and that we ought to hang on to them. It's also clear that the lesbian and gay movement has exploited them more successfully, perhaps, than any other group.

I wish to make a further point, and that is this. Conventionally, outrage and revolutionary absolutism have been posed against gradualist reformism, consensus against conflict, Marxism *and* fascism against liberal humanism and even the kindlier forms of conservatism. Perhaps in the general struggle against the dreaded binary oppositions, we ought to question whether these pairings are really so opposed after all; or whether the success of movements such as the suffrage struggle and, in recent years, most strikingly, the lesbian and gay movement (and there I think one can't use the term 'queer'), which in a curious way has managed to advance when all around were in retreat,[9] is not due to the fusion of such opposites. So that rather (in this case) than, say, OutRage and Stonewall being in opposition, or being alternatives, lesbians and gays are on the agenda because these opposites have combined – or at least it is their combined effect that is, in fact, effective.

Finally, while I would never reject the importance or impact of transgression, it can only be a tactic, never a total politics. And anyway, at present, it seems often to act as a substitute for politics. While I have always been suspicious of utopianism, I believe that no political movement can develop or grow without some idea of how society ought to be. We transgress in order to insist that we are there, that we exist, and to place a distance between ourselves and the dominant culture. But we have to go further – we have to have an idea of how things could be different, otherwise transgression ends in mere posturing. In other words, transgression on its own leads eventually to entropy, unless we carry within us some idea of transformation. It is therefore not transgression that should be our watchword, but transformation.

Notes

1 Mervyn Hartwig, Ann Junor and Rachel Sharp, (Macquarie University), 'Marxism, Science and Poststructuralist Fairy Tales', paper given at the Socialist Scholars' Conference, Sydney, 1990.
2 Walter Benjamin, 'The Work of Art in the Age of Mechanical Production', *Illuminations* (London: Fontana, 1973), pp243-244.
3 Benjamin, *Charles Baudelaire: A Lyric Poet in the Era of High Capitalism* (London: New Left Books, 1973), p13.
4 Deborah Cameron and Elizabeth Frazer, 'On the Question of Pornography and Sexual Violence: Moving Beyond Cause and Effect', in Catherine Itzin, ed., *Pornography, Women, Violence and Civil Liberties* (Oxford: Oxford University Press, 1992), pp359-83.
5 Michel Foucault, 'A Preface to Transgression', *Language, Counter Memory, Practice: Selected Essays and Interviews by Michel Foucault*, ed., Donald F Bouchard (Ithaca, NY: Cornell University Press, 1977), pp29–52.
6 Carol A Queen, 'Strangers at Home: Bisexuals in the Queer Movement', *Outlook*, 16 (1992), p33.
7 Camille Paglia, *Sexual Personae* (Harmondsworth: Penguin, 1992).
8 Richard Shusterman, 'Postmodernist Aestheticism: A New Moral Philosophy?', *Theory Culture and Society* 5:2-3 (1988), pp337–55.

Is Transgression Transgressive?

[9] Some will find this contentious, and disagree that the 1980s could possibly be seen as a period of advancement for lesbians and gays, since it saw the catastrophe of AIDS world wide, and in Britain an ideological attack culminating in Section 28 of the Local Government Act, 1988. Yet the lesbian and gay movement has a higher profile now than it did ten years ago, and at least some lesbians and gays are increasingly open about their sexuality. There are many flourishing lesbian and gay cultural activities and events (e.g. the growth of lesbian and gay film festivals), and the British government has recently (so far) resisted demands definitively to close off fostering and adoption to lesbians and gays, nor did it act explicitly to prevent lesbians from having A.I.D. There is a continuing process of struggle. Lesbians and gays may suffer more attacks, but this is partly because they have won a higher profile, in part as a result of their own political activities. Thus it is a rather extreme case of 'uneven development', but the lesbian and gay movement has at present more vitality than other sections of the 'left'.

Resituating the Bisexual Body: From Identity to Difference

CLARE HEMMINGS

The chapter begins to address the question of what it might mean to theorize bisexuality. First of all, I shall ask which theoretical and political positions inform the search, desire and need for a *definition* of bisexuality and a separate bisexual identity. My starting point is the belief that bisexuals have been marginalized within the lesbian and gay movement. Lesbian and gay theories leave little room for bisexuality, rarely taking account of it other than as aberrant or non-existent. To insist on a definition of bisexuality, as some lesbians and gay men have done, denies the way in which bisexuality already has been, and is, shaping the discourse of sexual politics and theory. I wish to advocate the need for a bisexual theory, which not only sheds new light on bisexual behaviour, but also has the potential for challenging the traditional boundaries of heterosexual and homosexual relations. In the second part of this essay I suggest that new theories of diversity need to be developed that take account of bisexuality as both politically and theoretically viable. Drawing on contemporary theories of the body and queer performance – particularly the work of Elizabeth Grosz, Monique Wittig and Judith Butler – this discussion enables the bisexual body to emerge as a figure of subversion and disruption. The double agent will serve as my metaphor for the subversive bisexual body for two reasons: (i) to challenge the negative connotations of 'transition' so often used against bisexuals, and (ii) to question the adequacy of current theories of sexual difference for accomodating a bisexual body. How does the bisexual body extend our understanding of the relationship between sexes, genders and sexualities? What might a new theory of erotic difference look like?

Although my title does not make it explicit, I am writing from a position of bisexuality – writing *as* a bisexual woman rather than *for* bisexual women. Throughout the essay I shall be using examples of the positioning of bisexuality within the Activating Theory: Lesbian, Gay and Bisexual Politics conference at the University of York in October 1992. This will serve as a focus for examining contemporary debates in sexual politics and theory, and for presenting new possibilities for theorizing bisexuality.

Identifying Bisexuality

Many bisexual delegates at the conference felt intimidated by direct forms of abuse, either personal or aimed at bisexuals in general. A number of interesting issues arose out of this, centring on a structure of inclusion and exclusion. It seemed to be assumed that (i) only those identifying as bisexual would be offended by biphobic comments; (ii) only those seen to be associating with the 'bisexual caucus' were bisexual-identified – hence adverse comments in an informal context (bar or workshop, for example) were not deemed to be offensive; (iii) no lesbian-identified woman will ever have slept with a man, identified other than as lesbian, or practised bisexual behaviour at any point. In her opening plenary of the Activating Theory conference, Lisa Power directly confronted the issue of opposite-sex relations for lesbian and gay-identified people, speaking for a more honest appraisal of who we have sex with and why, only to be 'greeted with what felt like uncomprehending silence. In the ensuing questions no-one picked up on many of the important points that she raised'.[1]

Bisexuals have felt minoritized within the lesbian and gay

community for a long time, yet our claims to this effect have often been met with scorn or disbelief. There seems to be an underlying assumption that if lesbians and gay men are oppressed, then bisexuals cannot be a minority, as this would presume that the latter are more oppressed than the former. Being positioned as a minority, however, is not related to *only one* hierarchized form of oppression. A model of oppression that takes institutionalized and internalized heterosexism as the only valid means to understanding inequality implies that bisexuals are oppressed only according to how far they share the same oppression as lesbians and gay men. To my mind there are a number of difficulties with taking heterosexism as *the original* form of oppression. What tends to follow are the assumptions that (i) bisexuals are less oppressed than lesbians and gay men by heterosexism, and, hence, cannot be a minority within that group; and (ii) since bisexuals are not a minority, we have no identity. Our exclusion from lesbian and gay communities simultaneously promises integration into the same. If we relinquish notions of difference, both in what oppresses us, and in our experience of oppression, bisexuals can be accepted into the lesbian and gay fold.

It is not only lesbians and gay men that assert that it is only on the basis of bisexuals having same-sex partner that we may be accepted within lesbian and gay communities. Lesley Mountain – a bisexual woman – proposes that it is only 'when we express the lesbian or gay part of our sexuality that we will suffer [from oppression]'.[2] Ara Wilson, in her rather vitriolic attack on bisexual identification in *Outlook*, goes further still: 'It seems irrelevant to create a distinct bisexual identity – what bisexuals have in common with lesbians and gays is their experience as homosexuals'.[3] To put it another way, bisexuals can be accepted into queer communities only if we deny our difference, or if we position ourselves as lesbians or gay men. It is not only bisexuals that fall short of the 'hierarchy of oppression' ideal, of course. Susan Ardill and Sue O'Sullivan note, in describing a discussion within the *Spare Rib* collective around whether a particular article was anti-lesbian or not, that those who objected to a ban on the article 'didn't display the requisite pain.' 'The *expression* of anti-lesbianism in whatever form, from whoever', they add, 'became the *oppression* of lesbians, full stop'.[4]

Written into the idea that identity can only be formed in relation to oppression is the expectation that it will always be the 'other' that is problematised, never the dominant, presumed hegemonic, idea. If heterosexism is the structuring factor of oppression, it is always the construction of the 'homosexual' that is debated, is 'up for grabs'. The 'heterosexual' is assumed to have a fixed meaning, the oppressor, against which the 'pervert' identifies her or himself. Of course, this issue is not one for queer theory alone, black feminists – notably Gayatri Chakravorty Spivak[5] – have also advocated the examination of the dominant category, in this case 'white'. If the privileged position is never problematized, if identity is seen to be formed in relation to oppression alone, the dichotomy of subject/object in the moment of struggle is still maintained. The boundaries of the binary opposites may be challenged and even modified, but the terms of the paradigm itself will remain intact.

There is a particular school of thought, exemplified by Monique Wittig's work, that states that it is only through identifying as lesbian that the heterosexist dominant ideology will be exposed for what it is. Such a model insists that there is an original, univocal and therefore privileged oppressive structure, containing and informing other models of power. But what about the *various* forms of oppression, complex and interrelated, that manifest themselves as historically specific, *in time*? There are no *ahistorical* binary structures that act as grids imposed upon our lives, and lend them meaning. Unequal power oppositions exist only in the precise forms that they take. 'Power must be understood in the first instance', argues Foucault, 'as the multiplicity of force relations immanent in the sphere in which they operate and which constitute their own organisation'.[6] Foucault's work is useful for examining the influence of multiple power-relations in the formation of identity. Yet his often abstract formulations fail to account adequately for the relationships *between* manifestations of power. Most power relationships are informative, if not palpably manifest, in all human situations, given that the individual will certainly have been directly influenced by heterosexism, racism, sexism, and so on. These manifestations of power shape both the individual's subjectivity and the meanings that subjectivity is imbued with. Thus, one cannot be free of heterosexism (even as an 'escapee lesbian')[7] or of racism, or of sexism. These things are, so to speak, remembered or incorporated in the particular situation of the self.

I identify two further difficulties that arise from the premise that sexual identity is only formed in response to confronting monolithic heterosexism: (i) the ways in which one is positioned as white or black, man or woman, rich or poor, are seen to have either *no* relevance, or separate relevance, to the formation of a particular sense of identity; (ii) the complex identifications an individual experiences that are not *directly* related to the situation of power one is involved in are trivialized. There are all sorts of experiences that lead the individual to a sense of her own identity, not all of them to do with being oppressed. Without wanting to be flippant, I like spicy food and drawing with pastels. The issue of taste or preference is one that is too easily overlooked in discussions about sexual identity. A woman is most likely to decide to label herself lesbian as a result of acknowledging same-sex desire, not as a result of acknowledging heterosexist oppression (political lesbianism is the obvious exception to the rule). It is a mark of the trivialization of bisexuality that those of us involved in opposite-sex relationships are often positioned as heterosexual for that time span. Seeing us in this respect as straight does not take account of the way the individual perceives herself, or how that relationship is understood or represented in a wider context. I am not suggesting by this that there is something innately 'me', pre-social and ahistorical, nor that identity is simply personal and apolitical. The point is that our unique identities, our unique genealogies, and our many and various group and community identities are formed through a variety of different influences, exchanges and experiences.

In fact, to say that we are all oppressors and oppressed in different forms and at different times is probably a more helpful way of looking at forms of oppression. Without a doubt the bisexual movement has come out of the lesbian and gay movement in many ways. But there are issues that exclusively affect bisexuals. For example, a recent ruling by the Church of England allows lesbians and gay men to be part of the Church (as long as they remain celibate, of course), but condemns bisexuality as the ultimate perversion that does not even have an excuse in sexological notions of inversion. In this instance, homosexuality is categorized as biologically determined. Presumably, the supposition is that bisexuals *could* have opposite-sex relations, but are perverted as an act of will. Only recently have many lesbian and gay groups and centres positively welcomed bisexuals. For example, the University of York Lesbian and Gay Society did not change its name to Bisexual, Lesbian and Gay Society until 1988. A union motion to (i) recognize the bisexual community (ii) change the student union's lesbian and gay officer to lesbian, gay and bisexual officer, and (iii) to change the officer's responsibilities to include bisexuals, was not proposed until 17 February 1993. While, on the one hand, bisexuals are often seen to share a common (but watered down) oppression, on occasions we are denied even that. When asked what constitutes bisexual oppression, Wilson claims it to be merely 'the dominant objectionable representations of bisexuals and bisexuality, notably the stereotypes of promiscuity and indecisive immaturity'.[8] In other words, we are either oppressed as lesbians or gay men, or not at all.

Interestingly, it is not just bisexuals who have experienced exclusion from some lesbian and gay communities. In the run up to the opening of the now defunct London Lesbian & Gay Centre (LLGC) in 1985, there was a series of heated debates about whether or not to allow sadomasochists access to it. In their analysis of events, Ardill and O'Sullivan isolate the issue of 'moral purity' as being of particular significance in the objections levelled against SMers:

In the LLGC battle, for example, speeches made by women who were opposing SM often began with a declaration of identity: for example, 'I am a lesbian mother and I think ...' In this context the words 'lesbian mother' are meant to convey a specific moral weight, not just that of personal experience. What was being invoked was a particular feminist ideology.[9]

This discourse of 'purity' and 'pollution' is one that runs through many of the debates about who does or does not have access to lesbian and gay communities. What begins as a survival strategy, in order for lesbian and gay communities to be seen as a viable alternative to straight communities, and to counter the negative prescriptions by the same, is eventually the cause of much discontent and resentment within the lesbian and gay communities themselves.

Defining Bisexuality

A recurrent theme around bisexuality throughout the Activating Theory conference was that of definition – the need for lesbians and gay men to be presented with an absolute definition of bisexuality and bisexual identity. At the workshop on women and bisexuality, Sue George, responding to questions about the research for her book on bisexuality and feminism,[10] read out a list of the various women who felt that they were sufficiently identified as bisexual to fill in a questionnaire aimed at bisexuals. The list included those who were celibate; had mainly female partners; had mainly male partners; had female and male partners simultaneously; alternated in terms of the sex of their partners; were monogamous; were non-monogamous; were married; were single; had previously identified as lesbian or as heterosexual; had always identified as bisexual; were confident about their sexuality; were unsure about their sexuality, and so on. The list was apparently endless. Some women who identified as lesbian also filled in the questionnaire because they had or were having sexual relationships with men, and saw that as important. What a bisexual is, or is not, becomes still more difficult to establish when male bisexuality is also considered.

Yet any sign of unwillingness to define bisexuality often results, yet again, in the trivialization or ignoring of bisexuals and bisexuality. And yet to provide such a definition – do we want one? what if we all take *my* definition then? – or to attempt to provide it, is still feeding into a banishment syndrome of sorts. A single definition will deny the variety of those people who consider themselves to be a part of the bisexual community. Definition comes to equal intelligibility – no further need to discuss or theorise what meanings bisexuality might have. One underlying assumption is that if a definition for bisexuality is not provided, it cannot be understood, cannot be slotted into the existing paradigm of sexuality that divides human sexuality into heterosexual, homosexual, and somewhere in between. But as I mentioned earlier, bisexuality is *already part* of the discourse of sexuality – it is constituted within that discourse, and, in turn, affects the very forms of that discourse. The meaning of bisexuality shifts historically and culturally, as do the meanings of lesbian and gay. It is ironic that bisexuals are still expected to come up with a self-definition in order to be welcomed within lesbian and gay communities that do not exist as a single entity in any case. Personal and political definitions, of self and of community, are both social and political ways of positioning oneself, and of being positioned. They are extremely important both for political expediency and a personal and communal sense of worth. But I would stress that, in terms of the conference, and in the majority of other situations where a bisexual is pushed to account for her- or himself, the demand for a definition is often an attempt to integrate bisexuality into a grid of intelligibility, rather than an acknowledgment of the variety of personal and political positions that a person may choose to occupy.

There are, of course, a number of other problems with the search for identity or definition as much recent lesbian and gay theory has shown. Being able to say 'I am a bisexual/a lesbian/a gay man' relies on a sense of both common and shared identity with others who label themselves in the same way, and (at least temporarily) a fixed and enduring sense of self. And here Judith Butler's remarks are especially pertinent:

> To claim that this is what I *am* is to suggest a provisional
> totalization of this 'I'. But if the I can so determine itself, then
> that which it excludes in order to make that determination
> remains constitutive of the determination itself ... What, if
> anything, can lesbians be said to share? And who will decide this
> question, and in the name of whom?[11]

What appears to be outside of one's self becomes the very
foundation of one's own ability to speak as subject. This is the
paradigm that the construct of heterosexuality relies on. It is
no doubt difficult to acknowledge that lesbian or gay identities
may have been constructed in a similar way.

A more acceptable framework for thinking about sexual
identities is, perhaps, in terms of their genealogies. In the
same way as the term 'homosexual' has taken many forms in
the late nineteenth and twentieth centuries, and has been
extensively documented, the term 'bisexual' has been
employed in different circumstances, and has consequently
come to signify a variety of things. Malcolm Bowie writes:

> This term [bisexuality] has at least three current meanings, and
> these can easily produce confusion. As used by Darwin and his
> contemporaries it represented an exclusively biological notion,
> synonymous with hermaphroditism, and referred to the presence
> within an organism of male and female characteristics. This
> meaning persists. Secondly, bisexuality denotes the co-presence
> in the human individual of 'feminine' and 'masculine'
> psychological characteristics. Thirdly, and most commonly, it is
> used of the propensity of certain individuals to be sexually
> attracted to both men and women.[12]

Further definitions include the following: 'Bisexuality is the
root of all human sexuality, and the matrix of all bio-physical
reactions, be they passive or active. Bisexuality is expressed
first and foremost in bi-gender identity, which may or may not
lead to bisexual orientation;[13] and a variation on the third
category enumerated by Bowie: 'Bisexuals are people who
experience the desire of emotional, sensual and/or sexual
relations with people of both sexes, though not necessarily to
an equal extent or at the same time'.[14]

Resituating the Bisexual Body

As suggested by Bowie's three uses of the term bisexuality, it is only recently that bisexuality has emerged as a chosen political and social identity. The 'we're all bisexual really' maxim constructs bisexuality as passive, and assumes that a sexual (and hence identity) choice will be made at some point. Only then can an active sexual identity be formed. Bisexuality is also not seen to have any bearing on *non*-sexual aspects of identity. As Jay P Paul points out, 'the attempt to render the homosexual identity as a higher order construct than the bisexual identity by emphasising its meaning for non-sexual aspects of self necessitates a belief in a biological or fixed basis for these non-erotic components.'[15] Such perceptions of identity formation can also be seen in the traditional 'coming out' narrative, one that involves a reconstruction of one's past to fit one's present identity. Such a narrative may create a linear history or fiction that attests to the 'truth' of one's sexual identity, and which perpetuates the conception of sexuality as innate, as pre-destined or genetic. Yet even that narrative is unstable, needing to be reinvented in each moment in order to create the fiction of solidity. It assumes there is such a thing as *repressed* sexuality that has managed to surface despite social conditioning to the contrary, and which must therefore be innate. In other words, the truth will out. I am not trying to suggest that narrative reconstructions are not important – to a certain extent I think they are probably inevitable – but rather they could be conceived of as multi-dimensional, fluid and subject to change.

At this point in time, we could do no more than seek to understand the cultural and historical reasons why bisexuality is being spoken of now, and why it is that one is able to identify as bisexual. Valverde says that 'Bisexuality does not exist as either a social institution or a psychological "truth". It only exists as a catch-all term for different erotic and social patterns whose common ground is an attempt to combine homo- and heterosexuality in a variety of ways'.[16] Perhaps it is in this definition that we might begin to think about how bisexuality changes the way in which we think about sexuality and identity, and, further, as I will argue in the second part of

127

this essay, how bisexuality challenges the constructions of gender and sex categories, and opens up a potentially subversive bodily space from which to proceed.

Embodying Bisexuality

I propose that a bisexual body might provide a theoretical site for breaking down binary conceptions of sex as the foundation of gender and hence sexuality. Bisexuality cannot be fully contained within a heterosexual matrix. The expression of same-sex desire for self-identified bisexuals simultaneously expresses potential desire of a 'heterosexual nature' – that is, with people of the opposite sex, defined in terms of their external genitalia. It is not that sex difference is never operative, nor that it does not inform our sense of identity, or result in material and qualitative differences between men's and women's lives. Nor do I wish to give the impression that bisexual men and women are all out there, consciously dismantling conventional frameworks of desire. Rather, I am proceeding from the belief that sex difference is not 'real', in the sense of related to an 'origin', or an essential truth about bodies and their relationship to gender and sexuality. In this part of my essay, I examine a possible new metaphor for a bisexual body. I also consider an alternative to the sex-gender-sexuality models of understanding our own eroticism.

The metaphor of the bridge (or, less kindly, the fence) has frequently been used to describe bisexuality. In 'Sorties ...', Hélène Cixous conceptualizes the bisexual as the bridge between two poles, which brings together opposing ends of the sexual spectrum.[17] The bisexual, then, is figured as *un*real, not interactive, but rather the facilitator for interaction. Cixous' metaphor creates the bisexual as inert, as dependent upon the reals of homosexuality and heterosexuality, rather than as a component in the act, as active and interactive. The inside/outside, heterosexual/homosexual, construction, which has recently been challenged by queer theorists,[18] is complicated still further in bisexuality. The bisexual is set outside compulsory heterosexual perform-ance[19] through the expression of same-sex desire, yet is simultaneously within it. Hence she is the 'outside' (which is also 'inside'), and the 'inside' (which is also 'outside'). From 'inside and outside at the same time' to 'inside and outside, and outside and inside at the same time'. The 'I' in 'I am bisexual' is not simply an insubstantial assumption of fixed identity, as in 'I am lesbian' – rather, it signifies transition and movement in itself. To say 'I am bisexual' is to say 'I am not "I" '.

My aim is to re-present the process of being/becoming bisexual as one that is ever re-centring, re-emerging and re-creating the 'I'. In another essay, Cixous revises her view of bisexuality when she asserts:

> To a self-effacing, merger-type bisexuality ... I oppose the other bisexuality on which every single subject not enclosed in the false theatre of phallocentric representationalism has founded his/her erotic universe ... [a] vatic bisexuality, which doesn't annul differences but stirs them up, pursues them, increases their numbers.[20]

The main difficulty with Cixous' presentation of the bisexual in this passage is its reliance on a sense of mysticism and ahistoricism. I find it impossible to know how to embody Cixous' bisexual vision. Perhaps what is needed is a metaphor for bisexual bodies that signifies both the specific cultural interpretation of bisexuality and its potential for political and theoretical subversion.

Butler describes the process of identity formation as 'the mode by which Others become shit'.[21] Taking this 'shit' analogy together with the familiar coding of the bisexual as the 'missing link', the figure of the *double agent* may serve a particularly useful function here. A double agent appears to be part of one camp but is also strongly identified with another. The implication is that one can never quite be sure where her allegiance actually lies. Cixous' bisexual bridge links the straight and queer worlds. The double agent, by contrast, is set up as a link between the two worlds, yet actually disrupts the very boundaries of the worlds we assume to be separate.

The double agent is the figure of political shame and personal amorality. She embodies personal and general confusion, with an often frightening and sinister knowledge of both the inside and the outside. It is as if the double agent becomes both the expellor and the expelled, the excreting and the excreted. The double agent is metaphorically covered in filth, is inseparable from that filth. The language of exclusion from within lesbian and gay communities relies on such a language of contamination: 'I'd never sleep with a bisexual because they bring men into the lesbian community/ are responsible for the spread of HIV/always leave you for someone of the opposite/same sex/can't be trusted, etc'. The figure of the double agent may seem an unlikely metaphor for the potentially subversive process that bisexuals – consciously or unconsciously – are involved with.

Traditionally the double agent sells her services to the highest bidder. The double agent is seen as immorally unconcerned with ethics or politics. Similarly, bisexual women have been accused of 'selling out' to men when, in the lesbian imagination, they leave a lesbian for the 'enemy', or 'pass' for straight. The implication is that no lesbian ever left her lover for another woman (or man, for that matter), or passed for straight. The currency exchanged in this scenario is pleasure (and one of its moral aspects, fidelity). The popular conception of a bisexual is that she will leave you when things get tough (pleasure principle), that she is always on the look out for another lover (pleasure-fidelity), and that when she finds one (male), she will have no qualms about relinquishing you and the lesbian community as a whole (fidelity). I am not suggesting that bisexuals *never* 'sell-out', pass for straight, or show less than one hundred percent commitment to women's and lesbian emancipation. Some bisexual women are, of course, apolitical, and not at all interested in feminism, just like some lesbians. I think that to a large degree the fear of bisexual women is the fear of infiltration, the fear that the secrets of a lesbian subculture will be sold to the dominant heterosexual culture at the price of a one-night stand.

And, of course, what is most powerfully inscribed in the figure of the double agent is that she is miserable – despised and despicable. She knows both sides, and yet she cannot be unaware that her own relationship to them is a sham. Only if you remain faithful to your identity (lesbian or heterosexual) can you ever be happy with yourself, and be part of a community. Not only, the story runs, is transition dangerous, it won't bring you *real* happiness either. My thesaurus gives as one of many possible synonyms for the word *transition* (commonly used to discredit bisexuality) the word *revolution*. Is it possible to begin to see the possibility of bisexuals as 'revolutionary double agents', whose 'transgressions' have political importance other than secrecy and production of multiple meanings? In the arena of sexual politics a revolutionary double agent may have a key to disassembling fixed gender relations, and the fixed dependent parallels of sex, gender and sexuality. She may have new insights into the tenuous nature of those oppositions.

In terms of parodying the imitation that sets itself up as the original,[22] namely heterosexuality, a bisexual double agent could serve to expose heterosexual shamming in a way that does not simply set up another opposition. Despite her theorizing to the contrary, Butler's disavowal of a bisexual body as potentially subversive in challenging notions of sex difference only too clearly reveals her reliance on the categories of male and female. Butler highlights the potential of male drag to parody heterosexuality, since it shows the assumption of 'an original or primary gender identity'[23] to be an illusion. In a drag performance, Butler contends, the false conflation of sex and gender, and the imitative structure of gender itself, are revealed. But if, as Butler insists, there is no real sex and no real gender, then we are all in drag of a type (though some forms of gender performance may be more 'encouraged' than others). By focussing on gay male drag as the privileged site of subversion, Butler is implying that it is when men dress and act as women that the intelligibility of gender and sex is questioned most transgressively. Surely,

131

such an assertion relies on the oppositional sex categories of man and woman that it seeks to undermine? A drag performance would be rendered meaningless, were it not for fixed notions of gender and sex. It seems to me that a 'bisexual performance' might employ different means to parody the structure of sex and gender and sexuality. As Carol A. Queen writes:

> Heterosexual behavior does not always equal 'straight.' When I strap on a dildo and fuck my male partner, we are engaging in 'heterosexual' behavior, but I can tell you that it feels altogether queer, and I'm sure my grandmother and Jesse Helms would say the same.[24]

If the heterosexual gains meaning in performance, such bisexual opposite-sex performances *shift* the meaning of the same, if only incrementally. The fact that a bisexual double agent does not construct her 'I' on an exclusive diet of heterosexual acts or suppositions means that the cohesive structure of heterosexuality is undermined from within that performance, rather than in opposition to it. Heterosexual behaviour is forced to expand to contain the 'other' that it excludes to found its sense of self. Of course, as a delegate at the Activating Theory conference pointed out, it is not just bisexuals who might enact heterosexuality queerly. Straight couples could be strapping on dildos in suburbia at this very moment.

Erotic Difference

Contemporary theorists have been concerned with examining the category of sex in order to disrupt conventional assumptions of the relationships between sex, gender and desire. Yet although Grosz, Wittig and Butler have started from the premise that 'sex' is naturalized rather than natural, they have not challenged assumptions of sexual object choice as determining of sexuality, and therefore do not take on board any possibility of a bisexual body.

In challenging Western philosophical constructions of a

mind/body dichotomy, Grosz proposes that we begin to move away from the concept of *the* body, to understanding that 'there is no body as such: there are only bodies – male or female, black, brown, white, large or small – and the gradations in between. There is always only a specific type of body, concrete in its determinations, with a particular sex, race and physiognomy.'[25] Yet although Grosz goes on to suggest that we must move away from a Western intellectual heritage of mind/body splits and dependencies, to viewing bodies as 'a site of social, political, cultural and geographical inscriptions, production or constitution',[26] she still maintains sex difference as being a mark of/on the body which is visibly male or female. This would suggest that although the body is a site for inscription, the specific body is still concrete in terms of its anatomical sex. In this respect, Grosz is rejecting sex difference as socially, politically and culturally constituted per se. Rather she is stating that the *kind* of male or female body one has, and the meanings that it thereby signifies, are culturally and historically specific. In Grosz's theory, the body is surface, or raw materials – a sex-differentiated blank sheet inscribed upon by culture.

Wittig, too, appears to reject any essential notion of sex difference when she says that 'there is no sex'. 'There is', she argues, 'but sex that is oppressed and sex that oppresses. It is oppression that creates sex and not the contrary'.[27] Because 'man' and 'woman' are components of a heterosexist paradigm, and gain meaning only within those terms, Wittig advocates being 'lesbian' as a way out of heterosexist prescription. Her now notorious statement, 'Lesbians are not women',[28] is the result of such an argument. Wittig's comment gave rise to the subsequent dialogue. 'Do you have a vagina?' – delegate, 'No' – Wittig. Lesbians, it would seem, are a separate class from other women. Yet how is a lesbian defined other than through the social construction of man/woman? Wittig's lesbians rely on the categories of sex difference they wish to escape from, unless they are suggesting that men *or* women can be lesbians. I am unsure how Wittig would see the bisexual fitting into her political

133

model. Not a runaway wife, not a lesbian, but not defining herself as heterosexual either, the bisexual must surely pose a problem for Wittig. The instability of a bisexual identity modifies and re-writes both the 'heterosexual contract' and the 'lesbian contract'. Again, I would stress that this is not always the case, and not always conscious. Bisexuals, as I have said, come in a multiplicity of forms. However the categories of heterosexual and homosexual cannot contain the constant movement of a bisexual process easily. This is why I believe that the 'contracts' must be re-written.

In the work of both Grosz and Wittig, sexuality is still defined in terms of the genitalia of the object of desire. If a woman feel sexual desire for another woman she is said to be making a 'lesbian' sexual choice, and her sexuality is defined as lesbian. In forefronting bisexuality, and the possibility of a bisexual body, these constructs are shaken in their assumptions. If a woman makes a sexual object choice of another woman, and on another occasion of a man, she cannot be said to be either lesbian or straight. But our sexualities, we are told, come from the sexual object choices we make. In that case can there be such a thing as *bisexual desire*? This question need not reflect notions of a Freudian 'polymorphous perversity'. Rather it could be understood in terms of object choices made in adulthood, based on something other than sexual difference within a framework of compulsory heterosexuality. If there is no such thing as bisexual desire, how can sexual object choices of both men and women be made? On this question, lesbians and gay men have claimed, in line with traditional Freudian thinking, that apparent adult bisexuality is, in fact, the surfacing of a repressed homosexual instinct.[29] The difference between these contemporary lesbian and gay and Freudian explanations for bisexuality is that the first blames heterosexual culture (for the bisexuals incomplete homosexuality), and the second blames the individual's failure to negotiate the Oedipus complex (for her incomplete heterosexuality).

Perhaps if we shift the enquiry slightly, from asking whether or not there can be such a thing as bisexual desire, to challenging the notions of sex difference that define our object choice (and hence our sexuality) in the first place, we can begin to disrupt existing paradigms of sex, gender and sexuality in an altogether different way. To my mind we need to theorize the positioning of bisexuality in different frameworks, to avoid being left with a collapse. I propose a system of *erotic difference* as one way of challenging a Freudian structure of desire, without being left with a mass of tangled signifiers. Difference has generally been understood and examined in terms of the divisions between bodies, genders and sexualities – 'I am not, because I haven't got or don't do ...' Differences in this sense – sex, 'race', class – are viewed as static, as definite markers that carve a space between two or more people. In this respect, differences are what claim our attention, what cannot be transgressed. In an attempt to overcome the boundaries of difference, Luce Irigaray, in *Parler N'est Jamais Neutre*,[30] battles with the possibility of joining the positive aspects of the concepts of 'sexual difference' with those of 'sexual sameness':

> Two qualitative differences remain to be discovered, to be placed in relation to each other – that which arises from sexual difference and that which can be lived in a sympathy between women. They are no doubt not separate but they do not correspond to the same feeling. To fold them in on to each other or to efface one within the other would be to reduce both to something quantative.[31]

A bisexual erotic difference might focus on internal rather than external parallels. How are our similarities embodied in different ways, or how are our differences made similar (culturally, historically and specifically)? The answer might be to introduce the term *difference as*. I am not advocating the removal or glossing over of difference per se, but rather hoping to invest sexual difference with new meaning not entirely based on or informed by power, and not signified by genitalia and object choice alone. 'Erotic difference' does not always have sexual difference between men and women, or sameness between women and women, and men and men, as its marker. Sometimes this may be the case, sometimes not.

135

This proposed view of shifting similarity and difference does not need to de-politicise the individual and group experience of sex, 'race' or class oppression. I am not suggesting that the ways in which we are culturally gendered, sexed, oppressed are not important, but rather that the ways in which we embody gender, for example, create a variety of differences and similarities that are not fixed, and the meanings of which may be infinite. I am also proposing that it is not always anatomical sex that informs our sexual object choice. Heterosexuals are not attracted to everyone of the opposite sex, lesbians and gay men are not attracted to everyone of the same sex, and – though some would have us believe otherwise – bisexuals are not attracted to 'anything that moves'. A sense of erotic difference – that, I maintain, informs our desire – is created by a whole range of differences and similarities, many of which may be to do with power, but not all of which are to do with constructions of sex and gender.

The erotic for a bisexual theory could become bodily sites and bodily behaviours that seek actively to dismantle binary means of identifying difference. The conceptions of a bisexual *difference as* is in no way intended to suggest that, erotically, lesbians and gay men perform their sexualities along straight lines of 'same as', or heterosexuals as 'difference between', or that bisexuals perform 'bisexually'. The 'bisexual body' is intended to stand both as a signifer of the possible reconfigur-ation of the relationships between sexes, genders and sexua-lities, and as the site of possible bisexual political activity and community – not exclusive to bisexual-identified people by any means. Of course, Elizabeth Wilson has reminded us that 'transgression' may be translated other than in terms of trans-gressive tranformation,[32] but we may have to take that risk.

Notes

[1] *BIFROST: A Monthly Magazine for Bisexuals* 17. (1992), p3.
[2] Lesley Mountain, 'Letters', *BIFROST: A Monthly Magazine for Bisexuals* 17. (1992), p7.
[3] Ara Wilson, 'Just Add Water: Searching for the Bisexual Politic', *Outlook* 16. (1992), p28.

Resituating the Bisexual Body

[4] Susan Ardill and Sue O'Sullivan, 'Upsetting an Applecart: Difference, Desire and Lesbian Sadomasochism', *Feminist Review* 23. (1986), p38.

[5] Gayatri Chakravorty Spivak, *In Other Worlds: Essays in Cultural Politics* (New York: Methuen, 1987), pp92, 117; and *The Post-Colonial Critic* (New York: Routledge, 1990), pp62, 68, 72. Richard Dyer, 'White' *Screen* 4. (1988), pp44, 45, 64, also focuses on the construction of the dominant category in this case.

[6] Michel Foucault, *The History of Sexuality, Volume One, An Introduction*, trans, Robert Hurley (London: Penguin, 1978), p92.

[7] Monique Wittig, 'One is Not Born a Woman', in *The Straight Mind and Other Essays* (Hemel Hempstead: Harvester Wheatsheaf, 1992), p20.

[8] Wilson, 'Just Add Water', p26.

[9] Ardill and O'Sullivan, 'Upsetting the Applecart', p33.

[10] Sue George, *Women and Bisexuality* (London: Scarlet Press, 1993).

[11] Judith Butler, 'Imitation and Gender Insubordination', in Diana Fuss, ed, *Inside/Out: Lesbian Theories, Gay Theories* (New York: Routledge, 1991), p15.

[12] Malcolm Bowie, in Elizabeth Wright, ed., *Feminism and Psychoanalysis: A Critical Dictionary* (Oxford: Basil Blackwell, 1992), p26.

[13] Charlotte Wolff, *Bisexuality – a Study* (London: Quartet, 1977), p1.

[14] Off Pink Collective, *Bisexual Lives* (London: Off Pink Publishing, 1988), p90.

[15] Jay P Paul, 'Bisexuality: Reassessing Our Paradigms of Sexuality', in Fritz Klein and Timothy Wolf, eds, *Two Lives to Lead: Bisexuality in Men and Women* (New York: Harrington Park Press, 1985), p30.

[16] Mariana Valverde, *Sex, Power and Pleasure* (Toronto: The Women's Press (Canada) 1985), p114.

[17] Hélène Cixous, 'Sorties', in Helène Cixous and Catherine Clement, *The Newly Born Woman*, trans. Betsy Wing (Manchester: Manchester University Press, 1987), p2.

[18] For example see Fuss, *Inside/Out: Lesbian Theories, Gay Theories* (New York: Routledge, 1991), p2, and Butler, *Gender Trouble: Feminism and the Subversion of Identity* (New York and London: Routledge, 1990), pp133–34.

[19] Butler, *Gender Trouble*, pp25 and 31.

[20] Cixous, 'The Laugh of the Medusa', in Elaine Marks and Isabelle de Courtivron, eds, *New French Feminisms* (Brighton: Harvester Press, 1981), p254.

[21] Butler, *Gender Trouble*, p134.

[22] *Ibid.*, p18.

[23] *Ibid.*, p137.

[24] Carol A Queen, 'Strangers at Home: Bisexuals in the Queer Movement', *Outlook* 16. (1992), p3. Elizabeth Wilson quoted this passage in her paper 'Is Transgression Transgressive?', University of York, Activating Theory Conference, October 1992, as an example of where it is not. When a delegate pointed out that the passage was written by a bisexual woman, and

that she found Wilson's use of it insensitive, the delegate was accused of
guilt-tripping.

25 Elizabeth Grosz, 'Feminism and the Body', paper delivered at the
Centre for Women's Studies, University of York, 1992, p14.

26 Grosz, 'Feminism and the Body', p18.

27 Wittig, 'One is Not Born a Woman', p2.

28 Wittig, *The Straight Mind*, pviii.

29 See Paula Rust, 'Neutralizing the Political Threat of the Marginal
Woman: Lesbians' Beliefs about Bisexual Women', paper delivered at the
Lesbian and Gay Studies Conference, Cincinnati, Ohio, 1991, p4.

30 Luce Irigaray, *Parler N'est Jamais Neutre* (Paris: Editions de Minuit,
1985), p294. My own translation.

31 Irigaray *Parler N'est Jamais Neutre*, quoted in Christine Holmlund, 'The
Lesbian, the Mother, the Heterosexual Lover: Irigaray's Recodings of
Difference', *Feminist Studies*, Vol 17. No 2. 1987, p289.

32 Wilson, 'Is Transgression Transgressive?', in this volume, pp107–17.

Activating Bisexuality: Towards a Bi/Sexual Politics

JO EADIE

Rather than embrace an idealist faith in the necessarily, immanently corrosive efficacy of the contradictions inherent to these definitional binarisms, I will suggest instead that contests for discursive power can be specified as competitions for the material or rhetorical leverage required to set the terms of, and to profit in some way from, the operations of such an incoherence of definition.

Eve Kosofsky Sedgwick[1]

Bi Way of an Introduction

Like all sexualities, 'bisexuality' has a history. A double history: of the ways in which there are and have been sexual subjects who desire both men and women; and of the ways in which that word has evolved and been deployed relatively recently. Its current deployment is bringing it into a series of conflicts with lesbian and gay communities.[2] This essay looks at the nature of those conflicts, argues for some ways out of them.[3] I will be suggesting that the problem – and also the solution – is bound up with fights over definitional incoherence, whereby the instabilities of sexual identity become a battleground.

In speaking of bisexuality, I am trying to attend to its different histories. When I refer to bisexuality I am therefore gesturing towards a range of sexual-political phenomena:

self-identifying bisexual people; people experiencing both same-sex and opposite-sex desires or practices who choose positively to identify as lesbian, gay or straight; people who have non-bisexual identities which struggle to contain outlawed bisexual feelings; people who desire both men and women, for whom the term 'bisexual' is anachronistic or culturally inappropriate. Those parameters in themselves mark some of the issues of definitional incoherence.

Danger and safety will be continuing themes in this essay, and many of the current conflicts involve calls by lesbians and gay men for safety. There are three main arguments for the need for safe spaces, and all have been used to exclude bisexual people:

(i) The need for a space free from the oppressive behaviour of the group in power. Bisexual people are said to have 'heterosexual privilege': they are therefore assumed to behave in heterosexist ways.

(ii) The need for a group to be together to share experiences and define an agenda, free from the imposed interpretations, norms and contempt of dominant groups. Bisexuals are said to have different interests and therefore threaten the possibility of free discussion. They will also dilute the common experience, and because they have not shared them will be uninformed.

(iii) A place to be free of the fears and feelings of anxiety caused by being around members of an oppressive group. Some lesbians and gay men do not feel comfortable around bisexuals.

Even where personal safety is not such an immediate issue, bisexuality is dealt with in ways that are closely tied to such thinking. My aim is to undermine those positions. I shall not simply be arguing against them, but disputing the sexual epistemology on which they are premised, and the forms of identity politics which follow from that.

For me, the most recent airing of these arguments was in a discussion between the Nottingham Bisexual Group[3] and The

Outhouse Project, a local group which is working to establish a 'lesbian and gay community centre' in Nottingham. It was the content of that name that was being contested. Would they, we asked, include bisexual people among their users? While they referred to such arguments largely as examples of what they did *not* think, the sticking point of the discussion (for a while) was that they did not actually see the need for a name change. Since their full charter stated that 'the co-operative welcomes members of both genders and all sexual orientations', they felt that it was unnecessary to mention bisexual people in their title. Against this, we were arguing that the absence was a very powerful one for us. A crucial point in the discussion was around bisexual history. We pointed out that historically places that have said 'lesbian and gay' in their titles mean very specifically 'and not bisexual'. Lesbian and Gay Switchboard in London did at one time not accept bisexual volunteers; the London Lesbian and Gay Centre had for many years policy excluding bisexual users; the NUS Lesbian and Gay Campaign was not open to bisexual students. We also pointed out that the bisexual community had now reached a point where 'bisexual' was no longer simply a diagnostic or classificatory term, but a positive, self-chosen, and political identity. Prospective users would therefore assume that if this were not explicitly recognised by an organisation then this was a deliberate exclusion.

What is perhaps most interesting in this event is the constitution of a bisexual 'we' at all – itself symptomatic of the very changes that were being discussed. It was not so long ago that I was involved in such discussions as a sole bisexual 'I', arguing for policy changes which would make organisations in which I was involved reflect my needs. Now I am part of a community.

Negotiations such as this with lesbian and gay communities mark a return to the point at which many of us have left it: feeling that there were no spaces in which we could mix, or where we were accepted, we have built our own communities. Now we are back. But that return is not a simple negotiation between separate parties. Much of the work of building a bisexual community has involved producing collectivities which have no secure borders. For instance, many have predominantly lesbian, gay or heterosexual lives and identities, either by choice or under duress.

Given this, the work of a bisexual politics is at least as much about dismantling the entire apparatus which maintains the heterosexual/homosexual dyad as it is about creating a third term to add to it. Such a dismantling questions the grounds on which a separation of sexual orientations is assumed to be possible – and it is perhaps this which makes the work of creating a bisexual community so contradictory. The 'we' which was able to speak in the discussion was the product of a great deal of time and energy, enabling a group of us to develop a bisexual community in Nottingham. That work was itself predicated on the existence of a larger bisexual community spread through the country, which is dependant on the last twelve years[5] of intensive activism, generating groups and events which could make the affirmation of bisexual practice and desire, within whatever identities it circulates, a very real option. For many of the people coming to the Nottingham Bisexual Group it is the fact of such a larger context that makes it possible for them to validate their sexualities. And it does so by offering the possibility of a community where there is an ongoing discussion of these issues, rather than a pre-established identity to take up.

What this suggests is the need for a form of sexual politics which is always attentive to the collapse of the categories with which it operates. Too much activism draws its energies from the anxieties attendant on that collapse, and is primarily motivated to defend those borders. More productively, we can think of strategies whereby, to quote Judith Butler, 'without the presupposition or goal of "unity" ... provisional unities might emerge in the context of concrete actions that have purposes other than the articulation of identity'.[6] Such unities are not generated by themselves: this is not a voluntaristic call for a form of activism which can simply be adopted at will. While the basis of community work is that forms of activism and campaigning are chosen and negotiated, the ground on which such negotiations take place is densely structured by existing debates, problems and opportunities. To risk some sociological generalisations, there are a series of historical changes which have facilitated the growth of a bisexual community, not least the rise of lesbian and gay politics. While that politics has increased the languages and opportunities for addressing same-sex desires, and has thereby encouraged bisexual visibility, it has also pushed bisexuality onto the agenda by its hostility towards it. Alongside this, capitalism's increasing commodification of desire has lent the logic of the market to sexuality, so that even as the right strengthens its 'family values' agenda, sexual pleasure becomes, paradoxically, an ever more acceptable purchase. The rise of the New Right in general, and perhaps the AIDS crisis in particular – a crisis generated by the wilful neglect of governments – has mobilised lesbian and gay communities into action. The intensification of gay pride in response to this increasing homophobia, and the tightening of the boundaries of the queer nation that has accompanied it, has led to an increased stigmatisation of bisexuality, and therefore a greater need for supportive bisexual spaces. And it is this experience of past exclusions which so strongly marks the bisexual community's commitment to a more diverse model of sexual oppressions.

By being non-prescriptive around sexual desires, practices, relationships and identities, bisexual collectivities undermine the very ground on which they gather. It is often that non-prescriptiveness which then comes to form the basis of our gathering. Some groups established by bisexual people have chosen not to centre on bisexuality, but on a wider sexual diversity, on the grounds that it is an inclusive sexual agenda which will best serve our interests, rather than an attempt to set up pure bisexual spaces.[7] Thus the discussion with The Outhouse Project, also included questions of transsexuality and sexual diversity. This addresses the inclusion of bisexual people not simply as 'the bisexual issue', but as part of a shift in the picture of sexual dissidence so that activism can embrace more than just the needs of lesbian and gay-identified people.

This approach is not without its problems: the major one is that throughout the bisexual community there are fears about not being bisexual 'enough'. With alarming regularity I encounter people who feel that, in the absence of a coherent (which would also mean policed) bisexual identity, their expression of bisexuality is wanting. Monogamous people feel they should be having more relationships, and people in multiple relationships feel they are perpetuating a stereotype. People who have had primarily same-sex relationships feel they are expected to have opposite-sex relationships, and people in opposite-sex relationships feel they have not proved themselves until they have had a same-sex relationship. This persistent insecurity is generated by the absence of any normative identities which might provide the security of being bisexual in 'the right way'.[8] However it is this very absence which, when valued, enables the growth of communities where a range of sexual subjectivities are articulated with one another.

My concern in this essay is to suggest the conditions under which such a valuing can taking place, and to explore how dominant lesbian and gay sexual epistemology has obstructed such a valuing because it has been structured not only to exclude bisexuality, but also to cement a heterosexual/homosexual dyad.[9] What are the investments in such a structuring, and what are the consequences? What might be formulated in its place? What conditions are available for such a change to occur? In pointing out the problems of prevalent sexual epistemology, I am not arguing that there is any true or final model which might have been set in place at some mythical starting point of all sexually dissident communities. I am also not denying the effectiveness of the strategic decisions that have been taken in the history of sexual politics, and which have shaped the epistemologies we now have. Nor am I ignoring the shaping presence of hostile cultures within whose shadows our histories have been made. But I hope to show why it is time to change now, and to find ways not only to give up old certainties, but also to profit from that incoherence.

Bisexual Lives

To suggest how bisexuality is marginalised by existing sexual epistemologies, I will begin with a reading of *Modern Homosexualities*,[10] a recent anthology of contemporary lesbian and gay social theory which has been described as setting 'the parameters of lesbian and gay studies for the 1990s'.[11] I was not sure how I would find bisexuality represented in a book called *Modern Homosexualities*, still less in one subtitled 'fragments of lesbian and gay experience'. The bad news was that we did not make it into the index (although the word 'bisexual' appears twelve times in the book). The good news was that where we did – and for that matter did not – appear makes for very illuminating reading. The problems highlighted by a bisexual reading of this text fall into five broad categories, which are representative of other cultural-political phenomena arising from a lesbian/gay engagement (or not) with bisexuality. These five fields – or symptoms – are: the ignoring of documented changes, the language of the homosexual act, collapsing distinctions, unspecified instability, and the love whose name dare not be spoken.

1. *The ignoring of documented changes.* A first warning sign in the book might be the absence of bisexuality from sites of enquiry where its presence is very well known. Beth E. Schneider's 'Lesbian Politics and AIDS Work' addresses safer-sex information for lesbians, noting that 'in all the guidelines for women, sado-masochism is included, despite the considerable controversy about these practices'.[12] There is another controversial issue which also always makes it into lesbian safer-sex guidelines, and that is sex with men. This goes unnoted, along with an earlier significant absence: 'many lesbians have important relationships with gay men, as friends, co-workers, or political colleagues'.[13] And....?

Another moment of non-documentation is in Judith Schuyf's suggestions for future areas of research on western lesbian life-styles. 'To the five life-styles recognized in the 1950s at least three have been added: the lesbian-feminist, the lesbian mother, the lesbian anarcho-squatter'.[14] Not the lesbian-identified bisexual or the lesbian who sleeps with men.

2. *The language of the homosexual act.* It is standard practice to use 'homosexual desire/behaviour/experience/ practice' to describe sex between men or between women. This, supposedly, does not impose assumptions about the identity of the people involved. But the word 'homosexual' is still dependent on the model of sexuality which divides the world into 'heterosexual' and 'homosexual' populations. Thus one writer refers to 'both heterosexuals and homosexuals'[15] as if this covered the entire population. The continued use of 'homosexual' in anthropological or sociological research, such as the essays by Stephen O. Murray on Mesoamerica and Huseyin Tapinc on Turkey, in spite of careful disavowals about applying identity-based models of sexuality, eclipses the possibility of bisexuality. Bisexuality simply cannot exist as a category in discourses which name all male-male and female-female sex 'homosexual' and all male-female sex 'heterosexual'. Thus while Tapinc observes that ' "What is homosexuality?" and "Who is homosexual?" will be answered in very different ways according to the diverse cultural meanings and practices',[16] he has already framed the question within a heterosexual/homosexual paradigm. My chosen terms, throughout the present essay, will be same-sex and opposite-sex (which remain problematic in that they are dependent on a reification of sex).

3. *Collapsing distinctions.* As a counterpart to this supposedly identity-neutral langauge there is also 'identity positive' language, which explicitly identifies subjects as lesbian or gay. This renders bisexuality invisible by imposing an assumed shared identity on all the people in a specific setting. This is not a simple call for a 'bisexual history' where Langston Hughes, and Oscar Wilde are reclaimed as bisexual figures (although there is obviously a place for that work). It is rather to insist on the participation of self-identifying bisexual people and the existence of bisexual desire, in spaces that are called 'lesbian and gay' – a fact which is being excluded from

analysis. So, for instance, Vicki Carter describes Queer Nation and OutRage as 'made up of lesbians and gay men',[17] in spite of the commitment of many of the groups bearing those names to the involvement of bisexual people, and other sexual dissidents who are not lesbian or gay.

There are two particularly interesting moments of tension in this move to collapse bisexuality into other categories. One is Peter M. Nardi's study of gay friendships which finds that 'the majority (82%) of gay men have a gay or bisexual best friend and the majority (76%) of lesbians have a lesbian or bisexual best friend'. Any question of difference is banished by the interpretation of those figures as identifying 'a best friend who is of the same gender and *sexual orientation*'.[18] The sudden appearance, and equally sudden disappearance, of bisexuality marks an interesting historical point where it is becoming harder to ignore the fact of bisexuality, but still lesbian and gay-identified researchers do not really understand how to theorise it.

The other sign of this history is in Ken Plummer's preface and introduction. Neither piece addresses bisexuality except for, in each case, one promise of a tripartite sexual movement. The preface states that 'the essays will be of direct, practical, and continuing relevance to the lesbian, gay and bisexual communities over the next few years';[19] the Introduction closes with the announcement that 'a space has been created for many and diverse voices to make claims and counter-claims as to what the lesbian, gay, and bisexual experiences were, are, and will become in the future'.[20] These unexpected utopias come suddenly, saved for the last paragraphs (and in the case of the Introduction, for its final line!) in a pair of symptomatic – almost convulsive – moments out of which the entire present confusion can be read. Their positioning as closing remarks signals an awareness of the key place of bisexuality in the changes that are happening, and addresses that by giving it a rhetorical weight which is unfortunately belied by the failure to give it any theoretical attention.

4. *Unspecified instability.* Another avoidance of the necessity of theorising bisexuality is the way that the

contributors to *Modern Homosexualities* address the inadequacy of the labels 'homosexual', 'lesbian' and 'gay'. They raise this issue repeatedly: '[these terms] may in fact neglect many same-sex experiences which are not organised this way';[21] 'are the conceptualizations of lesbianism emanating from gay and lesbian studies and remaining in common currency currently rendering invisible certain types of women, women's experiences, and women's relationships?';[22] 'we need more and more ways of thinking about same-sex sexualities'.[23] But this acknowledgement of the limitations of terms never goes so far as to name bisexuality as an issue.

5. *The love whose name dare not be spoken.* Coming at it from the other side, there are several encounters in the book with the facts of opposite-sex sex within a lesbian or gay identity, where the theoretical implication simply go unremarked. Maggie French's 'Loves, Sexualities and Marriages' (a trio of promising plurals) opens with an even more promising quotation: 'I can understand that it is perfectly possible to love someone of the same sex and opposite sex ... one can do both',[24] a quotation attributed to the 'wife of a gay man'. The chapter looks at 'married couples who discovered that one partner's sexuality was gay or lesbian'.[25] It is never made clear whether those terms are chosen by participants or imposed by the researcher. There is also no indication of any inquiry as to how participants in the study identified themselves, although the claim that 'they or their partner was gay or lesbian'[26] is the researcher's unquestioned interpretation of what has happened in these marriages.

The already quoted 'wife of a gay man' with her implicit bisexual perspective returns. After her husband came out to her she began 'a woman-to-woman relationship [and] her identity shifted to a lesbian married to a gay'.[27] But this is not a marriage of convenience. She says of the shifts in identities and relationships: 'it's added a great deal of knowledge and colour to our sex life ... he enjoys his sex life with me ... he enjoys his sexual encounters with his fellers'.[28] And I think one can legitimately ask: what is going on here? French never asks that question, or even poses this situation as a limit-case for the meaning of 'lesbian' and 'gay'. The only conclusion she can draw is that 'marriage is neither inevitably heterosexual nor a validation of heterosexual identity'.[29] But then what exactly are these transgressive marriages a validation of? Could it be – dare one say – of bisexuality?

Modern Homosexualities operates with a structural exclusion of bisexuality, so that its emergence, and the questions it raises, cannot be accommodated or theorised by these essays. The writers register bisexuality only in their attempts to exclude or rewrite it. In this sense, the promise that the book 'sets out the parameters of lesbian and gay studies for the 1990s' may prove all too depressingly true for a range of lesbian and gay spaces. These evasions of bisexuality do nothing to address the serious implications of the facts of opposite-sex desires for dominant lesbian and gay self-understanding, political action, and community norms. Some of the implications have been theorised in Elisabeth D. Daumer's[30] recent argument for bisexual practice as that which 'reactivates the gender and sexuality destabilizing moment of all politicized sexual identities'[31] and disarticulates comfortable identity-positions. She describes bisexuality as 'a sign of transgression, ambiguity and mutability'[32] which prises open 'radical discontinuities between an individual's sex acts and affectional choices, on the one hand, and her or his affirmed political identity, on the other'.[33] She refuses to set up bisexuality as a stable identity itself, to avoid resolidifying the boundaries she is trying to erode. For Daumer, bisexuality is rather a disruptive potential, which haunts and unsettles lesbian, gay and straight identities, by keeping open the possibility of dissident desires: 'What if, by mistake, one forgot that the person holding one's hand was a man – or a woman – and if one [as a woman], equally by mistake, were to slip into a heterosexual relationship with a woman, a lesbian relationship with a man?'.[34]

While I agree with her analysis, what she overlooks is the centrality of a hostility to opposite-sex desires and practices in lesbian and gay culture. Daumer's hope is that bisexuality will facilitate links between those currently identifying as lesbian or gay, and those currently identifying as straight, by eroding their separateness. But a recent comment in *Gay Times* reveals the capacity of those communities to transform – or to contain – bisexual practice, so as to forestall any such rapprochement. Graham McKerrow writes:

> Sex between gay men and lesbians is also coming out of the closet ... Now people talk openly of their opposite-sex-same-sexuality lovers and at the party after the SM Pride March a gay man and a lesbian had sex on the dance floor, but it wasn't heterosexuality. You can tell.[35]

There are two pieces of disavowal in those few lines. The most obvious one is that ominous 'it wasn't heterosexuality' and its accompanying appeal to a gut-level awareness of difference: 'you can tell'. I am reminded of Elizabeth Wilson's assertion at the Activating Theory conference that bisexuality just 'isn't the same'. This is not something that is up for discussion: these issues are decided by being referred to a deeper, supposedly instinctive, sense of otherness. It might be important – but it should never have been necessary – to remember all the other regimes of oppression, inequality and persecution that have been propped up by the words 'they're just not like us'. The other telling phrase is 'opposite-sex-same-sexuality'. Earlier, I outlined the collapse of 'bisexual' into 'lesbian' and 'gay' in Nardi's essay. What is being collapsed here under the words 'same-sexuality'? Does this cover relationships between gay men and bisexual women? It certainly ignores those opposite-sex relationships between lesbians and straight men, or bisexual men and heterosexual women. The word 'same' hermetically seals the boundaries of gay and lesbian communities, banishing the awkward questions of what else is going on in such instances of opposite-sex sex. Bisexuality seems caught between a position where it is completely other to lesbianism or gayness, so that no connection or alliance – let alone more intimate relationship – is possible, or so similar that it doesn't disturb current thinking at all. As another gesture towards keeping the heterosexual/homosexual binary intact, and thickening that slash to the point of impenetrability, Bernard Devlin, Alex Laski and Shimonn McKenzie recently wrote an article in *The Pink Paper* entitled 'Deconstruction Into Heterosexual Oblivion'. They stated categorically that:

> no evidence exists to substantiate ... [the] claim that it 'has been a noted phenomenon for about ten years' that lesbians are having sex with straight men, or that gay men are having sex with straight women, or (more ludicrously still) that lesbians and gay men are having sex with each other.[36]

Returning to *Gay Times*' assertion that 'it wasn't heterosexuality', underpinning these ways of dealing with bisexuality is the positioning of the straight world as a monolithically privileged and hostile force ('stop the straight war against queer love', read the stickers). This drawing up of the battle lines is nothing new in sexual politics, and the demonization of the straight world is certainly nothing new in lesbian and gay communities. The creation of an enemy performs a cleansing ritual, whereby the embattled community is totally free of the disgusting traits of 'them'. The expurgations of lesbian and gay culture have included identifying the straight world as the sole possessors or practitioners of, among other things: heterosexual privilege, eroticizing difference, old age, boring clothes, gender role conformity, bad dancing, cross-gender desire, bad looks, and breeding. Along with the exclusions which each of these terms performs is a purging of the 'straight' lesbians and 'straight' gays who have children, do SM, enjoy gender roles, or have opposite-sex relationships. All such deviants can be represented as symptoms of the invasion, or persistence, of straight ideology in the queer world: to be repelled, persuaded, or ignored. In Ara Wilson's memorable phrase these are 'heterosexual incursions into our cosy but fun little world.'[37]

To put itself at ease, the body politic rids itself of all those dis-easing (for which read 'diseased') subjects, practices, pleasures and attitudes which trouble it. Discourses of normalisation produce what Erving Goffman has called spoiled identities. These are the irredeemably tainted identities, produced in the name of a world which might be easy, habitable, comfortable for some by excluding certain groups from legitimation, rights or power. In anti-oppressive practice one manifestation of such a 'politics of ease' is the 'safe space', a space purged of power and prejudice – which often amounts to a space purged of those people who do not share assumed norms. *Gay Times* articulated this position in a review of BBC2's *Open Space* documentary 'Bi' by asking: 'How can a person really know how badly a group is oppressed unless s/he's at least a member of that group? But if a bisexual can't fully comprehend the oppression of lesbians and gays, the reverse is also true.'[38] Can't fully comprehend? Does a lesbian lose all her memories, insights and awareness the moment she fantasizes about a man? How many years of living and loving is erased by the first shade of opposite-sex desire? The ease with which those comments draw up a line between 'us' and 'them' is frightening. I have already indicated how bi people can be presented as no different at all: no need for change, questioning, adaptation. At the other end of the spectrum there is a talismanic power to the word 'bisexual' whereby it can invoke an entirely separate, discrete, dissimilar, self-contained group. It is sometimes said that bisexuals don't exist – we are 'really' gay, or 'really' straight. Now we are 'really' different.

The *Gay Times* comment is the soft end of lesbian and gay communities' policing of bisexuality within their space. In Manchester's 'Flesh' nightclub people are asked at the door if they are lesbian or gay – the bisexuals are refused entry (including those bisexuals in same-sex relationships). The straights have the sense to lie: pride costs these days. In many lesbian and gay telephone helpline organisations bisexuals are seen as a group who cannot be dealt with: 'we haven't shared their experience'. The same people who will confidently take calls from heterosexual transvestites give apologies and brush-offs to bisexual people. I recently had a call passed on to me by a well established helpline: it was from a straight man who had just discovered letters to his partner from her girlfriend. So great was the halo of difference attached to the very presence of bisexuality in this equation that *trained gay workers* saw it as appropriate to pass the call on, in breach of the organisation's own rules on confidentiality, rather than deal with it.

So much disavowal suggests a very strong anxiety. And the anxiety is, very simply, this: if there is not a discrete group of people who only ever experience homosexual desire, then *what if we are not so different from the straight world after all*? While the fight is on to ward off bisexuality's presence as a 'heterosexual incursion' by consigning it to its own space, the basic anxiety persists: what if the rituals of exorcism fail? What if the enemy turns up in our own community, erupts – like the scene in *Alien* – in our own flesh?

Now none of this is to suggest that there are *no* differences. There are clearly legal and institutional pressures on us which do not affect straight-identified people (and yet there are still straight men being arrested for cottaging). There are social spaces which are ours rather than theirs (and yet increasingly straight-identified people are dancing in gay clubs). There are cultural products and sub-cultural conventions which originate, or circulate, particularly within our communities (and yet always find audiences beyond them). While it would be foolish to deny the specificity of lesbian and gay communities as they have developed, their borders are permeable. And among the differences which constitute them, the one difference which it might be assumed would most strongly delineate lesbian and gay space from straight space – that is, same-sex desires and sexual practices – is definitely not confined to them. Nor are opposite-sex desires and practices confined to the straight world. Thus while there may be a range of differences, there is no transcendent difference upon which to establish the heterosexual/homosexual binary.

I do not mention *Alien* casually. The drama of *Alien* is the confrontation between Them and Us (on the surface). Human crew against non-human monster. While the alien's eruption from John Hurt's stomach marks the unnerving fact that the non-human can inhabit the human, it also dramatises something much more reassuring: the two cannot, ultimately, coexist. The Other cannot be inside our own space: its birth destroys the host, so that where 'them' begins, 'us' has to stop. John Hurt is the sacrificial victim in this particular exorcism ritual – much as bisexual people are sacrificed by ostracism from lesbian and gay communities, for not being 'one of us'. To acknowledge, to *give birth to* the other in us is supposedly to cease being who we were altogether. The reality, of course, is very different.

Dangerous Politics

If the main obstacle to the acceptance of bisexuality, in all its meanings, is the construction of 'lesbian and gay' around an opposition to opposite-sex desire, then the key issue for a theorisation of bisexual politics is the dissolution of those boundaries. I want to begin that work with Mary Douglas' book *Purity and Danger*,[39] an anthropological enquiry into the ways that certain practices and people are declared dangerously polluting to an otherwise 'pure' state. She defines dirt, that which menaces purity, as 'matter out of place' and therefore 'dirt is the by-product of a systematic ordering and classification'.[40] Pollution exists only where there is strong categorisation, and where 'eliminating ... [is an] effort to organise the environment'.[41] Douglas comes down firmly in favour of pollution as a process of social change: 'purity is the enemy of change, of ambiguity and compromise'.[42] By a close study of attempts to foresetall such change, she produces a theory of the function of purity and stigmatised dirt. These analyses attend to forms of separation and demarcation which serve particular social interests. Douglas sees ritual danger as marking a real danger to a particular set of assumptions, which is then represented as dangerous to mental or physical health.

Hence the anxieties centred on bisexuality can be read as expressing a very real fear of the collapse of a symbolic system: the heterosexual/homosexual dyad. Douglas presents a picture of paranoid societies, where 'people living in the interstices of the power structure, [are] felt to be a threat to those with better defined status. Since they are credited with dangerous, uncontrollable powers, an excuse is given for suppressing them.'[43] That statement makes interesting reading in the light of current myths about bisexuals, many of them shared by gay and straight people: that if you get involved with them they convert you; they always leave you for a partner of the other sex; they drain the vital energies of gay politics; they are an HIV risk; they are psychologically unstable. You only need to watch *Basic Instinct* to see a range of straight anxieties cohere in the figure of a bisexual woman who is, quite simply, a threat to life – a set of images which was deployed to almost identical effect in Alison Maclean's 1993 New Zealand film *Crush*. Similarly, in 1983 in the USA *Gay Community News* printed a now infamous cartoon advertising 'bisexuality insurance' to protect lesbians and gays from the dangers of a bisexual lover.[44]

A second important focus for danger is territory. The creation of spaces that are safe from heterosexism has been a successful, and often very difficult, enterprise. It has included the creation of clubs, support groups, phonelines and magazines. But the equation of heterosexism with heterosexuality now fuels mostly a ghetto mentality which impedes political alliances and which is a luxury of those whose oppression is apparently so restricted to sexuality that alliances are not an issue. It also generates a constant fear of discovering 'heterosexuality' in your own lesbian/gay body, or in a lover, or friend – which is, for instance, behind the assertion that 'it wasn't heterosexuality' in *Gay Times*. The demonization and othering of heterosexuality polices the sexuality of those within such spaces at least as effectively as it keeps anyone straight-identified out of them. For while heterosexist abuse poses a very real danger to all of us, a disproportionate amount of energy is being expended on 'the enemy within', via a range of discursive engagements every bit as invasive, and final in their judgements, as the x-ray pictures which capture the enemy within Sigourney Weaver's body in *Alien 3*.

155

Douglas cites three approaches to the threatening impact of category violations:

1. Consign them to another fixed category: bisexuals are really gay, or really straight. The anomaly doesn't exist.
2. State that they are dangerous, and should therefore be avoided or controlled. Pass on the phone call, keep them out of the club, don't have relationships with them.
3. Find some way of acknowledging them, in order to disrupt existing limited patterns.

Pursuing this last option requires models of a non-devouring relationship to difference, which operate by miscegenation and hybridity, in a celebration of boundaries transgressed and never simply unified.

Miscegenation has been explored as a metaphor for political practice in the work of Donna Haraway, as part of her project to produce a postmodern feminism which both undoes fixed binaries, and preserves radical difference. Haraway's use of such a charged word makes analogies between the violence generated by white racist desires to maintain separateness in the face of the collapse of black/white boundaries, and the consequences of other attempts to keep categories separate. Haraway is in effect arguing for the inevitability of miscegenation, in spite of such attempts, and highlighting the oppressive function of the horror that has been attached to that fact (the horror of *Alien* – the horror of letting the other into our bodies).

For Haraway the projects of domination practised by a range of systems of oppression are explicable as 'a search for a common language in which all resistance to instrumental control disappears and all heterogeneity can be submitted to disassembly, reassembly, investment and exchange'.[45] A world in which we are all compatible and reconciled – where there is only 'self' and no 'other' – enables a system of monolithic values to co-ordinate us in a single (capitalist) economy, a single (white) culture, a single (patriarchal) gender system, and a single (heteronormative) sexuality. Against this is her dream 'not of a common language, but of a powerful infidel heteroglossia'[46] where networks of resistance are not coherent – which would involve submission to a central organising principle – but productively conflictual. Underpinning this form of politics is Haraway's insistence on the partiality and locatedness of every subject. We are situated in specific places and speak from there, shaped by them. She argues for 'situated and embodied knowledges and against various forms of unlocatable, and so irresponsible, knowledge claims. Irresponsible means unable to be called into account'.[47] Here, to be called into account is to be called to account for the specificity of one's vision, the contexts, histories and power differentials which produce it. Questions of knowledge then become, from a Foucauldian perspective, a question of the dangers and abuses of any particular epistemology.

If any transcendent, omniscient position is irresponsible, we can learn to relinquish the search for a single, total explanatory politics, in which conflicts of understanding are regarded as inefficient, and disagreement with any project is understood by that project as a threat to its liberatory trajectory. As we reject the image of the pure and integral self, defending itself against contaminating incursions, we can develop new models in which, as Haraway puts it:

> The knowing self is partial in all its guises, never finished, whole, simply there and original; it is always constructed and stitched together imperfectly, and therefore able to join with another ... we do not seek partiality for its own sake, but for the sake of the connections and unexpected openings situated knowledges make possible.[48]

Knowledge, then, is partial in two senses: it is incomplete, and it is biased. Haraway argues that once we accept this partiality, our knowledge becomes a resource for coalitions. For participants in coalitions, the acquisition of new knowledge does not simply mean locating others within our framework, but requires an acceptance of contradictions and discrepancies. Within the coalition we encounter other perspectives which cannot simply be subsumed into our own but which must negotiate with them in order to form a viable political force. Politics involves a mapping out of a web of abuses – not organised as simple hierarchies of who has power and who does not – which can be communicated and addressed in mutually transforming 'power-sensitive – not pluralist – "conversations" '.[49] We can then move beyond embattled positions of mutual blame and pure/dangerous dynamics, where the name of the game is to prove who oppresses whom and there is only one winner. For Haraway the consequence of such 'conversations' is miscegenation.

Bisexuality is a miscegenate location. On the one hand, it raises the need for a sexual politics where queerness can positively embrace opposite-sex desires. On the other, it is itself a place where there is a difficult mixing of supposedly incompatible orientations. These meetings are dangerous exchanges, which disrupt the identities we have built up, and lead to unpredictable places. 'Conversations' of lesbians and gay men with bisexuality include: defining agendas for shared actions; sexual relationships; angry debates on adding 'bisexual' to the names of 'lesbian and gay' organisations, books, conferences; the inclusion of information about safer sex with women in HIV education aimed at gay men. They also include internal 'conversations' about and between the contradictory and perhaps never unified positions within ourselves: gender identities, sexual practices, sexual fantasies, sexual identities, sexual orientations, sexual politics. None of this is comfortable or easy. Reading Douglas and Haraway together, then we may gain a picture of a sexual-political epistemology whose categories defend deeply partial visions with strong emotions. Such a defence holds lesbian/gay politics in a particular place, resistant to articulation with other sexual politics.

I want to use one other writer to look at some of the specific historical concerns which shape these resistances, and to suggest some of the directions of transformation that our current situated positions open up. Homi K. Bhabha has used 'hybridity' as a tool to analyse the specific material, symbolic, and psychic imbrications of certain cultural histories. His work has focused on issues of race and colonialism, and I am interested in examining how far it is also useful for accounts of sexually dissident communities. For Bhabha, cultural difference is the produce of active 'cultural differentiation'.[50] Systems of separation and organisation – such as those outlined by Douglas – create difference as a function of power, with rights and privileges inhering in certain specified cultural identities (taking us back to 'they're just not like us'). 'Hybridity', writes Bhabha, 'puts together the traces of certain other meanings or discourses',[51] by reconfiguring existing cultural material. It supplements dominant terms, and signals their limitations by finding new uses for them. That insinuation of the supplement into the dominant means that the processes of differentiation falter, no longer achieving what they did. Consequently hybridity effects 'a disturbing questioning of the images and presence of authority'[52] and the terms on which authority declares its supremacy.

Bhabha suggests two ways in which hybridity challenges authority – one orientated towards the future, one towards the past. As new communities form out of the old, they indicate that the old material-symbolic regime of authority cannot go on forever: they are no longer encompassed by the existing system, even as they inhabit it. Any authority's own practices slip away from it, and it is no longer self-identical in what were its own secure spaces. One piece of bisexual hybridity effecting just such an intervention is the call for the adoption of the title 'Lesbian, Gay and Bisexual Pride' – which has already taken place in parts of the USA. A slogan which has been integral to lesbian and gay communities, and which has shaped them in ways which homogenised them so as to exclude bisexuality, now crops up in the centre-stage of bisexual politics, as part of a hybrid politics. The hybrid does not seek a radical break with its past. Rather, the hybrid acknowledges the part that the past has played in constituting new cultures and identities, and then displaces the dominant (and dominating) culture's attempt to enshrine itself in 'an eternity produced by self-generation',[53] by supplementing it and thereby rewriting the future.

159

The other process of hybridity is the rewriting of official history, and the forms of present culture which supposedly perpetuate it. Any normative culture enacts 'a continual displacement of its irredeemably plural modern space'.[54] It repeatedly disavows its own differences from itself in appeals to a construction of the nation – or of the queer nation – which claims a homogeneous past. One particularly strong symbol in the production of a narrative of gay homogeneity is the pink triangle, deployed in ways that make a claim for a gay identity, analogous to ethnicity, where the gay community is read as the cultural manifestation of an inherent sexual orientation.[55] The triangle situates gay people as grouped in a distinct culture or community, our own separateness proven by the separation of gay people for extermination in the concentration camps of Nazi Germany. The circulation of the triangle as a badge, an earring, a T-shirt design, makes it operative in maintaining such a community by acting as an element of a putative gay ethnicity. But the production of that community is seen to be based on a shared sexuality which is already, and invariantly, in place.

The stakes in changing such a history are high. The bisexual use of pink and black triangles was recently described to me as 'cultural theft'. When bisexual people take up those symbols it is as a marker of the fact that the history of bisexuality is – and has always been – densely bound up with homosexual identity. The collectivity of queers marked by the Third Reich included people who experienced opposite-sex as well as same-sex attractions. And so do the contemporary collectivities of lesbian and gay communities. The hostility to bisexual use of these symbols marks a defence of a history which supposedly proves gay collectivity and similarity, but which in fact is a history of differences which have never been fully contained.[56] When the other voices start to inhabit this history 'a hybrid [queer] national narrative' emerges to turn 'the nostalgic past into the disruptive "anterior" '. The historical fixing points of present regimes of differentiation prove unstable, and this 'displaces the historical subject – opens it up to other histories and incommensurable narrative subjects'.[57]

Bhabha argues that 'the paranoid threat from the hybrid is finally uncontainable because it breaks down the symmetry and duality of self/other, inside/outside'.[58] As well as bisexuality insinuating itself into collective histories and collective futures, it comes to inhabit the personal histories and futures of many lesbians and gay men. The adoption of a lesbian or gay identity currently involves the rejection of past opposite-sex experiences, and the denial of any such possibilities for the future. The lesbian and gay activist group OutRage advertised one of its events as a chance to 'rejoice at being saved from HETERO HELL'. With 'hetero' standing uncompleted, it remains unclear whether this hell is the social structure of heterosexism, or the very fact of heterosexual desire – so that an escape from the former seems to require an escape from the latter. While the two are in many ways implicated in one another, the conflating of all heterosexual desire with the destructive mechanisms of heterosexist and heteronormative oppression does nothing to enable people to accept their own sexual diversity. Indeed, it produces a mirroring of that hellish structure of exclusion and sexual purism from which it claims to effect an escape.

Bhabha offers a model for the incorporation of otherness in a way which does not deny its disruptive potential. I have opened his theory up to a more nuanced model of the distribution of authority and difference, for his tends to rely on a clear-cut division between the central and the marginal, rather than a multiplicity of centres and margins around different issues. Bhabha's choice of 'irredeemable' to describe modern plurality acts as a powerful counterweight to such salvationist rhetoric as the example from OutRage. There is no redemption from plurality. Deviance persists in the culture which is trying to expel it, thereby disrupting the myths of any authority's heritage as an always homogeneous past, and its peristence as an always identical future.

In spite of our best efforts, then, we are those people we always warned ourselves about. The narratives, identities and spaces which we have, contain other histories, selves and places, which make of us very different people. And we require a sexual politics which can adjust to that. Making such changes means, for me, putting 'bi' into the 'sexual' of 'sexual politics', and for others means making other hybrids by putting their bodies and desires into a 'sexual' that has increasingly meant only 'lesbian and gay'.

Sexual Citizens

While hybridity makes a liberating model for activist politics, the question still remains: what needs to happen in order for it to be taken up? Under what conditions can such activism take place? One fruitful site for the collapse of borders, as suggested by Haraway, is the coalition. Central to the operation of a coalition is an end to the politics of ease. Commenting on nationalism, and equally true for other calls for safe and pure spaces, Bernice Johnson Reagon has argued that: 'At a certain stage nationalism is crucial to a people if you are going to ever impact as a group in your own interest. Nationalism at another point becomes reactionary because it is totally inadequate for surviving in a world with many peoples'.[59] I want to change Reagon's emphasis slightly: there are not two consecutive stages of a need to be separate, and a need for coalition. Rather the two needs are concurrent, and both must be met at different points, in a dynamic of separation and confluence. The loss of ease is traumatic to all of us who suffer because of our differences, but Reagon states the need for that loss in no uncertain terms: 'You don't go into coalition because you like it. The only reason you would consider trying to team up with somebody who could possibly kill you, is because that's the only way you can figure you can stay alive'.[60]

One important factor in coalitions is that the range of inequalities means that we are all taking risks: unilateral privilege is rare. But what is also difficult for any of us to face is that those oppressive others with whom the oppressed might make coalitions, have the same fears, however unfounded they may be. White fears of black violence, heterosexual fears of AIDS, men's fears of castrating lesbians:

fears usually expressed as hostility. When we are faced with those unreasonable fears – which have been used to legitimise our oppression – we inevitably respond with anger. Coalition then involves acknowledging all those incensing fears which get in the way of working together – and which need to be addressed in separate spaces, before we hear them in the raw (and which, it needs to be said, bisexual people are faced with whenever we work with lesbians and gay men).

The communities we have built are very comfortable, and in this brutal world we need all the comfort we can get, but they also insulate us from the facts of power exercised against us, of which we are always reminded when we leave. To choose to live in a safe space (which may not be safe for everyone in it) is to settle for less than we deserve, by neglecting the possibility of working in coalitions whereby the whole world might be safe for everyone. As such, coalitions are not simply the coming together of otherwise antagonistic groups, but also offer a new site of comfort. In order to maintain this sort of coalition we need to attend to the processes of our politics as much as to the goals. The questions must constantly be asked: how is this group functioning? what is everyone feeling? where are the tensions, the hostilities, the resentments? how is power operating here? (A search through books on conflict resolution and groupwork yields hundreds of practices to address them). However, I am arguing for a process not of harmony, which is another totalizing gesture, but of productive anxiety, where our clashes are not seen as unacceptable (in the name of homogeneity), signs that we cannot work together (in the name of spaces free from oppression), or distractions (in the name of a final goal). Rather, their difficulty is the sign that we are getting somewhere worth being.

But given the difficulty of such alliances, what can stitch them, however provisionally, together? I see three central issues which coalitions have to address in order to survive. Firstly, how do we recognise that we are different, without attempting to accommodate our differences under any overarching interpretative framework? Secondly, how do we

163

recognise that not all difference is comprehensible? As Iris Marion Young has written, in a critique of the hope for communities of direct connection and shared understanding: 'politics must be conceived as a relationship of strangers who do not understand one another'[61] – and sometimes never will. Thirdly, how do we prevent an acknowledgement of shared oppressions from occluding the reality that we operate within our own relations of domination, privilege and inequality?

In responding to these questions, and taking up the model used in bisexual community work, a mode of articulation which does not erode our differences – but does erode our separateness – is that of citizenship. In a description of citizenship which is resonant with hybridity, Simon Watney has argued that:

> An ethically grounded practice of citizenship has the great initial advantage of being posed to, and on behalf of, the entire population – no longer pictured in crude parliamentary terms as a majority surrounded on all sides by distinct and possibly threatening minorities, but rather as a complex unity of many overlapping and interrelated groups and identities.[62]

Here, citizenship is presented as a means to undo oppositions. Such a model locates us all as subjects in need, linked in relationships of interdependence and responsibility. Perhaps the defining issue on progressive and reactionary invocations of citizenship is how far such responsibility is seen as individual (with the proposed remedy being individual altruism, attendant on calls for personal morality), and how far it is seen as structural (with state and institutional responsibilities for undoing established systems of inequality).[63]

I want to raise three main criticisms of the efficacy of citizenship. Firstly, citizenship can be underpinned by a model of cultural assimilation, whereby 'the good citizen' is one who conforms to a particular set of norms, and is only entitled to recognition from the state – and, by implication, from other citizens – on those terms. Secondly, citizenship can assume shared needs across all citizens. It therefore serves to erode any notions of different vulnerabilities. In particular, it erodes notions of communities, with their own different locations in a web of oppressions, and replaces them with an array of individuals who all have identical requirements. Lastly, citizenship can prescribe the needs of the citizens it envisions, creating an agenda of what freedoms are important. When it sets out a model of specific rights, and ignores others, citizenship produces a model of apparent liberty when it in fact closes off whole areas of unmet needs (for example, citizenship-based politics often asserts a right to work, but rarely a right *not* to work).

These models very clearly inform the right's current interest in citizenship, where a single 'Citizens' Charter' prescribes for everyone, regardless of their positioning, and assumes an invariant, and selective, set of needs. Against this, it is possible to argue for a differentiated model of citizenship, where the notion of entitlement requires attention to the specificities of different communities and individuals. For insofar as we are entitled to common rights, and varied expressions of them, we all require different interventions and forms of empowerment in order to secure them.

As lesbian, gay and bisexual people, we often speak as if from outside a monolithic heterosexual hegemony, and replicate that positioning of 'us and them' in our self-construction. Might we not instead speak in a way which disrupts that model, by positioning ourselves, *and others*, as deviating from an unattainable sexual ideology, situating all the marginals as *outside* and *beyond* – that is to say, as the *successors to* – a hegemonic sexual standard? And I mean this not in the sense of us as the already-written and stable future, but rather as the urgently needed collectivity through whom, in multiple ways, change can be hastened. We do not know where we will go, or what else we might need to take into account (therefore acknowledging our partiality), and we cannot expect agreement, consensus or comfort in our perverse body politic. If we can get beyond the rhetoric of the embattled minority standing self-righteously against the enemy, how else can we position ourselves?

Activating Theory: Lesbian, Gay and Bisexual Politics

If we ask seriously the question of who is oppressed in the name of a sexual standard, the list is extensive. Lesbians, gay men, bisexual people, transgender people, SM practitioners, old people, sex workers, disabled people, fetishists, people with HIV and AIDS, children, people with learning difficulties. Anyone having sex in public, in groups, with objects. White racism continues to view all expressions of black people's sexuality as disgusting or exotic. And while 'heterosexual privilege' is a phrase much in use in lesbian and gay politics, for straight women, being sexually active counts as evidence against them in cases of rape and sexual harassment. For all these groups, sexuality is a target for discriminatory intervention.[64]

In this sense we already have a culture of 'sexual citizenship' on an assimilationist model: straight, white, married, monogamous, adult, able-bodied, gender-euphoric, vanilla males are full citizens. The rest of us are not. Against such a system of exclusive citizenship it becomes clear that we need to turn our political focus from a single issue of homosexual desire, to an agenda of *inclusive* sexual citizenship, where a diverse range of citizens have an entitlement to pleasure and where no consensual sexual practices are grounds for legal, institutional or interpersonal harassment.

The formulation of a citizenship agenda around sexuality raises again the problems of normative identities. For insofar as models of sexual citizenship are proposed by communities which already have their own models for who does and does not count as having entitlement, they replicate those processes of exclusion. Instead, I think it is helpful to develop a citizenship agenda that is generated by coalitions around specific issues, where the creation of identity is not the pre-requisite for a collectivity which can articulate its rights. Rather, as I outlined for the growth of a bisexual movement, mobilisation on particular issues creates commonality on the basis of different affiliations to a shared campaign. I am thinking for instance of the 'Countdown on Spanner' campaign, where SM practitioners of different sexualities

166

worked together on the issue of a court case brought against a group of gay men for their SM activities; or the recent march on Washington in the USA which was – after much debate – in the name of lesbian, gay, bi and transgender people.[65]

Sexual citizenship opens up more opportunities for such campaigns by widening our awareness of the different exercises of power on sexual expression. The productivity of such campaigns is precisely that while they require a form of consensus on one issue, there is no need for consensus on many others. They then become generative of debates which are possible because they do not undermine the basis of the collectivity, which lies elsewhere than the identity of participants. These points have a particular inflection for an agenda of sexual citizenship. For it would be easy to use it as the basis for a system which seemingly co-ordinates a range of sexual subjects into a comfortable harmony, their differences all explained and understood. Citizenship is not itself an overarching concept which can conquer differences. Within a citizenship-framework the specificity of groups will go on producing different debates around citizenship and its implications. Sexual citizenship, like sexual identity, is most powerful as a mobilising force, when it raises new questions rather than providing final answers.

For bisexual people its strength is that it opens up the hold that lesbian and gay identities have had on sexual politics. It carries the promise of our participation, by setting out an agenda in which our sexual difference is a reason for articulating our interests, and not grounds for our exclusion. Insofar as it does so by opening up a wider agenda it raises the same problems as that of building a bisexual community: with no normative sexual identity, on what terms are we to feel secure? And, in much the same way, I am arguing that our security lies in our sharing a space where our needs are all different and yet imbricated with one another. It is by building on those imbrications, which are already in place, that we can take our activism in these new directions.

Notes

1 Eve Kosofsky Sedgwick, *Epistemology of the Closet* (Hemel Hempstead: Harvester Wheatsheaf 1991), p11.

2 Given that distinctive social, geographical and economic lesbian and gay spaces do exist, it seems unfair to put every use of 'community' in scare quotes. However, I am noting here that it is a term which is predicated on the very fixity of boundaries that I will be disputing.

3 I am focusing on these conflicts, rather than straight conflicts with bisexual people for three reasons. Firstly, my own involvement with lesbian/gay communities makes this my area of experience. Secondly, in a classic example of Foucault's reverse discourse, it has been lesbians and gay men who have said the most, and been most hostile, towards bisexual people *as bisexual*, and so it is around that that we have organised. Heterosexual hostility has targeted us as if we were lesbian or gay – just more of those perverts. As bisexuality acquires an identity which is visible to the straight world, this is changing. Thirdly, I feel that we belong together, and I am writing out of that desire.

4 The Nottingham Bisexual Group, which I was involved in setting up in October 1992, provides spaces for support and discussion for people exploring issues around bisexuality. It also arranges training for a range of organisations, and is involved in various activism projects, the major one of which is hosting the Eleventh National Bisexual Conference. It is one of the largest bisexual organisations in the UK.

5 This figure is based on the establishment of The London Bisexual Group in 1981, the first bisexual group in the UK.

6 Judith Butler, *Gender Trouble: Feminism and the Subversion of Identity*, (London: Routledge, 1990), p15.

7 For instance, the Freedom of Sexuality groups in Liverpool and Bristol. Obviously this non-prescriptiveness does not extend to abusive behaviour or harassment.

8 This is not the only source of these anxieties. Gay and straight discourse alike are concerned with disputing the 'credentials' of people describing themselves as bisexual. One particularly strong and offensive instance was offered by the *The Pink Paper* commenting on singer Brett Anderson's announcement of his bisexuality: 'a "bisexual who's never had sex with a man" … stinks as bad as a white boy blacking up': 18 April, 1993, p14.

9 Politicised lesbian and gay sexual epistemology is obviously not 'dominant' when compared to heterosexism. However, within lesbian and gay communities, various forms of the epistemology I am describing dominate – and they are also a replication of that dominant division of heterosexual from homosexual in which the straight world has so much invested.

10 Ken Plummer, ed., *Modern Homosexualities* (London: Routledge, 1992).

11 Elizabeth Wilson, quoted on the book's cover.

12 Plummer, ed., *Modern Homosexualities*, p165.

13 *Ibid.*, p161.
14 *Ibid.*, p63.
15 *Ibid.*, p182.
16 *Ibid.*, p39.
17 *Ibid.*, p223.
18 *Ibid.*, p114, my emphasis.
19 *Ibid.*, pxviii.
20 *Ibid.*, p25.
21 *Ibid.*, pxv.
22 *Ibid.*, p73.
23 *Ibid.*, p15.
24 *Ibid.*, p87.
25 *Ibid.*, p87.
26 *Ibid.*, p92.
27 *Ibid.*, p94.
28 *Ibid.*, p95.
29 *Ibid.*, p97.
30 Elisabeth D. Daumer, 'Queer Ethics; or, the Challenge of Bisexuality to Lesbian Ethics', *Hypatia* 7:4 (1992), pp91–105.
31 *Ibid.*, p98.
32 *Ibid.*, p103.
33 *Ibid.*, p99.
34 *Ibid.*, p97.
35 *Gay Times*, January 1993, p29.
36 *The Pink Paper*, 14 March 1993, p10.
37 *Outlook* 4:4 (1992), p28.
38 *Gay Times*, August 1992, p66.
39 Mary Douglas, *Purity and Danger* (London: Routledge, 1966).
40 *Ibid.*, p35.
41 *Ibid.*, p2.
42 *Ibid.*, p162.
43 *Ibid.*, p104.
44 Reprinted in Loraine Hutchins and Lani Kaahumanu, eds., *Bi Any Other Name* (Boston: Alyson Publications, 1991), p224.
45 Haraway, 'A Manifesto for Cyborgs: Science, Technology and Socialist Feminism in the 1980s', in Linda J. Nicholson, ed., *Feminism/Postmodernism* (London: Routledge, 1990), p206.
46 *Ibid.*, p223.
47 Haraway, 'Situated Knowledges: The Science Question in Feminism and the Privilege of Partial Perspective', in Haraway, *Simians, Cyborgs and Women* (London: Free Association Books, 1991), p191.
47 *Ibid.*, pp193, 196.
48 Haraway, 'The Actors are Cyborg, Nature is Coyote, and the Geography is Elsewhere: Postscript to "Cyborgs at Large"', in Constance Penley and Andrew Ross, eds., *Technoculture* (Minneapolis: University of Minnesota Press, 1991), p23.

[49] *Ibid.*, p23.

[50] Bhabha, 'Signs Taken for Wonders: Questions of Ambivalence and Authority Under a Tree Outside Delhi, May 1817', in Francis Barker et al., eds, *Europe and Its Others: Proceedings of the Essex Conference on the Sociology of Literature*, 2 Vols (University of Essex, 1985), I, p99.

[51] Bhabha, 'The Third Space', in Jonathan Rutherford, ed., *Identity: Community, Culture, Difference* (London: Lawrence and Wishart, 1990), p211.

[52] Bhabha, 'Signs Taken For Wonders', p98.

[53] Bhabha, 'Dissemination: Time, Narrative, and the Margins of the Modern Nation', in Bhabha, ed., *Nation and Narration* (London: Routledge, 1992), p299.

[54] *Ibid.*, p300.

[55] For a summary of such arguments see Steven Epstein, 'Gay Politics, Ethnic Identity: The Limits of Social Constructionism', *Socialist Review* 17:3/4 (1987), pp9–54.

[56] For another critical account of the deployment of the pink triangle, see Stuart Marshall, 'The Contemporary Political Use of Gay History: The Third Reich' in Bad Object-Choices, eds., *How Do I Look: Queer Film and Video* (Seattle: Bay Press 1991), pp65–101.

[57] Bhabha, 'DissemiNation', p318.

[58] Bhabha, 'Signs Taken for Wonders', p100.

[59] Bernice Johnson Reagon, 'Coalition Politics: Turning the Century', in Barbara Smith, ed., *Home Girls: A Black Feminist Anthology* (New York: Kitchen Table, Women of Colour Press, 1983), p358.

[60] *Ibid.*, p357. The discomfort of the coalition has also formed the basis for many rejections of it, on the grounds that it is simply too painful to work with people who behave oppressively towards you. Work to make coalitions more comfortable is essential – and sacrificing ease does not simply mean sacrificing rights! But a commitment to anti-oppressive practices within a coalition does not end the discomfort.

[61] Iris Marion Young, 'The Ideal of Community and the Politics of Difference', in Nicholson, ed., *Feminism/Postmodernism*, p317.

[62] Simon Watney, 'Practices of Freedom: "Citizenship" and the Politics of Identity in the Age of AIDS', in Rutherford, *Identity*, p184.

[63] 'Progressive' and 'reactionary' are slippery terms – all the more so as calls for voluntaristic self-transformation are as likely to be found in radical sexual politics as in the Conservative Party Manifesto.

[64] Gayle Rubin gives a more extensive account of some of these issues in 'Thinking Sex: Notes for a Radical Theory of the Politics of Sexuality' in Carole S. Vance, ed., *Pleasure and Danger: Exploring Female Sexuality*, second edition (London: Pandora 1989), pp267–319.

[65] Bi rather than bisexual: the 'sexual' was seen as undermining the work of lesbians and gay men to insist that they shared a culture more than just a desire.

Which Equality? Toleration, Difference or Respect

ANGELIA R. WILSON

The difficulty with revolution is that it is motivated by the need to revolt but often unaccompanied by a coherent alternative which is completely supported by every revolutionary. The need for revolution is easy to arouse by simply giving a voice to the unspoken, or perhaps unheard, experiences of oppression. And indeed it is my experience of oppression as a lesbian in a homophobic, heterosexist society which fuels my desire for change, for revolution. But, perhaps unfortunately, my desire for change is tempered by a desire to know exactly what this might be a 'change to'. Like the experience of socialism by some women, my own encounter with fundamentalist religion has left me with both caution and scepticism about the prospect of complete reformation, not least my own position in it. And so the plea for lesbian and gay equality, which I have heard from my own protesting mouth, stirs my desire for change and then leaves me silent with only a nagging doubt. Any brief encounter with activism cannot but make me both wanting more, and wondering where it will all end. This ever-illusive equality is but a tease, in form and in practice. I know I want change; I know I want the all too familiar face of inequality to disappear. But I am unable to sketch in the face of the equality I desire. Indeed, I am only comforted in knowing that others, even more trained and able than myself, also struggle in creating and then identifying with this desired equality. My caution, indeed my scepticism, of revolution insists that I plot and plan, that I consider the alternatives. What might this equality look like? Which of its attractive features might satisfy my desire for empowerment? What in its manner might calm my fear of oppression? And · what of its touch might give realism to my practical needs?

The need to identify this equality then leads me to the remnants of legislation, and to the dominant liberal theories which offer a glimpse of the shape 'equality' has taken in the past and the shape it could take in the future. While toleration of our deviance in the Sexual Offences Act (1967) was to placate our desire for change, it simply teased us, drawing us out of the closet, onto the streets. And in offering a private space for our sexual desire, it aroused a public desire for change. This desire both collectively and individually gave us an identity. And with this solidarity we began to hammer away at the shackles of inhibition, those laws and social norms that had silenced our desire for so long. Our desire became our identity, our identity became our politics. Yet as our desire for change became public we began to realize it was not one but many. Our revolution was not about change but changes. And now, in the struggle to create and to identify this equality our desire for change must sense every desire. It must, in fact, attempt to sketch in a face of equality that satisfies every desire. And that is my attempted task in this essay. I begin by considering the impact of liberal toleration, and its inherent inability to provide a foundation for equality. I then turn away from a focus on tolerant legislation towards the possibilities of a politics of difference found in liberal political theory. But the essentializing group identity required by a politics of difference does not seem to offer a satisfactory notion of equality which speaks to the varied differences within the lesbian, gay and bisexual community. And so, finally, my search retreats to the fundamental lesson we, as a liberation movement, have learned during our struggles together. Despite our differences, in fact *because* of them, we have learned the lesson of respect. In offering a framework for respect, I am attempting to capture the common links we have discovered as a community, as well as solidify

172

those which become necessary for the continued success of our revolution.

To Tolerate

Perhaps the most notable façade of equality in contemporary British history is the Sexual Offences Act of 1967. Decriminalizing sex, in private, between men, over twenty-one, this Act was seen at the time by supporters as a realisation, if only partial, of legal equality. But even as the ten-year battle to implement the Wolfenden Report ended, heterosexual supporters of the Act quickly warned that it was not a mandate for equality but 'an act of toleration'. Such toleration, a cardinal virtue of western liberal thinking, is both in theory and in practice an accommodating minimum, and can only be seen as a substitute for equality. And while liberal political theorists may pronounce the social value of toleration, the experience of those tolerated is not, as we learned in the 1980s, that of equality.

In his reflections on liberal political theory, Will Kymlicka observes that 'tolerance is considered a cardinal liberal virtue, throughout the whole tradition'.[1] Indeed, since the time of Locke's 'Letter Concerning Toleration' (1689), this ideal had held prime importance in conceptualizing the relations between individuals who espouse different concepts of 'the good'. Toleration of another's existence or actions is held by liberal political theorists to be virtuous in that it does not prescribe moral values. This neutrality respects, they argue, individual choice. For example, Joseph Raz defines toleration as follows:

> the curbing of an activity likely to be unwelcome to its recipient or of an inclination so to act which is in itself morally valuable and which is based on a dislike or an antagonism towards that person or a feature of his life, reflecting a judgement that these represent limitations or deficiencies in him, in order to let that person have his way or in order for him to gain or keep some advantage.[2]

In this instance, then, toleration is what stops one from acting

173

on the basis of dislike for another's existence or choice of lifestyle. It is a virtue because it restrains action which would show 'disrespect' for another's choice or identity.

Similarly, John Rawls, in his essay entitled 'The Priority of Right and Ideas of the Good', specifies that his 'political liberalism' places the 'right' over the 'good'.[3] In their commentary on Rawls, Chandran Kukathas and Philip Pettit explain that this version of liberalism 'stresses the importance of toleration, and argues that the polity should be governed by principles which do not themselves presuppose that some particular form of the good life is best'.[4] This concept of toleration as either 'putting up with' someone or some action found repugnant or as simply 'non-prescriptive morality' might challenge the homophobe and the bi-phobe to 'put up with' with gays, lesbians or bisexuals. But is this enough?

In her important critical analysis of liberalism, Susan Mendus proposes that the concept of toleration is quite problematic:

> the circumstances of toleration are circumstances in which there is diversity coupled with disapproval, dislike, or disgust, and where the tolerator has the power to influence the tolerated. In cases where toleration involves more than mere dislike, and has moral force, a paradox arises, which involves explaining how the tolerator might think it good to tolerate that which is morally wrong. In other words, we need to show how we can consistently claim both that toleration is a virtue in individuals and a good in society, and that (strong) toleration necessarily and conceptually involves reference to things believed to be morally disreputable, or evil.[5]

Toleration, in other words, necessarily rests on a bed of disapproval. And it is this underlying theme which is most frightening. With a history so dominated by social, political and moral outrage at the very mention of homosexuality, toleration cannot be welcomed as a virtue of liberal character as much as a warning of eventual unrest. Mendus' words pinpoint that fear which informs the power relation between the tolerated and the tolerator. Toleration has limits. When

174

those limits are reached the tolerator has the power to criminalize and punish the tolerated.

Since the 1967 Sexual Offences Act, homosexuals have been standing at those limits of toleration.[6] After all, homosexuals had been warned not to go too far. Indeed, Lord Devlin had argued in 1967 that it was merely an act of toleration which protected homosexuals and that legislation was not a stamp of approval.[7] Lord Arran, himself a supporter of the Act, asked homosexuals to 'comfort themselves quietly and with dignity and to eschew any form of ostentatious behaviour or public flouting'.[8] But the 1960s and 1970s were hardly a time for expressing sexual desire in private, or remaining safely in the closet. The 1970s *Gay Guide* listed over 200 gay venues in the United Kingdom; the first Gay Pride march was held in London on 1 July 1972; and the first out lesbian Member of Parliament, Maureen Colquhoun, publicly identified herself in the autumn of 1977.[9] However, while the 1970s saw an increase in local council funding for support services for lesbians and gay men, the tables were turned with the financial cutbacks of the 1980s and the impact of the moralistic New Right. The AIDS crisis, which silenced many of our desires and added fervour to those remaining desires, was intensified by the damning backlash not only from the New Right, but from most government officials, and legitimated by the medical community. Lesbians and gay men became the targets for moral outrage and the scapegoats for social problems and political ideologies. Sensing a threat to the traditional nuclear family, and probably the stability of heterosexuality itself, supporters of the now infamous Section 28 of the Local Government Bill wanted to ensure that public monies would not be used to 'promote homosexuality' or 'pretended families'. The widespread support for this Conservative-initiated bill simply became the voice of those who believed homosexuals had stepped beyond the limits of toleration. It was believed that homosexuals had broken some sort of unwritten agreement that homosexuality would be tolerated only if family values were affirmed. And church officials argued that 'as a result they've got the backlash they

175

asked for'.[10] The bed of disapproval had become increasingly irritated, if not volatile, and the tolerator had no option but to act.

So can toleration be a virtue? Perhaps it is a virtue of the privileged. But to the oppressed it is experienced as a hidden untrustworthy vice. Toleration is untrustworthy because it is accompanied by predetermined limits of what does and does not constitute acceptable action. Once these moral limits are violated, toleration lapses into moral prescription and legal alienation. As a prescription for social interaction, toleration is based solely on the tolerator's willingness to 'put up with' what she or he finds morally repulsive. Only those with a particular morality, and in this case a particular sexuality, will ever be tolerated. This leaves the desire for equality not only unsatisfied, but even more aware of the need for change.

To Identify, To Differentiate

By the beginning of the 1990s lesbian and gay identity in Britain had emerged as an engaging power on the political scene. The energy given through the public identity of groups like the Homosexual Law Reform Society, the Campaign for Homosexual Equality (CHE), and the Gay Liberation Front (GLF) continued as a new age of activism began. ACT-UP, formed in 1989, confronted head-on government and public agencies to fight the spread of AIDS and support those living with HIV. OutRage, established in 1990, focused the anger of our desire for revolution through a confrontational challenge to homophobic authorities. And Stonewall, set up in 1989, gave our desire for change a consistent voice questioning every legislative authoritarian move. The need to satisfy our desire for change was taken into the streets, into Parliament, and into the face of inequality. But while the identity emerging in the 1990s expressed our desire for revolution, for change, it also reflected the different desires we had discovered among ourselves. Even the formation of the above mentioned groups signalled our different understandings of activism. Revolution, for some, is a call for the complete

176

overthrow of existing oppressive social structures. And its realization can happen only through an 'in your face' activism which presents a confrontational challenge to the oppressors. Revolution, for others, is a form of change that involves altering oppressive legislation and social norms. And this type of change is seen to be possible only through traditional modes of negotiation with those in power. But as the realities of these different ideological approaches to activism were played out, the individuality of our experiences of oppression led to questioning the legitimacy of each person's desire for change. And thereby fragmentation threatened the movement as a whole. Our desire for revolution, for change, is now striving to know every one desire, to listen carefully to the different descriptions of equality so that we might sketch in, and recognise, its face. The politics of our identity is seeking to reflect the politics of our difference. And in that struggle, as part of that struggle, I once again find myself searching for the theories of difference which might enable equality to be realised.

In her pioneering study of the politics of difference, Iris Marion Young contrasts an ideal of assimilation – or what might be called transcendence of group difference – with an egalitarian politics of difference. 'The assimilationist ideal', she writes, 'assumes that equal social status for all persons requires treating everyone according to the same principles, rules and standards. A politics of difference argues, on the other hand, that equality as the participation and inclusion of all groups sometimes requires different treatment for oppressed or disadvantaged groups.'[11] She points out that 'traditional politics that excludes or devalues some persons on account of their group attributes assumes an essentialist meaning of difference'. Alternatively, the egalitarian politics of difference espoused by Young reflects 'difference more fluidly and relationally as the product of social processes.'[12] While this politics of difference still recognises equality as the participation and inclusion of all groups, it also acknowledges that sometimes these groups require different treatment because of the wide variety of oppression experienced in

177

diverse social, cultural, and economic conditions. Young notes that increased urbanization and the extension of equal formal rights to underrepresented groups, such as women, and racial and ethnic minorities, has not led to the assimilation of groups into a particular (stable) form of western, white, male-dominated, able, heterosexual culture. 'Attachment to specific traditions, practices, language, and other culturally specific forms is a crucial aspect of social existence. People do not usually give up their social group identifications, even when they are oppressed.'[13]

Set in opposition to assimilationist policies, Young's notion of recognised group difference, in which groups define themselves, may sound quite appealing to those groups whose identity has historically been essentialized by mainstream society. In fact, Young's distinction between a group defining itself and being defined by the oppressor does hint at the possibility of group empowerment. It also suggests that public or legislative recognition of difference on the group's own terms may be achievable. But can this be equality? I may be overly sceptical but the idea of an egalitarian society which reflects every group's difference is very hard to imagine. Maybe I am wrong, maybe I am just not imaginative enough. Utopias are not necessarily beyond imagination, but they are often beyond what can be seen as the realm of practical possibilities. And, in fact, Young herself foresees the difficulties of realising this utopia. And in light of this, she points the direction for public policy. She argues that 'a democratic public should provide mechanisms for the effective recognition and representation of the distinct voices and perspectives of those of its constituent groups that are oppressed or disadvantaged.'[14] This account of a democratic public would be supported by institutional structures and public resources supporting:

(1) self-organization of group members so that they achieve collective empowerment and reflective understanding of their collective experience and interests in the context of the society;
(2) group analysis and group generation of policy proposals in

178

institutionalized contexts where decision makers are obliged to
show that their deliberations have taken group perspectives into
consideration; and (3) group veto power regarding specific
policies that affect a group directly, such as reproductive rights
policy for women, or land use policy for Indian reservations.[15]

She continues to flesh out this framework, and in the final
chapter readers are told that an example of this society of
egalitarian difference can actually be found in the
contemporary city. It is in the city that a variety of social
groups both interact and have a separate identity – or, in
Young's words, where difference is more 'fluidly and
relationally' the 'product of social processes'.[16]

But is a city really an example of egalitarian difference? If
there is one thing most cities are known for, it is the
sectioning off of areas for particular cultural groups or classes
– 'China Town', 'suburbia', and 'the other side of the tracks'.
This may appear to some as a natural or chosen geographical
identity for a group, but arguably it can be seen to reflect
simply the ghettoization of deviant groups who are not
accepted into, or can not afford, the more affluent
neighbourhoods. Young's view of the city as the embodiment
of positive social group interaction fails to question the
overarching social and economic structure which itself
separates groups through borders such as poverty and racism.
Moreover, reasons for membership to those spearately
defined groups differ, and 'community' boundaries often are
not clearly delineated. For example, it may be difficult for an
individual of particular ethnic minority to feel a part of a
predominantly white, British neighbourhood, even if they
share similar economic, educational and class status. Young
may be right to question assimilationist understandings of
difference, but the impact of that project alone can only be
miminal because it fails to question the deeper structural
divisions of society. Although her somewhat courteous
recognition that groups need to define themselves – for the
purposes of empowerment, access to services, and so on – she
fails to provide the analytic tools needed to question the

structural prejudices that shape and define the internal boundaries that section off parts of the city from one another.

The second difficulty I find with Young's politics of difference stems precisely from the way in which she believes groups must define themselves. Young explains that, 'in the objectifying ideologies of racism, sexism, anti-Semitism, and homophobia, only the oppressed and excluded groups are defined as different. Whereas the privileged groups are marked with an essence, malleable subjectivity, the excluded groups are marked with an essence, imprisoned in a given set of possibilities.'[17] She observes that this understanding of difference means 'absolute otherness'. And she continues:

> the group marked as different has no common nature with the normal or neutral ones. The categorical opposition of groups essentializes them, repressing the differences within groups. In this way the definition of difference as exlusion and opposition actually denies difference. This essentializing categorization also denies difference in that its universalizing norms preclude recognizing and affirming a group's specificity in its own terms.[18]

While Young's aversion to this type of essentializing difference highlights the need for a group-determined identity, she fails to consider the possible inability of some groups to offer a coherent account of exactly who they are. And, consequently, her conception of a politics of difference cannot answer the problems resulting from the group's 'identity crisis'.

Throughout her work, Young routinely lists social groups like women, people of colour, ethnic minorities, and lesbians and gay men, as if they were entirely coherent for and in themselves.[19] One of her key words is 'affinity', which serves to establish a sense of belonging. She defines a social group as 'a collective of people who have affinity with one another because of a set of practices or way of life; they differentiate themselves from or are differentiated by at least one other group according to these cultural forms'.[20] Elsewhere she states: 'Groups ... constitute individuals. A person's particular sense of history, affinity, and separateness, even the person's mode of reasoning, evaluating, and expressing feeling, are constituted partly by her or his group affinities.'[21] Given her emphasis on 'affinity', I am not sure why she posits lesbians and gay men as a cohesive social group. The differences within the lesbian, gay and bisexual 'community' – and the quotation marks are necessary here – may be loosely held together by a shared oppression experienced in our heterosexist society. But do we all share the same 'way of life'? The fundamental tensions that arose in the early days of activism between gay men and lesbian separatists undoubtedly prove that we do not, and do not wish to, share a 'way of life'. More recently, similar tensions can be seen between lesbians around the censorship debate. Lesbians are increasingly aware that 'sisterhood' does not mean, if it ever did, a shared 'way of life'. We may fall broadly under the category of people who desire the same sex but the acting out of that desire, the choice to act or not, the way in which we perceive that act as defining one's self, even the motivation of that desire are all different for each individual. We may differentiate ourselves from the heterosexual cultural forms which inform a heterosexual way of 'reasoning, evaluating, and expressing feeling'. But do we offer a coherent alternative for a homosexual – or bisexual – way of doing these things? Surely it is that coherence that we are revolting against?

Furthermore, the inability of groups to determine a coherent identity causes theoretical difficulties for Young's ambitious politics of difference. The main problem here hinges on the ability of a social group to identify itself by coherently expressing commonalities within the group. And those groups unable to do so are thereby unable to move towards practical changes. The theoretical complications which result can be seen by contrasting Young's work with that another liberal feminist, Susan Moller Okin. In her study of justice and the family in liberal political theory, Okin uses a form of the 'difference' argument to make a stronger case for women's equality. Like Young, Okin spends the last chapter of her book offering examples of this difference-based equality.[22] The scope of her argument, however, encompasses only the oppression faced by women and, in particular, career women as part of a heterosexual family. By limiting her scope, Okin is able to find enough commonalities between these women to present a powerful argument for special legislation which meets their economic and childcare needs.

Young, by contast, simply throws her net too wide, largely because she is careful to include most oppressed groups within contemporary society as if they had coherence in their group-defined identity. But her theoretical model obscures the fact that these groups are oppressed for different reasons. And, given her definition of a social group, those reasons do not always offer enough commonalities for an identity, especially in terms of the lesbian and gay 'community'. Young's politics of difference is torn between two conflicting demands. On the one hand, she wishes to reject essentialist categories that dominant forces use to otherize subordinated groups. And, on the other, she realizes the need for group commonalities which become essentialist categories generated by the group for itself. Those of us challenging the inequalities we experience because of our sexual identity certainly need, like Young, to reject the former, but are increasingly incapable of establishing the latter. The politics of difference, then, proves difficult to translate into a practical framework, and any attempt seems to be underpinned by some notion of essentialism – one that is either identity-determined by the oppressor or by the group itself.

The conception of difference found in Okin's work, by comparison, requires us to clarify a specificity of *need*. Exactly what do we need to change? For Okin, the economic dependence of women could be overcome by sufficient arrangements for child care, and by re-evaluating care roles within the heterosexual family which would enable women to participate in the work force more easily. Women, then, can unite around this specific need and work towards change. Alternatively, can we, as a lesbian, gay and bisexual 'community' articulate a specific need which unites us all? Should lesbians work for a change in the age of consent laws which, at present, only effect gay men? Can gay men support campaigns around

182

breast and cervical cancer in the way lesbians support the AIDS campaign? If our desire for change is motivated by different needs, can we, as a revolutionary 'community', support every change that is needed? Even if a few of us can coherently express specific desired changes, can those desires be claimed by the 'community'? Or do our different desires for change unavoidably stem from different, and often conflicting, oppressions? These questions are not new – indeed, their history is intertwined with the birth of our liberation movement itself. The division between lesbian separatists and gay men has been a constant source of conflict and pain, as well as dialogue. And while time may have made us familiar with that division, it has also served to make us aware of other divisions. So if our jointly acknowledged difference from heterosexuals spurs us on toward change, will the differences among and between ourselves frustrate our revolution? Possibly. But not necessarily. Perhaps it could even be argued that if fragmentation to the point of complete ineffectiveness was a necessary outcome of our fundamental differences, the split between lesbian separatists and gay men at the beginning of the liberation movement would have thwarted any possibility of social change. Fortunately, that was not the case. But I would propose here that our future achievements must be firmly grounded upon a *respect* for our differences. This has to be a respect for the different and particular experiences of oppression that fuel our specific, and our more general, desires for change.

To Respect

In my attempt to plot and plan what a desired equality might look like, I want to sketch in an outline for respect. And although it is just a sketch, it is never the less a prerequisite for a coherent alternative to current oppressive social structures. The outlines consist of four basic tenets of respect. First, if we understand sexuality to be intertwined with our well-being it is important to respect each person's own interpretation of her or his particular desires as they relate to her or his own self-determined sexuality. In other words, if sexuality is important to my own understanding of who I am, then I should give similar respect to another person's understanding of who she or he is. Raz makes a comparable argument in which he explains that well-being depends upon one's ability to make sense of her or his own life and of the surrounding social forms. Well-being, according to this definition, consists of comprehensive goals which play a conscious role in one's life, like ambitions, commitments, relationships, and so on.[23] So the idea here is simply a respect for the ways that other people will interpret their own life and surroundings differently. Each individual will interpret – understand or negotiate – biological needs, socially constructed norms and personal choices differently. And that interpretation might include a self-determined sexuality which is then important to their own well-being.

The second closely related point involves respecting the individual's acting on her or his interpretation of desire – in other words, respecting the action that results from one's individual interpretation of personal well-being. This general idea is quite straightforward, since it means that if I am going to respect a person's interpretation of her or his sexuality, I should generally respect the way she or he acts upon that interpretation. Now this view by no means necessitates that I respect every possible action that might be taken. And, in the liberal tradition, I would employ a version of the harm principle to regulate such action. Again, Raz provides a concept of harm that is at least a starting point. The prevention of harm includes 'harm to anyone (himself included) as the only justifiable ground for coercive interference with a person.'[24] While male-stream political theory has introduced the divide between 'private harm', which has legitimated many forms of private abuse, and 'public harm', which has failed to question many forms of social oppression, this divide and its interpretation are not the only possible interpretation, or even a partially acceptable one. In fact, Raz's work strikes a rather unique balance between neutrality and perfectionism. For Raz, harm includes not only physical harm, but also coercion, manipulation and even socially harmful attitudes such as racism.[25] Moreover, harm at the hands of society or government involves, according to Raz, 'depriving a person of opportunities or of the ability to use them is a way of causing him harm ... harm to a person may consist ... in frustrating his pursuit of the projects and relationships he has set upon.'[26] Now while I would not accept this brief sketch as complete or wholly acceptable, it does represent a rather interesting interpretation of harm that, when fleshed out, could offer some practical guidelines for respecting more forms of sexual identity than are currently found in heterosexist society.

My third point is that respect for someone must include an awareness of the conditions needed for that individual to realise her or his well-being. While the harm principle may offer general rules for social interaction, the conditions needed for well-being require positive action. For example, these conditions might include anti-discrimination legislation, or parity between contractual negotiations for heterosexual marriages and homosexual partnerships. But, like the aforementioned harm principle, this would not be the only possible interpretation. It could include a more radical restructuring of the social institutions which support, maintain, and reproduce hegemonic conceptualizations of sexuality.

Fourth, and finally, respect must be aware of the power differentials which enable some to fulfil their well-being and while oppressing others. Given the above framework, respect must be consistent with empowerment. The power needed to interpret one's own well-being – and, for the argument here, one's sexuality – must be encouraged rather than accompanied by stringent social codes of prescriptive sexuality. Again, Raz notes the importance of pluralism and a range of options available in a society and the freedom to experiment – even to transgress – social norms. The idea that personal well-being may be understood in the light of social norms is, Raz explains, 'to be consistent with experimentation'.[27] Elsewhere he adds that people can, by developing

185

their own 'variations and combinations, transcend the social form'.[28] This final tenet of respect should ensure that individuals have the power to experiment and transcend social norms.

So if this sketch of a politics of respect becomes a precursor to equality, what might be considered as practical objectives? Besides the respect which *should* exist among the lesbian, gay and bisexual 'community', this framework can be used to identify specific changes needed in society. Because of the shared experience of disrespect in heterosexist society, all of us can advocate certain changes. In her rather poignant, if not directive, criticism of the liberal state, Shane Phelan articulates the debilitating disrespect we have all experienced:

> Lack of protection against social and economic harassment demonstrates, not that the liberal state is failing to live up to its standards, but that its standards leave huge loopholes in the most intimate, most defining areas of our lives. The cost to people of growing up hearing that they or others like them are sick, warped, in need of a good fuck, or otherwise defective, is a cost that can be seen only when one makes the judgement that these things are not true.[29]

In order to eliminate the disrespect at the hands of prejudice, and indeed to have any hope of equality, we must focus on at least three primary targets. First, non-discrimination laws must include sexuality/sexual orientation and be supported by education and monitoring structures for hearing grievances and punishing those offenders. Second, because of the historical categorization of homosexuals as mentally or physically 'ill' or 'deviant', legal institutions should be made particularly sensitive to claims of 'disrespect' at the hands of the medical community. And third, if sexuality can be seen to be intertwined with a person's understanding of her or his own well-being, options for making choices about sexuality must be supported by the government as a valid social form. As Raz states, in terms of the options available within society, it is 'clearly not number but variety [that] matters'. For example, he notes that 'a choice between hundreds of identical and identically situated houses is no choice, compared with a choice between a town flat and a suburban house'.[30] Likewise, I would argue that choice between accepted heterosexual social forms is not variety. It is not respect as I have outlined above. And, what is particularly relevant to this essay, it is not anywhere near the equality we desire.

To Be Equal

So if respect for the different experiences among us is a prerequisite for the continuation of the revolution, are we any closer to creating, to identifying, that desired equality? As I have shown in this essay, equality cannot be the result of toleration. The very definition of toleration rests on disapproval. And this disapproval is indicative of a power relationship which is not experienced as equality, but only hidden disgust and inequality. Alternatively, the politics of difference found in contemporary liberal theory offers an equality based on group identity. But the essentialism required by either a group-defined identity or specificity of need is simply beyond the reach of a lesbian, gay and bisexual 'community' which has fundamental internal differences.

Equality, Raz argues, can only be a quantifying term which is associated with a particular 'sphere of application'.[31] He notes that 'pure concern for equality may be expected to be separate from the independent recognition of the value of the matter in question (hunger, for example). It may be expected to serve as an independent source of value.' But instead, he continues, equality itself rests on other valued principles: 'Equality is said to matter where it affects what is valued for independent reasons; it matters only because what is to be distributed is valuable for independent reasons. Principles of equality always depend on other principles determining the value of the benefits which the egalitarian principles regulate.'[32] In other words, Raz is arguing that you cannot hold up equality as an independent ideal. Rather, equality must always be seen in relation to other political values. We cannot therefore posit equality. We are, instead, obliged to ask: Which equality?

If we understand equality as a quantifying term, it must be accompanied by a coherent list of valued benefits to be distributed equally. Without an accompanying principle, equality is left to the interpretation of those in power. And those in power may assume that equality means 'with them' rather than 'revolution'. For example, perhaps we need to learn from the difficulties faced by women which resulted from an 'add women and stir' approach to altering the patriarchal system. Surely we desire more than to be equal with heterosexuals – or to be considered as heterosexuals with 'alternative' private lives. Our struggle for liberation has not been a struggle for a conforming equality. It has been a struggle in which we as a community, and as individuals, have grappled with difference. And the equality which satisfies us must reflect not monolithic, repressive heterosexual values, but instead must respect the variety of values which result from our differences. The protesting cry for revolution, for change, cannot be one of equality alone. It must be accompanied by a politics of respect.[33]

Notes

[1] Will Kymlicka, *Liberalism, Community and Culture* (Oxford: Clarendon Press, 1991), p9.

[2] Joseph Raz, *The Morality of Freedom* (Oxford: Clarendon Press, 1986), p402.

[3] John Rawls, 'The Priority of the Right and Ideas of the Good', *Philosophy and Public Affairs*, 14 (1988), pp223-51.

[4] Chandran Kukathas and Philip Pettit, *Rawls: A Theory of Justice and its Critics* (Cambridge: Polity Press, 1990), p140.

[5] Susan Mendus, *Toleration and the Limits of Liberalism* (London: Macmillan, 1990), p20.

[6] Because this piece is largely historical, I have used the descriptive terms 'homosexual' and 'lesbian and gay'. The positioning of bisexuality within current theory and activism is yet another testimony to difference, and to the need for a politics of respect.

[7] Lord Devlin quoted in H. Kennedy, 'There is no case for the persecution of gays', The *Listener*, 12 March 1987, p7.

[8] Lord Arran quoted in Sarah Benton, 'What are they afraid of?', *New Statesman*, 11 March 1988, p14.

[9] Stephen Jeffery-Poulter, *Peers, Queers and Commons: The Struggle for Gay Law Reform from 1950 to the Present* (London: Routledge, 1991), pp97, 106, 136.

[10] Benton, 'What are they afraid of?', *New Statesman*, 11 March 1988, p14.

[11] Iris Marion Young, *Justice and the Politics of Difference* (Princeton, NJ: Princeton University Press, 1990), pp157-58.

[12] *Ibid.*, p157.

[13] *Ibid.*, p163.

[14] *Ibid.*, p184.

[15] *Ibid.*

[16] *Ibid.*, p157.

[17] *Ibid.*, p170.

[18] *Ibid.*

[19] For examples, see *Ibid.*, pp36, 196-97.

[2'] *Ibid.*, p186.

[21] *Ibid.*, p45.

[22] Susan Moller Okin, *Justice, Gender, and the Family* (New York: Basic Books, 1989), pp170-86.

[23] Joseph Raz, *The Morality of Freedom* (Oxford: Clarendon Press, 1986), pp290-91.

[24] *Ibid.*, p413.

[25] *Ibid.*, pp319-20.

[26] *Ibid.*, p413.

[27] *Ibid.*, p309.

[28] *Ibid.*, p312-13.

[29] Shane Phelan, *Identity Politics: Lesbian Feminism and the Limits of Community* (Philadelphia: Temple University Press, 1989), p18.

[30] Joseph Raz, *The Morality of Freedom* (Oxford: Clarendon Press, 1986), p375.

[31] *Ibid.*, p225.

[32] *Ibid.*, p240.

[33] My thanks to Susan Mendus, Davina Cooper, and Didi Herman for their comments on this essay, as well as to Joseph Bristow for guidance on points of style.

An Engaged State: Sexuality, Governance, and the Potential for Change[1]

DAVINA COOPER

In the 1986 council elections for the London Borough of Haringey, the leaflet announcing 'Labour's team for Crouch End' stated 'The election of Labour Councillors ... will mean that all [women, Black, lesbian, gay, and older people's] needs are met'. This statement crystallised the promise of Britain's new urban left, the vow that the local state would and could fundamentally transform social conditions for the most disadvantaged communities. It was not only at the level of local government that such a belief prevailed. Across the world, lesbians, gay men, feminists and other progressive forces engaged with state structures, many acting in the belief that state change offered hope for significant social progress.

Among different social movements and groupings, objectives and strategies varied: resisting police practices and repressive legislation through direct action; the development of municipal equal opportunities initiatives; campaigning for law reform; protesting against government inaction over AIDS. Out of these struggles, different perspectives and issues began to appear on state agendas; new social forces won access to state power. Yet can the state be deployed as a 'vehicle' for progressive change in the area of sexuality, or is it simply a force charged with the maintenance of the status quo?

An Engaged State

Much has been written, from an 'external' perspective, on the state as a regulator of sexual relations and, to a lesser extent, from an 'internal' position, on the state as a terrain across which different forces do battle.[2] In this chaper, I draw on both approaches to explore the prospects and limits of an oppositional state sexual politics. My focus is on the ways in which state practice steers sexual struggles and agendas in particular directions. I am, therefore, here, less concerned with normative questions as to whether oppositional social forces *should* attempt to deploy state power. I hope, however, that this discussion will be of relevance to more strategy-oriented debates.

Broadly, my argument is that to understand the current possibilities and limitations faced by oppositional sexual forces engaged with the state we need to understand the intimate relationship between state form and practices and the organisation of sexuality.[3] My second argument is that this is not a one-way relationship. It is not simply that the state affects the forms that modern sexuality and its struggles take but also that the nature of the state is influenced by sexual identities, ideologies and culture. Sexuality is not epiphenomenal but rather has a wider determinacy although the degree of its impact on the state may prove a moot point. In suggesting this, my analysis is at variance with that of writers such as Gayle Rubin who criticises those who burden sexual acts 'with an excess of significance',[4] and Joan Cocks who argues that 'disobedient eroticisms' in the bedroom need have no repercussions for social life.[5]

The State and Sexual Struggle

1. The State as Actor

For many progressive sexual forces in Britain, the state remains a key obstacle. Activists and theorists have pointed to the ways in which the state represses and penalises certain sexual practices and identities: homosexuality, prostitution, paedophilia, transvestism, transsexuality, sadomasochism, while privileging others.[6] This focus on the state as an entity that acts against particular communities I call the 'external' view. In relation to such a state, progressive forces can struggle and resist but such challenges are located on the 'outside'.

While state practice does regulate and shape sexuality in particular ways, I wish to briefly modify this 'external' view – first, by considering whether the state possesses enough unity and agency to act, and second, by examining whether sexual state policies are the outcome of consensus among dominant forces within the state. These questions are important to the discussion that follows since they foreground the ability of oppositional forces to deploy state power.

Traditional conceptions of the state among both Marxists and liberals have been fundamentally challenged by poststructuralist frameworks which emphasise fragmentation, and decentre agency.[7] Some poststructuralists have gone so far as to question whether anything as coherent as a 'state' exists at all.[8] While I would accept that the state does not identify a unified entity, I nevertheless agree with Zillah Eisenstein that it is a useful concept in highlighting particular linkages, connections and intensifications[9] that can be missed if the state paradigm is rejected altogether. Yet in adopting the concept of state, let me briefly outline what I mean by it.

Poststructuralist doubts have thrown into relief conventional, essentialist approaches which try to define the state in a single functionalist or form-oriented manner. However, as with sexuality, which I discuss later, the concept of the state is used in far too many varied and complex ways to make an attempt to 'fix' it with a single meaning of much value. In this chapter, I treat the state as a concept possessed of many identities: it is a set of institutions, a condensation of social relations, a national, corporate identity, and monopolist of legitimate public violence. These identities slide over each other, and the articulation between them, to the extent it exists, is temporary and contingent. The contested and context-dependent nature of identifying the state needs to be borne in mind when considering its 'terrain'. How do we decide where the borders or boundaries of the state lie? On what basis or bases is such a determination reached? This last question I return to later on.

Despite poststructuralist questions about the nature of the state, from an external view the state does appear to act both through individual institutions and as an overall entity. Moroever its actions have effects. In the context of sexuality, the state has played an important role in shaping identities, politics, and communities. Indeed, if we are to go on to understand the state as a terrain of struggle, we need also to understand the state's ability to help construct the players before, during, and after the game. For instance, notions of 'the paedophile' are intensely influenced by age of consent legislation, while prostitution practices and identity are shaped by state welfare policies, policing practices, obscenity legislation, and so on.

Yet the process of state agency is complex. It is not simply a matter of certain institutions, or dominant forces within them, making decisions that are then transparently implemented. For the making and operationalisation of such decisions will themselves be shaped and mediated by a range of state processes, practices, and ideologies. Moreover, even among dominant state forces there is conflict.[10] Rarely is there one set of instructions being issued forth. Rather, it is a process of negotiation, struggle and compromise. For instance, Conservative government legislation in the 1980s in Britain has been seen by many as articulating the Tory state's position on sexuality. However, legislation such as the Education Act 1986 s.46 on the need for school students to appreciate the value of family life, and the Local Government Act 1988 s.28 prohibiting local authorities from promoting homosexuality were both the outcome of struggles between neo-conservative and neo-liberal members of Parliament.[11] Conflict between dominant state forces over the regulation of sexuality is also evident in the House of Lords judgment, *R v Brown and others* (1993).[12] The majority decision held that consensual sadomasochism was against the public interest and should therefore be found unlawful under the Offences Against the Persons Act 1861. The dissenting judgments, on the other hand, claimed that questions of morality should not be presumed to fall within the remit of the criminal law unless explicitly stated by Parliament.

Although state agency in the realm of sexual politics has entailed struggles and disagreements among dominant forces, little of the friction seems to have involved conflicting sexual ideologies. Rather it has concerned other matters – the relative powers of state bodies, questions of political strategy, intra-party struggles for supremacy, and the demands of political allies. To the extent that sexuality has formed the reason rather than simply the terrain of struggle, conflict among dominant forces has been less over the unacceptability of homosexuality, or conversely, the privileging of heterosexuality than on the best way of dealing with sexual 'deviance' (or, perhaps, the *degree* of its deviance).[13] For instance, in the state debates around the Wolfenden Report and subsequent Sexual Offences Act 1967, the conflict between conservatives and liberals concerned the *possibility* of a private sphere of immorality rather than its content or nature.[14]

As a result, despite conflict and fragmentation, the British state has been able to project a relatively coherent outward approach towards sexuality itself. Internal disagreements have functioned within sexual, discursive boundaries so naturalised that they have remained largely unarticulated within the state. However, it is these two facets of state agency – coherence in terms of sexual ideologies, yet fragmentation and conflict in the process of their achievements – that have propelled oppositional, progressive forces to act. For without the former, there would be little need to take on the state, and without the latter, little opportunity to do so.

2. *Access to the Terrain of the State*

The notion of the British state as an actor in the 1980s needs to be complicated by an 'internal' perspective which explores the state as a terrain across which struggles between different forces take place. Such struggles do not only involve dominant state interests. Indeed, sexual legislation in the 1980s was in part a response to the entry of oppositional forces[15] onto the terrain of the state through municipal government, and the development of progressive policies there.

In different countries, progressive sexual forces have gained access to a range of state sites, practices, and forms of power including funding, policy-making, law reform and recruitment. To different degrees, these forces have attempted to challenge the naturalised, unacknowledged norms implicit in the state's treatment and regulation of sexuality. Yet the terrain of the state is not equally accessible to all such movements. Or to put it another way, different sexual interests may gain entry to different aspects of state practice and power. For instance, a paedophile group may gain entrance to a publicly funded community centre in which to meet; a campaign for prostitutes' rights may win notice or acknowledgement of their demands by government depart-ments or commissions; lesbian and gay equality groups may achieve law reforms or municipal policies. The relative impact or power of any of these gains is difficult to measure since it is contingent on the particular historical moment and on the aims of the groups themselves. However, differential access in Britain to the state's terrain creates uneven access to state power. Why have some groups been more successful than others in gaining such access?

One important factor or tendency in explaining the differential success of sexual forces concerns their relationship to the state's own 'drive' for stability and legitimacy. This is not the product of some abstract functional requirement. Instead, it emerges from an overdetermined process that combines the interests and agendas of politicians and bureaucrats, the hierarchical structures of decision-making and power, electoral considerations, state ideology (what is deemed suitable state activity), and cultures of governance.[16]

The need for stability and legitimacy means that state institutions may be more likely to respond to sexual social forces where ignoring them could arouse disruptive activity and a loss of credibility. However, such a response by the state may not be pre-emptive. While some state bodies

195

internalise the requirements for hegemony and, where they cannot construct the objects of legitimacy, act to contain or defuse demands before they are pressed; in other instances, the threat or reality of pressure may have to be made explicit.

This process was illustrated in the struggles between Labour local councils in the 1980s and lesbian and gay social forces.[17] In a context of emerging hegemony for equal opportunity policies, and of lesbian and gay municipal activism, some councils responded, without explicit public pressure, to lesbian and gay demands. In other instances, it took demonstrations, lobbies and support from heterosexual quarters to 'persuade' councils to include lesbians and gays, at least nominally, in their equal opportunity policies. However, although lesbian and gay rights groups were able to challenge the political legitimacy and stability of municipal left councils more than many other sexual movements, their 'success' was nevertheless geographically uneven. In areas where lesbian and gay forces were less organised, more detached from left-wing, community politics, and where politicians did not look to new social movements for credibility, their ability to enter the local state was limited. In some instances, Labour councils were prepared to weather the storm of lesbian and gay protest perceiving it as likely to be short-lived, at odds with their own political agenda, and almost certain to precipitate equally vociferous, and politically destabilising, activism from opposing quarters.

A second possible factor in explaining the differential access of sexual social forces to the terrain of the state concerns the congruence between movement discourses and those of the state, and between their respective 'modus operandi'.[18] Lesbian and gay rights groups, utilising the discourses of formal equality and citizenship, are more congruent with the explicit ideologies expressed by the British (or Western) state than are campaigns based on radical or revolutionary feminism. Similarly, groups who operate within hierarchical organisational frameworks and whose politics consists of motions, letters and meetings are more compatible with state practices than ad hoc, direct action projects.

Questions of congruence also have to take into account the variation between different aspects of the state. Thus, while a lesbian and gay law reform group may utilise broadly common discourses to parliamentary committees, in relation to other state bodies, such as the police, judiciary, prison service or military, there might be less ideological compatibility. In this latter context, it is difficult to imagine many progressive sexual movements possessing greater similarity. This does not mean, however, that such state apparatuses are entirely closed to progressive sexual forces. For while ideological differences may reduce access, organisational differences may be, in some instances, an advantage. The police force, for example, may find it easier to accommodate an informal lesbian and gay support group than a highly organised bureaucratic structure like itself.

It is also not simply a question of preferring the grouping that is easier to contain. In the case of state bodies with oppositional agendas, support may be given to grass-roots organisations that can carry out policies and campaigns closed to the state institution itself. For instance, some British left-wing local councils in the 1980s prioritised funding to small, relatively informal, community groups who were able to develop projects too politically controversial for councils themselves to engage in. However, the power and steer of state organisational forms is revealed by the fact that, in many instances, once such funding was established, the requirements on voluntary bodies to produce reports, have named chairs, constitutions, regular minuted meetings and so on imposed on them the same (politically disabling) bureaucratic structures as those faced by state bodies.

The third general factor I wish to consider concerns the nature of the state's hegemonic project. By this I mean the normative agenda constructed both to win popular consent and to deploy such consent for the achievement of particular goals. This third factor thus brings together the other two – the pursuit of discursive strategies to gain legitimacy, and the generation of legitimacy to facilitate particular ideological interests. Because of recent political differences in Britain between different state bodies – in particular, between local and central government – to talk of an overall political project is difficult. British local government in the 1980s, for example, gave access to very different forces to those welcomed or admitted by central government. However, in the battle to construct a state project, apparatuses are not equal as the 1980s clearly revealed. Moreover, even between different institutions some broad trends are apparent and certain intra-state social meanings prevail. These will shape groups' ability, if not to engage with the state, then at least to do so with invitation.

Although lesbian and gay groups operated in conflict with the state's dominant political emphasis on the nuclear family, marriage, monogamy, and traditional parental roles, they did articulate parallel social forms which, to a degree, drew them into the hegemonic project. Section 28 might refer derisively to 'pretended families' but at least they were families. Similarly, the gay movement's recent emphasis on marriage and partnership contracts suggests a tentative investment within such an enterprise.[19] This quasi-incorporation contrasts with the marginalisation in Britain of other sexuality movements or demands: sadomasochists, paedophiles, revolutionary and radical feminists. While the latter expressed ideologies explicitly at odds with probably all normative state agendas, the emphasis of sadomasochists and paedophiles on minority rights, liberty, and the private seem at first glance to be compatible with hegemonic liberal (or neo-liberal) discourse. Why did they then remain with minimal access to the state's terrain?

According to Rubin, a sexual hierarchy exists which places paedophiles, sadomasochists and other minorities at the bottom – constructed as dangerous in contrast to the relative acceptability of monogamous, 'vanilla' lesbians and gays.[20] While such a hierarchy does seem to reflect popular opinion, there are two provisos I would like to make. First, it says nothing about the nature of the individuals who possess state power. Many may practise sadomasochism, paedophilia and everything else on the sexual spectrum. Thus the subordination of certain sexual desires operates at the level of public legitimate discourse rather than social practice. Second, even at the level of discourse, there is much within our society which asserts the erotic potential of sadomasochist and paedophile practices: the construction of sexuality around domination and subordination; the gendered eroticisation of vulnerability and prepubescence; and other social and economic practices that condense gender, class, national and racial inequalities in ways which make sadomasochism and paedophilia imaginable, feasible, and viable.

The denigratory treatment of sadomasochism and pae-dophilia, then, reveals the complex ways in which different discursive elements combine to create a hegemonic project. In theory, paedophilia could be identified as an issue of individualism, of children's rights or, conversely, of legitimate adult authority, but it is not. Rather, it is publicly perceived as pathological, abusive, degrading and irrational. Similarly, dominant, public constructions of sadomasochism are not of privacy and individual capacity to consent (see *R. v Brown*, 1933) despite the arguments of sadomasochist (SM) advocates.

As the ongoing practice of maintaining hegemony and legitimacy reveals, entry onto the state's terrain is not a matter over which the state can exercise absolute control. This is not only because of its interest in retaining credibility and political stability. Within a context of ongoing social antagonism and struggle, new forces gain access as the balance of power shifts, while forces dominant within the state either change or have to respond to other demands. Lesbian and gay rights in Britain during the 1980s were more sucessful than sadomasochiist rights or lesbian feminism in obliging the state to open up, in part for the reasons discussed above, but also because they were able to mobilise effectively around an agenda which prioritised state practice.

The decision of a movement to focus on the state and its inability to mobilise effectively raise issues closely linked with those concerning state responsiveness. Let me take a couple of examples. First, the specific ways in which discourses combine, as I discussed above, will affect not only a movement's relative legitimacy (and, hence, the likely degree of state responsiveness), but also the extent to which a community, for instance, transvestites, is able or willing to publicly identify itself and assert its demands.[21] Similarly, state ideologies and practices, such as unequal treatment and discrimination, will influence whether social forces see the state as a central focus for their political activities. One influential aspect of state practice in this respect is the 'confessional'.[22] The state's practice of scrutiny – expecting social needs and demands to be presented for its detailed consideration – militates against communities or movements, such as paedophiles and sadomasochists, who may feel such a process will render them too exposed or vulnerable, especially, in the present climate, to legal regulation or prosecution.[23] However, what the effects of particular state discourses and practices will be on social movements cannot easily be predicted. For lesbian and gay rights groups in the 1980s, repressive and discriminatory state practices provided the motivation for engagement. For British revolutionary feminists, it reinforced their sense of alienation from the state and the prioritisation instead of other sites of activity.[24]

3. Limits and Contradictions in Engaging with State Power
For reasons already discussed, in Britain, lesbian and gay rights movements were more successful than other sexual minorities or more radical sexual campaigns in winning access to the terrain of the state and thus to the deployment of state power. In Britain, the main achievements were at the municipal level, in the development of equal opportunity, non-discriminatory policies.[25] Elsewhere, the focus was somewhat different. For instance, in Canada greater emphasis was placed by lesbian and gay reformers on law reform and litigation strategies to achieve equal treatment.[26] But despite the gains that have been made, attempts to resist, transform, and utilise state power have been limited. Here, I wish to consider several factors which may have stymied or reduced the impact of lesbian and gay activists working within and through the state. In considering the impact of such elements during the late 1980s and early 1990s in Britain, I in no way

wish to suggest that their existence or the particular effects witnessed are inevitable. Socially and culturally contingent, the influence of the factors described below depends, among other things, on the capacity and boundaries of state power, and the strength and strategies of oppositional forces within the state at any given historical moment.

Within British local government, lesbian and gay activists were successful in initiating anti-discriminatory policies, obtaining community funding, putting on cultural events, improving service provision and generally raising the profile of a multicultural sexual politics.[27] However, these 'gains' cannot be seen in isolation from the continuation of opposing state policies and presumptions. Even within local government, pro-lesbian and gay departmental policies were 'sabotaged' by contradictory working assumptions within those same services which treated heterosexuality and the nuclear family as the norm. Such conflicts functioned even more strongly across different state bodies. For instance, local councils might fund groups which supported sadomasochism or gay adolescent sexuality, while, at the same time, the courts, on grounds of public policy or statutory interpretation, convicted men for engaging in the same sexual activities.

The extent to which conflicting or contradictory state discourses and practices can undermine lesbian and gay policies depends on what the latter are attempting to achieve. If the aim is simply to remove particularly discriminatory provisions, for example, on the inheritance of council housing or in relation to adoption policies, then competing discourses or policies may not matter too much unless they stop such objectives from being achieved or from benefiting particular sections of the lesbian and gay community. For instance, the specific case-law proscription and regulation of gay sadomasochism might well limit certain lesbians and gays' ability to adopt, even if the formal, legal prohibitions on homosexual couples adopting were removed.

However, if the objectives of lesbian and gay social movements are wider, if they target the social meanings through which sexuality is constituted, if they aim to contest the (compulsory) reproduction of heterosexuality, then the contradictory nature of state discourse and practice will be a serious impediment. But the converse is also possible. Less sympathetic policies of the judiciary, police force, military and prison service might undermine more progressive approaches. At the same time, progressive policies, developed in education, voluntary sector funding, health care and so on may have a beneficial impact on state policies and practices in other institutions. While it is hard to judge the extent of this influence, small scale effects are apparent. For instance, the establishment within the police force of a lesbian and gay staff group mirrored comparable developments in local government.

Alongside this problem of contradictory state practice – the difficulty for lesbian and gay activists of controlling or deploying anything more than specific, micro aspects of state power – is a more general issue of actually using state power. Can unreconstructed state power be meaningfully utilised to achieve oppositional ends? Arguably, the form and nature of state technologies change as a result of being utilised for different objectives; but, if this is so, such changes seem not to be dramatic. In general, lesbian and gay law reform does not transform the nature of the legal process or of litigation, while lesbian and gay municipal policies still operate within the framework of a hierarchical bureaucracy.

One might argue that the existence and maintenance of state authority are important if lesbian and gay policies are to be at all effective – 'they' need all the power they can get. Yet, while this might be true for the achievement of formal equality, substantive equality may be impeded. First, because the structures themselves are 'sexualised' in ways that are barely challenged by such reform initiatives as I discuss below; and second, because it raises the paradox of a state hierarchy *imposing* equality with the potential resentment, backlash and opposition such a strategy frequently precipitates.[28]

But can't provoking the opposition be a good thing if it generates debate? Many activists and theorists writing about the state argue that one of its main attractions to new social movements is in providing an arena in which important

202

discursive struggles can take place. Battles over lesbian and gay reforms have taken place in many countries – Britain, Canada, the USA as well as elsewhere – and have undoubtedly played a useful role in giving visibility to lesbian and gay demands, and in denaturalising compulsory heterosexuality. At the same time, it is also important to recognise the limitations of such debates when played out on the *state's* terrain. First, hegemonic state discourse will impact upon and shape the arguments of all sides as competing forces strive to maintain ideological legitimacy as well as achieve political victory.[29] Second, such debates are frequently 'performed' in inaccessible venues – the courts, parliament, town hall – rarely attended other than by activists.[30] For most people their knowledge about the debates will come from the mass media, mediated by the press, radio and television's own ideological steer.

The dependence of progressive state actors on the mass media highlights a further, more general problem: the state's lack of omnipotence.[31] Foucault and others have examined the ways in which technologies of power, irreducible to state power, operate in relation to sexuality. Economic, familial, cultural, religious, medical as well as media discourses shape, control and regulate sexual practices, relations, and identities. Although linked to state practice, the organisation and expression of sexuality cannot necessarily be controlled by it. Thus the ability of the state to reshape sexual ideologies and practices is limited. Just as conservative forces cannot eradicate sadomasochism through criminal prosecutions and convictions, lesbian and gay forces cannot achieve social parity with heterosexuality simply by law reform and municipal policies. At the same time, the nexus, however tangential or precarious, between the state and different forms of power does enable state-initiated changes to produce ripples elsewhere, which in turn impact back upon state policy and practice.

State Form as Sexual Effect

The overdetermined nature of the state's relationship to other forms of power suggests that to change state practice it may be necessary to focus on transforming those processes and relations that shape and influence state form. In the context of sexuality, this means, among other things, considering the ways in which the state is sexualised – that is, the form of the state reflects and constitutes a particular sexual organisation. Without this form being changed, the potential to introduce sexual change through the state may be limited. As I stated at the beginning of this chapter, to talk about the determinacy of sexuality in relation to the state contests those analyses of sexuality which perceive it as epiphenomenal, that is as having little or no impact on anything else. Yet, in saying sexuality has determinacy, what exactly does this mean?

Sexual Determinacy
In addressing this question, we need first to consider what is meant by sexuality. People use the concept in a range of ways to identify particular practices, relations or identities, as a discursive structure, disciplinary framework and terrain. It can also be understood at the level of culture and metaphor, as a series of social practices which signify at a more general or abstract level. Recognising the multiple meanings sexuality possesses is important, and an attempt to reduce them to a common core appears to me misguided. Like any concept, the meanings accorded to sexuality depend largely on the context within which it is utilised. In the analysis that follows, I draw on these different meanings to show how sexuality impacts upon state activity. Here, I wish briefly to set out some possible ways in which sexuality can exert a determinacy beyond its own terrain.

First, at its most concrete – as a set of practices – sexuality impacts upon the individuals involved psychologically and socially. The ways in which people perceive themselves and others during sexual engagements leave traces beyond the performing of such acts. Similarly, since our desires are not restricted to the actual moment of (genital) sexual activity, they necessarily impact upon a range of social interactions and personal choices. For instance, people spend time, money and energy finding partners or setting up highly detailed sexual scenarios.

Second, the social relations through which sexuality becomes constituted as identity, in particular, gender, 'race' and class, affect a range of economic, political, and social arrangements. Lisa Adkins discusses how compulsory heterosexuality is a crucial aspect of many women's labour relations.[32] Unless women are prepared, she argues, to take on this particular sexualised role which subordinates them to men, they will not be employed within particular industries, such as, in her example, the tourist sector. There are many other instances where gendered, racialised, and classed sexual roles and identities help to constitute other social relations. For instance, meanings of 'criminal justice' are formed both through and against those on trial, intensely evident in the prosecution of Afro-Caribbean men for sexual offences. Similarly, white, male 'convenience' marriages to South-East Asian women are conditional on, and shaped by, particular stereotypical sexual expectations.

The idea that sexuality is a constituent aspect of other social relations can be understood, within a Foucauldian framework, by thinking of sexuality as a 'disciplinary technology of power'.[33] From this perspective, sexuality organises people into particular roles, constructs subjectivities in specific ways, and naturalises or enforces certain behaviour, attitudes and practices. Erotica and desire become the means of achieving these effects, assisted by norms, knowledge, and sanctions – formal and informal. Adopting this analysis, *homosexuality* can be seen not only as resistance, but also as an alternative form of disciplinary, sexual power. For, within gay and lesbian sexualities, organising principles exist that shape and systematise fantasy, behaviour and interactions. Indeed, only an entirely anarchic sexuality, lacking all predictability, which did not draw on current images, roles and fantasies, might escape.

If sexuality is seen as a form of disciplinary power, then it can shape practices and social relations in a range of terrains including, but not limited to, the state. As I discuss above, sexuality is constituted through social, cultural and economic relations of inequality. As a result, sexuality as disciplinary power is not stationary in form but historically and geographically contingent, a contingency which affects not only the nature of the disciplinary power itself, but also the sites through which it operates. For example, the practice of prostitution can be interpreted as a particular form of (heterosexual) disciplinary power where roles, knowledge and behaviour are shaped by (although not reducible to) participants' age, 'race', class and gender, at a particular legal, social, and economic conjuncture.[34]

If we are looking at the ways in which sexuality as disciplinary power helps to constitute state form, certain questions may arise. For instance, why does sexuality operate in certain ways rather than others? Who or what creates it or deploys it? These kinds of questions are difficult to answer since the notion of discipline in this context decentres and diffuses agency, focusing instead on the practices of those subjected to it. Perhaps, a more pertinent question concerns the nature of the power in question: is the state being constituted through progressive or conservative forms of sexual, disciplinary power? For lesbian feminist 'disciplinary' forms may look very different to 'patriarchal heterosexual' ones in terms of the culture, practices, role and boundaries of the state. If this is the case, is a transformation in the sexual, disciplinary power by which the state is constituted possible?

I return to this issue later, but first, if we abstract further from sexuality as practices, relations and disciplinary power, we come to the level of culture and metaphor. In describing sexuality in this way, I mean something linked but not reducible to ideology. Sexuality operates ideologically through the meanings by which it is constituted and conveyed. Within this process there are both dominant and marginalised matrices or meaning formations based on the articulation of different discursive elements. However, in talking about sexuality as culture, I want to highlight the ways in which elements of different sexual fantasies and imagery, such as the phallus, become detached to pervade other social practices and relations. Sexuality has a metaphorical shade, when it acts as the 'as if' of other phenomena – that is, we see the world through sexual analogies. Thus, our understandings of sexuality – the meanings by which it is constituted – will shape, through the process of metaphor, the meanings given to other practices or apparatuses such as the state.

Sexuality and the Constitution of State Form
In the final section of this chapter, I bring together the preceding discussions to explore the different ways in which sexuality impacts upons state form. To recap, my objective in doing so is to consider the ways in which this constrains or impacts upon the ability of oppositional forces to deploy state power for their own objectives.

Many feminists have argued that a key aspect of the state's role is in regulating the division between public and private.[35] Located in the 'public' realm, perceived as embodying rationality, due process, civic membership, impartiality, culture and intellect, the state is seen as the epitome of these qualities. As a result, some feminists claim the state is implicitly, but also fundamentally, gendered. It embodies the qualities defined as public and male, rather than those of the 'private' and female world.[36] To what extent could it be argued that the state in this way is also sexualised?

The qualities described above are not only those perceived as male, but also those perceived as asexual. For sexuality is linked with wildness, nature, irrationality, the body and partiality. Within this linkage we see the articulation of culture – the joining together of disparate elements – and the equation of metaphor – a bilateral process of signification. For not only does sex 'stand in' for the feral and the untamed, but both 'stand in' for sex. In this way, sexuality is the undomesticated excess contained within the domestic; it is nature's surplus that is both 'husbanded' and released within nature's asocial domain. Thus, the state is discursively constructed locating sexuality as 'other'.[37] Ostensibly unsexed, it governs the boundaries of the sexual and asexual worlds. The implications of this are several.

207

First, initiatives which seem to bring sexuality into the public, political sphere are frequently perceived as illegitimate. Sexual conversations, whether external or internal – about or for sex – along with their concomitant practices are deemed inappropriate within the polity. Yet, at the same time, the state and public generate a multiplicity of sexual discourses – the 'unspeakable' which they can never stop talking about. The effects of this contradiction are evident in the struggle between progressive and conservative forces over the exercise of state power in relation to sexuality. The right emphasises the importance of keeping sexuality out of the public sphere and therefore the need for intervention – for a proliferation of sex-talk – to ensure this is achieved. However, when progressive forces attempt to deploy state power to achieve a more liberal sexual politics, the right focuses on the illegitimacy of sexuality as a topic of governmental concern, reinforcing this argument with claims that progressive forces intend to turn public what has previously functioned as a private terrain. Yet while many on the right are willing for sexuality to remain private, others argue that there can be no private sexual domain.[38] All sexual practices impact upon the public sphere. Therefore, only those deemed to make a positive contribution – monogamous, marital, (procreative) heterosexuality – are acceptable.

Discussion of the public-private divide is complicated by critiques that question the meaningfulness and even the existence of such a division. Yet, even if we accept that there are not separate spheres governed by competing principles, the ideological and normative power of the conceptual division is important to recognise. Despite their eroticisation by certain sexual 'outlaw' communities for their prohibitive character, the state and the public sphere are perceived within dominant discourse as the antithesis of sexuality. Constituted within a culture which treats the heterosexual norm, and more particularly its institutions of marriage, courtship and divorce, as largely unsexual – hence the only acceptable form of 'sexual' expression within the public – one wonders how effectively the state can transform sexual meanings, in particular to bring homosexuality 'out'.

While there is a general, hegemonic liberal willingness to allow lesbians and gays greater freedom in the 'private', providing their sexuality is not 'flaunted' in public, lesbians and gays are at the same time discursively constructed as so sexual that even their mere presence is erotically saturated.[39] The threat of contamination means no space where others are present can be safe. Thus, problems arise in the case of state policies to do with parenting – donor insemination, adoption, fostering. For if children are within the gay home, what then is the private? Has it shrunk to the bedroom or even to the bedroom only at certain times of the night when children cannot reasonably be expected to be present?

This sense of a shrinking private and simultaneously expanding public sphere brings me to the second aspect of the state's form that I wish to consider: its institutional base and the articulatory principles which determine the practices and institutions within, outside or on the peripheries of its responsibility. Identifying state boundaries, as I said earlier, is not uncontested either by political actors or by political theorists.[40] Nevertheless, my argument is that the location of such boundaries is also affected by the ways in which sexuality is organised. Strong sexual norms in conjunction with weakening familial authority, greater economic individualism and rising social alienation have precipitated an expansionist state that regulates sexual behaviour through its education provision, health policies, police force, social services, and so on. The changing nature of sexual relations, identity and politics, in particular, the contestation of heterosexuality's monopoly on the normal, also impacts upon the remit of state apparatuses. Lillian Faderman describes the escalation in the state's interventionist role in relation to sexual practices in the USA during the 1950s.[41] While the penetration and surveillance of homosexual employees, clubs, and literary texts was largely a product of the right-wing panic of this period, such a panic in part emerged as a result of social changes that included greater sexual pluralism.

In exploring the capability of the state to be deployed by

oppositional progressive forces, the nature of state expansion or intervention plays an important role. While an expansionist, interventionist state may be a conservative reaction to contested sexual diversity, it may also assist those social forces who wish to use the state in more progressive ways. An illustration of this might be the educational and health work being carried out in relation to HIV and AIDS. The emergence of AIDS in Britain, and the West generally, has been used by the state to increase the regulation and scrutiny of sexual practices and identities, particularly of people known or defined as possible 'carriers'. Yet the expansion of the state into these areas has made possible, and increasingly legitimate, safe sex work which positively explores sexuality and lifestyles traditionally marginalised or invisible.

Whether progressive forces can legitimately extend state apparatuses in other areas depends in part on the nature of the articulatory principles that determine the basis for incorporation within the state. For instance, feminists who advocate greater regulation of pornography are placed in a position of having to justify this as a legitimate area for state intervention. The dangers of feminists engaging in campaigns for greater state control – demanding more restrictive legislation – has been well explored. Part of the problem concerns the power of existing articulatory principles for state intervention – public harm, corruption, undermining the family – which will appropriate and recreate feminist agendas in their own image. The ability to contest such principles from within the state is limited, for although generated there, they also take shape within other domains. A sexual culture which emphasises the private, the privileging of male sexuality, heterosexuality, and the nuclear family makes feminist articulatory principles for state intervention currently difficult to envisage.

The third way in which the form of the state is sexualised is through its hegemonic corporate identity. In this instance, viewed in relation to other states and entities, the state resembles a coherent actor. According to Wendy Brown, the 'late modern state bares an eerie resemblance to the "new man" ', ostensibly sympathetic to social movement demands and the needs of the subjugated but apparently able to do little.[42] One might go further and argue that the relationship between the state and its populace is, metaphorically, a heterosexual one of difference where the community – those subject to state power – become the feminised 'other'.[43]

The state may be a 'new man', but its relationship to the community is still an unequal one, despite this being increasingly hidden as the state depicts itself as vulnerable, with limited power, and open to the demands of its subjects/citizens. In relation to other states, more aggressive, paternalistic or authoritarian, the 'late, modern state' maintains a distance that is more apparent, perhaps, than real, for the homosocial relations between states remain. Other states – wild, irrational and lacking control – are feminised (or maybe *ef*feminised would be a better description), all the more disliked, feared and humiliated for revealing the possible ruptures within the contingent coherence of the masculine corporate identity.

What are the implications for sexual activists of conceptualizing the state in this way? The first is to treat with scepticism promises and commitments that are not actualised. 'New manhood' offers change but it has been characterised as a discursive strategy that often aims to appease rather than please, to change the surface form rather than any 'deeper' content. This is not to deny the value of altering state discourse; when Prime Minister Major met actor Ian McKellen, for instance, a message of sexual liberalisation was sent out. But change relies on more than offers of good will and promises that 'next time will be different'. Just as ironing may not the new man make, token gestures are only one aspect of state practice.

Second, if the state is constructed on a metaphorical, heterosexual relationship of otherness, working through the state will entail strategies which hierarchically *impose* change. A problem with this is that the state's own dominant status is not undermined. To what extent can sex-gender parity be achieved when the state's relationship to its communities is unequal? Do we need a lesbian or queer state before the state can effectively play a role in undermining heterosexual hegemony? What would such a state look like? How would it relate to its communities? And to what extent is its achievement possible while heterosexual hegemony remains?

Finally, the state's legitimate monopoly of custodial power, its right to use force against its populace is inextricably linked to a sexual imaginary or culture formulated around the eroticisation of domination. While many communities centre violence within their erotic imagination, the state deploys erotic desire within its production of force. This was illustrated in the news leaked that frontline USA soldiers in the 1991 war against Iraq were given pornography to read before sorties.[44] Yet, at the same time, the state's disciplinary power is deployed in *opposition* to 'uncontrollable' sexual desires, particularly in prisons, schools and the military-institutions that epitomise coercive regulation.

The apparently contradictory nature of these two processes – using sex to improve coercive efficacy, and force to render sex privatised – reveals itself in the police force's treatment of women working as prostitutes. Arrested, held and often imprisoned for sexual offences, prostitutes are also treated sexually by the state forces that regulate them. The impact of this articulation between sexuality and coercion on lesbian and gay state struggles depends on the sexual ideologies and aspirations of lesbian and gay movements, in particular, whether what is sought is a prefigurative nurturing sexuality antithetical to eroticised violence or one grounded in an open, multi-cultural pluralism. Yet, the central nexus of sexuality and violence also makes the attempts of oppositional sexual forces to deal with the disciplinary aspects of state policy, for instance, army and prison practice, difficult. For not only is sexuality seen as that which is most 'other', but, simultaneously, a particular form of sexuality shapes and generates state power at its 'heart'. The nature of this sexuality reflects a culture of brutality that belies discourses of consent, equality, nurturance and romance. It is the other

212

side of the 'new man' – those desires suppressed as unacceptable, yet which may better explain state actions than those on the discursive surface.

*

In this chapter, I have critically explored the limitations experienced by sexual struggles within the state's terrain. In doing so, I have not intended to suggest that such struggles are unworthwhile. My own experiences as a researcher and as a local councillor in Haringey, a borough that became temporarily famous for its lesbian and gay policies, suggest that entering the domain of the state may be a politically useful project. Not only is the state too pervasive to ignore, but, as well, some objectives may be more easily achieved from an informed, internal location, for instance, developing public sector employment policies, than solely by protesting from the 'outside'.

The trouble is that intra-state strategies often lead to the neglect and demotion of other approaches. Positioned within the state, they tend to attract public attention, resources, energy and status. As a result, external pressure groups may feel that they cannot compete or that they are placed in a secondary or supportive role to these more powerful state actors. The magnetic capacity of the state is difficult to control. However, those who choose, as politicians, government officials, lawyers, advisers, to act from within its terrain need to maintain a sensitivity to both the limitations of the arenas within which they operate and to the impact their actions may have on political forces less visible and less prestigiously located.

The politics of law reform and policy making frequently emphasise the pragmatic. Playing safe and eschewing risks may be, at times, necessary and inevitable. Yet there is a danger of this becoming the dominant mode of lesbian and gay engagement with the state. What can we do to ensure that other more subjugated, oppositional or grassroots voices are heard? How can we centre those social forces able to take

213

political risks? This question is crucial if we are to maintain the momentum for change.

This is not an argument for any one privileged positioning, but rather for the need to face and contest the pressures that exist, which place social forces in a hierarchy of legitimacy and political status. We spend a lot of time on the left denouncing and condemning the strategies of others, arguing their approaches are too reformist, ultra-leftist, Leninist, Trotskyist or Stalinist to succeed. Yet on what basis can such judgements be made? Rarely do we really know what the outcomes of particular projects might be, which will be effective, which will fail, and what will befall as a result. Would we, then, be better off *positively* pursuing a pluralist approach to political strategy, inside and outside of the state, one that recognises the uncertainty and contingency of possible achievements, and the precarious status of prediction?

But who is this 'we'? Among lesbians and gay men, does such an inclusive pronoun have any meaning? This is undoubtedly a highly contentious question, and the subject of extensive debate, particularly within current sorties over essentialism. In this chapter, I have referred to a number of different agendas within 'the' lesbian and gay community, primarily in the context of their relative access to the state. These differences are important, for they reflect ideological disagreements that cannot be simply brushed aside. The lesbian feminist-sex radical 'sex wars', for instance, are not the fault of one 'encampment' intent on making trouble. Reducing the issues, as some have done, to 'feminist policing' or 'false consciousness' fails to acknowledge or *respect* the ideological conflict that is present. The reality of political disagreement, I would argue, needs accepting if alliances and coalitions are to bridge the gaps.

Within this context, it is interesting that the tensions and battles that have arisen among lesbians and gay men have principally occurred over 'internal' community issues – SM, butch-femme, leather – rather than over the tactics and strategies for engagement with the state. While law reform has led to some polarisation over, for instance, pornography

214

and age of consent legislation, municipal policy-making, AIDS work, education initiatives have tended to bring different lesbians and gay men together, from liberal, civil rights activists to radical feminists. Disagreements have not vanished as conflicts on local government committees between community representatives reveal, but they have often been contained or mellowed by the more pressing problems posed by obstinate state bureaucracies and inadequate funding.

So, despite ideological differences, alliances and coalitions can be found on the 'ground', not only between lesbians and gay men, but also with other progressive actors as illustrated in the reciprocated support given to striking miners by the lesbian and gay community. This construction of 'equivalences', coming together within a broader counter-hegemonic movement is something that has to be worked at. It does not come easily. Nevertheless, it is an important strategy if relations between state and civil society are to be radically transformed. As lesbian and gay activists maybe we should be focusing more of our energies on creating solidarity in those arenas where it is both vital and possible, rather than on endlessly probing the issues and social terrains where we fall apart.

Notes

[1] I would like to thank Didi Herman, Helen Reece, and Carl Stychin for their helpful comments and suggestions. This essay is reprinted (with minor alterations) from the *Journal of Law and Society* (1993).

[2] See, generally, Carol Jones and Pat Mahoney, *Learning Our Lines: Sexuality and Social Control in Education* (London: Women's Press, 1989); Gary Kinsman, *Regulating Desire* (Montreal: Black Rose Books, 1987); and Jeffrey Weeks, *Sex, Politics, and Society: The Regulation of Sexuality since 1800* (London: Longman, 1981).

[3] The relationship between sexuality and the state does not exist in a vacuum. It is constituted and shaped by a range of other social relations, practices, and terrains. These are, however, decentred here is order to focus on the different ways in which sexuality and the state impact on each other.

[4] Gayle Rubin, 'Thinking Sex: Notes for a Radical Theory of the Politics of Sexuality', in Carole S. Vance, ed., *Pleasure and Danger: Exploring Female Sexuality*, first edition (London: Pandora, 1989), p279.

215

[5] Joan Cocks, *The Oppositional Imagination* (London: Routledge, 1989), pp172-73.

[6] Transsexuality and transvestism are arguably not sexual identities since they are more concerned with the performativity of gender. However, because they tend to have implications for the 'performance' of sexuality, I include them here.

[7] See, for example, Sophie Watson, 'Femocratic Feminisms', in Mike Savage and Ann Witz, eds, *Gender and Bureaucracy* (Oxford: Blackwell, 1992), pp186-205.

[8] See the discussion in Bob Jessop, *State Theory* (Cambridge: Polity, 1990), pp292-93.

[9] See Zillah Eisenstein, *The Female Body and the Law* (Berkeley: University of California Press, 1988). The links between state bodies lead to an intensification of power. This intensification and coordination is marginalised by poststructuralist approach that see the state as fragmented, disconnected, and erratic.

[10] By dominant state forces, I refer to those actors (collective and individual) who helped to shape or form the state's broad hegemonic project. Thus, within the context of Britain in the 1980s and 1990s, I do not include leaders of left-wing local councils.

[11] Davina Cooper and Didi Herman, 'Getting the Family Right: Legislating Heterosexuality in Britain, 1986-1991', *Canadian Journal of Family Law*, 10 (1991), pp41-78.

[12] Law Report, The *Independent*, 12 March 1992.

[13] Weeks, *Sex, Politics, and Society* (London: Longman, 1981), p242.

[14] See Tim Newburn, *Permission and Regulation* (London: Routledge, 1992), chapters 3 and 7.

[15] In this essay, I focus on *progressive*, oppositional forces engaging with the state. However, one might argue that other oppositional forces exist on the right of the political spectrum. Herman has explored this issue in the context of the new Christian right in Canada: *Reforming Rights: Struggles for Lesbian and Gay Legal Equality in Canada*, PhD dissertation, University of Warwick, 1993.

[16] None of this is to suggest that the British state actually *possesses* widespread legitimacy or stability but rather that the aspiration for both structures its work. Even radical British governments which either seek or anticipate disruption know that their political project will be difficult to continue if they cannot .create the necessary long-term stability to implement their objectives.

[17] Cooper, 'Off the Banner and onto the Agenda: The Emergence of a New Lesbian and Gay Municipal Politics 1979-87', *Critical Social Policy* 26 (1992), pp20-39.

[18] Jessop, *State Theory*, p260.

[19] Alternatively, it has been argued that lesbian and gay marriages, partnerships, and families are radical rather than conformist, since by adopting such institutionalised arrangements, the arrangements themselves

are deconstructed, denaturalised or transformed.

[20] Rubin, 'Thinking Sex', in Vance, ed., *Pleasure and Danger*, pp9, 267-319.

[21] This discursive production does not just happen to communities, for clearly their own activism and self-expression will help shape the discourses by which they are constituted and understood. However, such empowerment may be particularly difficult at certain historical junctures.

[22] Linda Singer, *Erotic Welfare: Sexual Theory and Politics in the Age of Epidemic* (London: Routledge, 1993), p150.

[23] To what extent is the 'confessional' an inevitable aspect of state practice? And to what extent do other ostensibly non-state bodies also require 'an explaining of oneself' before support is given? Is the problem to do with the particular nature of the scrutiny rather than the general process of scrutiny itself?

[24] Whether social forces can act politically without engaging with the state is a difficult question. Rape crisis centres, lesbian counselling phonelines, benefits in public venues, and consciousness-raising groups all have a state nexus, albeit an indirect and tangential one. Such a connection is, however, possibly different from that of forces engaging directly with the state from within, outside or on the boundaries of its practice.

[25] See Bob Cant, 'The Limits of Tolerance?', in Tara Kaufmann and Paul Lincoln, eds, *High Risk Lives* (Bridport: Prism Press, 1991), pp155-78.

[26] See Herman, 'Are We Family? Lesbian Rights and Women's Liberation', *Osgoode Law Journal 28* (1991), p789; and *Reforming Rights*.

[27] See Cooper, *Sexing the City: Community Politics and the Activist State* (London: Rivers Oram Press, 1994).

[28] See Martin Durham, *Sex and Politics* (Basingstoke: Macmillan, 1991).

[29] See Herman, *Reforming Rights*.

[30] Clearly, debate happens in other more accessible, less elitist arenas, such as schools, residential homes, and prisons. However, the participation of 'outside' voices in those arenas is often minimal. Demonstrations and grassroots actions may more effectively convey progressive discourse, although marches in poorly populated parts of town again rely on mass media.

[31] The new urban left in Britain, for example, found their work being interpreted and 'misread' by an extremely hostile tabloid press. In relation to lesbian and gay municipal policies, see Cant, 'The Limits of Tolerance?', in Kaufmann and Lincoln, eds, *High Risk Lives*.

[32] Lisa Adkins, 'Sexual Work and the Employment of Women in the Service Industry', in Savage and Witz, eds, *Gender and Bureaucracy*, pp207-27.

[33] Michel Foucault, *The History of Sexuality, Volume 1, An Introduction*, trans. Robert Hurley (Harmondsworth: Penguin, 1978).

[34] See Ann McClintock, 'Screwing the System: Sex, Work, Race, and the Law', *Boundary 2*, 19:2 (1992), pp70-95.

[35] Eisenstein, *Feminism and Sexual Equality* (New York: Monthly Review Press, 1984), p89.

[36] There is a tension in some feminist theory between perceiving women as

located within the private, and in perceiving women as private. White feminist analysis of the public-private dichotomy has also been criticised by feminists who argue that the private is something that many black women, as a result of slavery, historically never possessed. Today, for poor, homeless Americans, their residence is within the public. Thus, the private cannot simply be seen as a realm of oppression, but must also be viewed as one of privilege: Patricia J. Williams, *The Alchemy of Race and Rights* (Cambridge, Mass.: Harvard University Press, 1991).

[37] Clearly, there is a tension between the state being discursively constructed away from sexuality, and treating sexuality as a form of disciplinary power that not only shapes the state, but is also utilised by it.

[38] See, for example, Patrick Devlin, *The Enforcement of Morals* (Oxford: Oxford University Press, 1959); and the majority judgements in *R v Brown and Others*, 1993.

[39] This point is complicated by sexological and psychoanalytical developments that conceive of sexuality as healthy and positive. Within this framework, one particularly dominant in the 1970s and early 1980s (although, significantly, still evident in the 'virgin mothers' scandals of 1991), it is lesbians and gays who are desexualized and rendered dysfunctional.

[40] Antonio Gramsci, for example, worked at times with a very broad definition of the state that has subsequently been criticised as too inclusive.

[41] Lillian Faderman, *Odd Girls and Twilight Lovers* (New York: Penguin, 1992), chapter 6.

[42] Wendy Brown, 'Finding the Man in the State', *Feminist Studies*, 18 (1992), pp7-34.

[43] Defining the state's relationship as heterosexual, in a context of heterosexual hegemony, does not detract from the construction of the state as ostensibly asexual since, as I have argued above, heterosexuality's naturalised status renders it invisible as as a sexuality.

[44] 'Ethnic cleansing' through rape, as is happening in Bosnia as I write, is another glaring example. So too are the stories told of war where men – living and dying – get erections on the battlefield.

Unholy Alliances: The Recent Politics of Sex Education

RACHEL THOMSON

Sex education both constructs and confirms the categories of 'normal' and 'deviant' which it regulates, monitors and controls. Sex education is a particularly resonant intersection of power/knowledge.[1] Education reflects the dominant politics of a society's institutions and sex education reflects the sexual politics of those institutions. The debates that have surrounded the process of defining a 'national curriculum', particularly in the areas of English and history, illustrate the ways in which public definitions of education, culture and knowledge are contested. The processes that have contributed to contemporary definitions of sex education are also born of contestation. This chapter is about institutional sexual politics and hegemonic discourses. It is also about activism: the process by which the social movements of feminism, gay liberation and AIDS activism have impacted on the institutions and discourses that structure the aims and imperatives of school sex education. In particular, it focuses on the intersection and shifting configuration of two institutional discourses that address sex and sexuality in the public sphere, public health pragmatism, and the moral authoritarianism of conservative education philosophy.

1992 saw the publication of two important government policy documents of relevance to personal, social and sex education in schools. On one hand, the Department of Health published *The Health of the Nation*[2] which identified sexual health as one of five key areas to be targeted for intervention. On the other, the Department For Education published *Choice and Diversity: A New Framework for Schools*.[3] This document attempts to define the nature of the 'spiritual and moral development' of students, a quality that schools will be required to demonstrate to the newly reformed school inspectorate.[4] There is a fundamental dichotomy between these two approaches to the aims of school sex education held by government departments. Should school sex education be used as an opportunity to communicate knowledge and skills to enable young people to make their informed decisions or should it be used as an opportunity to impose a prescriptive model of sexual and personal morality?

I shall argue that these two approaches, sexual health and sexual moralism, are increasingly coming into conflict, the former stressing the distinction between sexually healthy and sexually unhealthy practices, the latter between the morally legitimate and the morally illegitimate. As Jeffrey Weeks notes 'sex is a contested zone, a moral and political battle field'.[5] School sex education is one of the key sites in which this battle is played out. State schools not only provide an environment enabling universal access to the under-16 'population', but schools are also public arenas in which hegemonic or 'official' representations of personal and public morality are expressed. As such schools are key sites for both social engineering and social control.

I shall also map some of the recent key moments in the development of public policy in the area of sex education and in doing so try to outline some of the tensions within this very public form of sexual politics. I will conclude by considering the opportunities that exist for contemporary sexual politics and activism to contribute to the politics and practice of school sex education. In particular, I shall argue that progressive sexual politics should be aware of the significance of 'unholy alliances' of discourse and be prepared to engage strategically in unfamiliar discursive territory.

Origins

Historically the evolution of public policy around sexuality mirrors wider social anxieties concerning nationhood, social change and social stability.[6] Historians have shown that the origins of school sex education lie in moralist and eugenic concerns around the breakdown of the family, the changing role and expectations of women, the purity of the race and the differential birth rate between social classes.[7] The aims of school sex education have never been to help young people have satisfying and fulfilling sexual relationships.

The biological legacy identified by all major studies of sex education[8] can be seen as a product of these origins. The imperatives of sex education were twofold, firstly to address the negative consequences of sexual behaviour (disease, pregnancy) and secondly to reinforce normative definitions of appropriate sexuality (sex within marriage). The biological model enables the pathology of sex to be explored while leaving the broader social dimensions unquestioned. Such an approach also focuses on the girl and the woman, both in terms of reifying her reproductive capacity and by placing upon her the responsibility for policing the 'natural' sexual excesses of men.[9]

Equal Opportunities: The Impact of the New Social Movements

During the 1970s and early 1980s the social movements of feminism, anti-racism and gay liberation began to make an impact on education in the form of equal opportunities and anti-racist philosophies.[10] In the absence of any constitution or bill of rights these philosophies helped to construct the rights of minority and oppressed groups in anti-discrimination and positive image strategies. In the area of sex education this was marked by a move beyond the biological model of sex education to social or rights based interventions which attempted to educate against prejudice. At this time we see initiatives such as the Inner London Education Authority

(ILEA) sexuality project, and a number of positive image exercises in the area of lesbian and gay sexuality such as the video *A Different Story*. Research undertaken at this time by the London Lesbian and Gay Teenage Group for the first time made visible the experiences of lesbian and gay pupils at school.[11] The underachievement of girls and ethnic minority students in the education system became increasingly acknowledged and tentative attempts began to be made to redress social inequality through education.[12]

Participatory and consciousness-raising models of education originating in the new social movements began to influence work undertaken with young people. We find an increase in group work and experiential learning methodologies and the genesis of anti-sexist work and girls groups in youth clubs. Attempts were made in a number of local education authorities for the curriculum and teaching methodologies to become more inclusive and to reflect the social diversity of the wider society. These methodologies were not necessarily widespread but they were gaining recognition as examples of good practice and informed the work undertaken in the pastoral curriculum. Teachers, influenced by the new social movements were undertaking anti-sexist and anti-racist work within the classroom. Schools, like the wider society, began to respond to some of the challenges and changes brought about by the sexual politics of the times.

During this time education about sex and personal relationships generally took place in an ad hoc way, there being no formal curriculum framework.[13] Yet there was a growing consensus in educational practice and philosophy as to the value of developing young people's, particularly young women's, critical abilities and communication skills. While formal 'biological' sex education usually appeared in science lessons, increasingly attempts were made to address broader decision making skills in Personal and Social Education (PSE) and other areas of the curriculum.[14]

Thatcherism, Parent Power and the Imposition of a Moral Framework

It is impossible to understand the policy changes that affected sex education through the 1980s in isolation from the general ideological project of Thatcherism within which we find the construction of new political constituencies and shifts in power from local to central government. One of the ideological centre-pieces of Thatcherism was the identification of the family as the unit of society and the construction of parents as a political constituency. This may be termed a 'discourse of familialism',[15] or what in education has come to be called 'parent power'. In Margaret Thatcher's own words: 'there is no such thing as society', only individuals and families. In effect, by giving mythical rights to mythical parents, real rights and powers were taken away from those who had been represented within the equal opportunities discourse. In education this meant an attack on the power and influence of local education authorities and the appearance of increased powers to school governors and parents. What actually took place was an unprecedented transfer of power to central government and the Department for Education.[16]

In many ways, the Thatcherite revolution in education was expressed as a revolution against the philosophy and practice of equal opportunities which itself became caricatured as 'the permissive society'. Anti-sexist and anti-racist education were targeted for amplification and vilification by sections of the media and the government in the lead up to plans for transforming education.

The two planks of the Thatcherite assault on the state of education were to undermine parental trust in the teaching profession and to discredit the role of Local Education Authorities. As others have noted, an appeal to popular racism and homophobia were key elements in the process by which some local education authorities acquired the stigma of loony left.[17] This label in turn played a critical role in galvanising public support for a generalised attack on the education system. The media circus that surrounded the children's book

Jenny lives with Eric and Martin, culminating in Section 28 of the Local Government Act which prohibits LEAs from 'promoting homosexuality', was essential in enabling the government to mobilise popular support for wholesale changes in the nature and organisation of the education system.

Sex education has not only been deeply affected by the changes that have swept across state education in the last few year, but, alongside anti-racist education, sex education has provided one of the focal points through which public support for these wider changes has been rallied. The press and the government together succeeded in convincing the public that the enemy within lay in the schools and the LEAs, and that political indoctrination if not sexual corruption was taking place in the classroom.[18]

Sex-tion 28: The Enemy Within

The two most significant pieces of legislation to affect sex education during this period were the Gillick ruling on contraceptive advice to under 16s and Section 28 of the Local Government Bill. Both of these pieces of legislation drew on public and parental fears concerning the sexuality of young people and questioned the degree to which teachers should be allowed professional discretion to respond to young people's needs for confidential advice and guidance. Significantly, neither Section 28 nor the Gillick restrictions on the giving of contraceptive advice to under 16s in fact apply to the teaching of sex education in schools.[19] Nevertheless, the media contribution to the Section 28 debate had the effect of undermining parents' confidence in the ability of teachers to undertake this task.

Section 28 in particular was a key cultural and symbolic event in the recent history of sexual politics. At a time of increasing public awareness of child sexual abuse and male violence within the home, the moral panic that surrounded the legislation helped to deflect attention from the 'health' and 'normality' of the family.[20] More directly, it played an important role in undermining the professionalism of teachers and in policing the politics of teachers. The phrase 'the promotion of homosexuality' had the insidious effect of constructing teachers as the potential corruptors of young people and of frightening teachers from saying what they thought was sensible and right out of fear of losing their jobs. Despite the popular rhetoric of familialism and the sovereignty of the family, the vast majority of parents were in fact keen for schools to provide teaching in this area.[21]

The Section 28 controversy also had a significant effect on the agenda of sex education itself. By constructing homosexuality as the symbolic 'other', a biological and reproductive model of sexual relations was reinforced. The inclusion of sexual identity in sex education potentially challenges the traditional biological approach that excludes a whole range of non-reproductives aspects of sexuality, masculinity and femininity. It could be argued that, by implying that a particular sexual identity could be 'promoted', Section 28 was, as Jackie Stacey claims, 'an implicit response to many feminist ideas and practices which had gained a certain foothold'.[22]

The net effect within education of both Section 28 and the Gillick ruling on contraceptive advice has been to create a climate of paranoia around the teaching of sex education. While neither should directly impact on the teaching of sex education they both encourage self-censorship and caution.[23] Progressive teachers who once took the lead in sex education and PSE have become increasingly nervous about what it is safe to teach, others see it as an opportunity to avoid discussing more challenging aspects of sex education.[24] We might also suggest that where 'homosexuality' is discussed it is likely to be in connection with disease. Ironically, research with young people suggests that they are more interested in questions of sexual identity than any other areas of sex education.[25]

Neither the Gillick ruling nor Section 28 were genuine responses to the educational challenge of sex education, nor to the needs of the young people whom education should serve. Rather they are examples of the way in which school sex education has been used to address the interests and anxieties of an adult society unable to contemplate the existence of adolescent sexuality. Throughout the 1980s sex education was the subject of a disproportionate amount of parliamentary and media attention.[26] By utilising the concept, if not the reality, of parent power and by mobilising parental fears concerning corruption in the classroom, sex education was effectively isolated from the rest of the curriculum. Educational professionals were no longer trusted to exercise their professional judgement in sex education, mirroring moves to undermine teacher autonomy in other curriculum areas. By rejecting teachers' professional expertise, the educational philosophies that informed their practice were also marginalised. Equal opportunities philosophies were replaced by a 'commonsense' discourse of family values, closely allied to the concept of parental choice and the centrality of the family as the unit of society. The final disbanding of ILEA in 1990 was a savage blow for equal opportunities philosophies in education. ILEA had been at the forefront of curriculum and staff development in PSE, health and sex education as well as in anti-racist and anti-sexist strategies for the classroom. With its demise the confidence and status that had slowly accrued to this area of the curriculum was dissipated. The focus and energy of activism by this point began to move away from education, and driven by the emerging crisis of HIV/AIDS, began to move towards health and the HIV/AIDS voluntary sector.

The 1986 Education Act: Governor Control

The 1986 Education Act removed from Local Education Authorities the responsibility for, or control over, school sex education, and placed it for the first time in the hands of school governors – an explicit attempt to provide sex education with inherently 'conservative' gatekeepers. Schools governors were required to consider whether sex education should form part of the curriculum, and if they decided it should, to produce a written statement on the form and content of that curriculum. This policy statement should then be made available to parents. Although parents were not granted the right to withdraw their children from sex education lessons, governors were given the discretionary power to allow students to withdraw if parents had religious objections. The 1986 Education (No 2) Act further required teachers, governors and Local Education Authorities to ensure that 'Where sex Education is given ... it is given in a manner as to encourage those pupils to have due regard to moral considerations and the value of family life.' Although school governors were entrusted with control over the sex education curriculum they were not trusted to develop a moral framework for that curriculum. In 1987 the Department of Education and Science issued guidance to school governors on their new responsibilities for sex education, setting out a moral framework within which sex education should be taught.

> Teaching about the physical aspects of sexual behaviour should be set within a clear moral framework in which pupils are encouraged to consider the importance of self-restraint, dignity and respect for themselves and others, and are helped to recognise the physical, emotional and moral risks of casual and promiscuous sexual behaviour. Schools should foster a recognition that both sexes should behave responsibly in sexual matters. Pupils should be helped to appreciate the benefits of stable married life and the responsibilities of parenthood.[27]

This guidance went further than the requirement to encourage pupils to have 'due regard to moral considerations' laid out in the 1986 Act. Circular 11/87 gives specific directives on the way in which sex education should be taught with particular reference to the teaching of 'controversial' subjects such as abortion, AIDS, homosexuality, contraception and the use of outside speakers:

It is important to distinguish between, on one hand, the school's function of providing education generally about sexual matters ... and, on the other, counselling and advice to individual pupils particularly if this relates to their own sexual behaviour. Good teachers have always taken a pastoral interest in the welfare and well-being of pupils. But this function should never trespass on the proper exercise of parental rights and responsibilities. On the specific question of the provision of contraceptive advice to girls under 16, the general rule must be that giving an individual pupil advice on such matters without parental knowledge or consent, would be an inappropriate exercise of a teachers professional responsibilities, and could, depending on the circumstances amount to a criminal offence.[28]

In effect, Circular 11/87 constructed a model for the teaching of sex education which was knowledge based, legalistic and excluded any understanding of inequality, diversity or social change. It was primarily concerned with delineating a 'traditional' model of family life and normative sexual relations and paid no attention to practical teaching methods or the reality of young people's needs and lives. By selectively defining 'controversial issues', the circular constructed sex education as inherently problematic territory and thereby provided a framework of surveillance rather than practical support. The language of the circular is deliberately exclusive, not only of lesbian and gay students or children of lesbian and gay parents, but of all those students who do not live in stable nuclear families.

Speaking of homosexuality, the guidance notes that

There is no place in any school in any circumstances for teaching which advocates homosexual behaviour, which presents it as the 'norm' or which encourages homosexual experimentation by pupils. Indeed, encouraging or procuring homosexual acts by pupils who are under the age of consent is a criminal offence. It must also be recognised that for many people, including members of religious faiths, homosexual practice is not morally acceptable, and deep offence may be caused to them if the subject is not handled with sensitivity by teachers if discussed in the classroom.[29]

While the guidance recognises the rights and sensibilities of conservative minorities it ignores the rights and opinions of those who hold more progressive, realistic or critical views of the 'value of family life'. In contrast to the inclusive nature of equal opportunities philosophies which aimed to embrace and respect the diversity of society, this framework prescribes an exclusive model of the family and sexual relationships in relation to which the majority are seen to fail.[30] It is a model that owes more to nostalgia for an idealised pre-feminist past than any serious educational attempt to explore health-related behaviour. Although the guidance did not have statutory status, and school governors were free to decide their own moral framework and policy guidelines, in the absence of alternative interpretations this circular had a significant impact on the way in which school sex education is perceived by school governors and teachers.

The National Curriculum: Discourses in Collision

The public health discourse, from which school sex education partly originates, was given renewed impetus in the late 1980s by the advent of HIV/AIDS. Although the public health discourse or the epidemiological model of sexual health has many hidden values,[31] it nevertheless takes a pragmatic approach to the issue of sex education. Where moral authoritarianism is primarily interested in securing a traditional definition of sexual relations within the educational institution, public health pragmatism is concerned to get information to students and to affect their behaviour. The present disjuncture between the Departments of Health and Education surrounding the implementation of *The Health of the Nation* (with the former setting statistical targets for teenage pregnancy reduction and the latter concerning itself with pupil's spiritual and moral development) is testament to the differing objectives of their respective ideologies.

These tensions can also be seen in the conflicts surrounding sex education within the National Curriculum. The 1986 Act succeeded in isolating sex education from the rest of the curriculum by giving school governors the responsibility to decide whether it would appear in the curriculum, and if so in what form. In doing so, education about sex and sexuality appeared to be excluded from the commitment in the 1988 Educational Reform Act to provide all students the entitlement to 'a broad and balanced curriculum' and to prepare 'pupils for the opportunities, responsibilities and experiences of adult life.'

The changes brought about to sex education in the form of the 1986 Act took place before widespread public acknowledgement of the threat of HIV and AIDS. With the introduction of the National Curriculum, some aspects of sex education, particularly the reproductive and disease components, were included in the science curriculum.[32] Although school governors supposedly had control over whether and what kind of sex education was taught in schools, their powers in this area were compromised. It was clearly felt that, irrespective of rhetoric about parental and governor control of the sex education curriculum, it was necessary to provide a safety net of basic information in the interests of public health. In 1991 the National Curriculum Science orders were revised to include HIV/AIDS at Key Stage 3 (11-14 yrs). The revision, made after consultation with key agencies in the field, recommended that HIV/AIDS was such a serious threat to public health that it could not be left to governors to decide whether it should be taught. This is another example of public health pragmatism overriding the rhetoric of parent power and the supposed sovereignty of the family.

Although the contradictions in the government's policy of governor control of sex education and the requirements of the National Curriculum had not attracted attention earlier, the inclusion of HIV in the National Curriculum was picked up by the right wing and by religious lobbies who began a concerted campaign for the right of parents to remove their children from National Curriculum classes:

In my view the order is yet another erosion of parental rights. It is the sacrifice of a parent's rights to guide the moral well-being of

230

their children and it is sacrificing it to the newest politically correct attitude. Members of this House and another place then wonder why parents want to slough off their responsibilities when the state tells them they may not have a conscience about what is taught to their children in our schools on matters of sex and sexual morality. As I say it is little wonder that parents are becoming concerned about the state's attitude towards their ability to bring up their own children. The parent's charter that was put before the electorate at the last election, specifically provides that there should be choice. Where is the choice here to the parents as to whether their children should be taught in accordance with their own views and concepts? The right is being taken away from them and there is no conscience clause.[33]

The following ambiguous government response illustrates the precarious balancing act that the DFE found itself performing in an attempt to negotiate the conflicting imperatives of public health pragmatism and moral authoritarianism:

There will occasionally be areas where those two interests, the secular and the religious, to some extent overlap. The current case is one. There are strongly held and irreconcilable views. After careful consideration of the issues, the Government have taken the line that they should follow the broad principles that parliament agreed should be enshrined in the 1988 Education Reform Act: that the curriculum should fully prepare all pupils for the challenges and problems, as well as the opportunities, which their adult lives will present; and that to this end all pupils are entitled to receive a broad, comprehensive curriculum. To create rights of exemption from the secular curriculum would not in my view be in the interests of securing an effective, broad education for every child. That must be our first concern. However I must repeat that the teaching of sex education and HIV within national curriculum science must, and I repeat must, have due regard to moral considerations and the value and promotion of family life.[34]

Under Thatcherism, sex education was politicised and used in an opportunistic way for broader political ends. The legacy for sex education has been, as Philip Meredith argues, that its 'recent evolution has been determined more by the consequences of 'moral panics than rationalisation'.[35] The instrumental deployment of the 'discourse of familialism' also brought into being a political alliance of the moral right. With the growing public health crisis of HIV/AIDS we find the government hoist on the petard of its own rhetoric and increasingly at the mercy of an unrepresentative moral lobby.

The Rise of Religious Moralism

The campaign to establish a parental right of withdrawal from National Curriculum sex education illustrates the conflicting and shifting forces at play in public policy on school sex education. The campaign, led by a fundamentalist Christian sect called the Plymouth Brethren, and culminating in the aforementioned debate in the House of Lords, also demonstrates the rising influence on the Government of a brand of religious moralism. In the absence of a discourse of equal opportunities, religion is playing an increasingly important role in educational debate over the nature of school sex education. The impetus for this rising influence is rooted in a number of factors including developments in multi-cultural politics, the close relationship between religion and education in the British education system, and the increasing influence of American style moral lobbies. The National Curriculum Council will shortly be publishing guidance to schools on 'spiritual and moral development' yet it refuses to publish the findings of the NCC Working Group on multi-cultural education. Increasingly, ethnic groups are becoming identified as religious groups and we slip semantically from a commitment to multi-culturalism to an awareness of multi-faith issues.[36]

The arrival of John Patten, practising Catholic and self-avowed moralist,[37] at the Department For Education has clearly encouraged the growth of this tendency. Secretary of State for Education Kenneth Clarke treated some four hundred letters of complaint from the Plymouth Brethren with indifference. To Clarke the Brethren were just a minority group to be ignored in the face of public health pragmatism.

232

With a change of Minister the same four hundred letters came to symbolise serious political pressure. It is clear that the conservative religious lobbies were aware of a powerful ally in Mr Patten. Baroness Phillips remarked in June 1992:

> I was delighted when my friend mentioned Sodom and Gomorrah. If you want to see evidence of global warming and all the other events which are happening, you only have to reread the Old Testament, the literature about the fall of the Roman empire, if you want to be a little more up-to-date, or the fall of the Greek Empire. Those accounts include greed, perversion and all matters which will become prevalent in our society if we are not very careful ... We do not want to become threatening, but parents feel very strongly about these matters. Rather unfashionably some of us have tried to voice these issues. I know that the Minister is a woman of great understanding. We hope that if she cannot give us the answers, she will at least pass on the questions to her noble friend. After all, Mr John Patten is a very good practising Catholic. How does a Minister think? Does one put one's conscience or one's job first?[38]

Baroness Phillips' hopes appear to have been well-placed. The recent white paper, now Education Bill, *Choice and Diversity: A New Framework for Education*, identifies the reduction of truancy and the spiritual and moral development of students as the future direction of educational policy.[39] Significantly, this document does not specifically address sex education yet it does address the development of moral values. The development of moral autonomy, decision making and social skills had previously been the territory of that part of the curriculum known as PSE. With the introduction of the National Curriculum, PSE disappeared, to be replaced by the non-statutory cross curricular themes. In direct contrast to the child centred methodologies characteristic of the PSE curriculum, *Choice and Diversity* argues that values should be imposed on young people and that these values are not negotiable. Where PSE aimed to enable young people to explore and define their *own* values *Choice and Diversity* actually proposes what those values should be. This prescriptive moralism goes beyond the 'familial discourse' of

233

Thatcherism where moral authoritarianism was tempered by radical liberalism. Parents, it appears, are no longer to be trusted to instil the correct set of values within the sphere of the family:

> In a variety of ways and across a range of subject areas, young people should always be taught that, in addition to rights and expectations, they also have important duties and responsibilities to their community. They should be encouraged to be involved members of those communities, to grow up as active citizens. They should be taught the importance of developing a strong moral code that includes a concern for others, self respect and self-discipline, as well as basic values such as honesty and truthfulness. Schools should have and should communicate a clear vision of those things they and the community hold to be important. The transition from dependent child to independent adult, imbued with these moral codes and values, should be the aim of every school and teacher. Most do this very well and are to be warmly congratulated on it. Some struggle to do it, or fail – sometimes because of the indifference of parents or the surrounding community.[40]

The tone of these passages point to a growing disjuncture between education and health philosophies in the area of teaching methods. Currently, teaching methodologies are hotly contested within education. The government has been forthright in its support for 'traditional' teaching methods despite near universal opposition from teachers and educationalists. Applied to PSE, or moral education, traditional methods will mean that students are to be *told* what is right and what is wrong. This not only flies in the face of what educational theory and practice knows of personal and social development but also of recent developments in health education which place importance on identification, participation and ownership in the learning process:

> Whatever the individual religious feelings of boys and girls, the ethos of any school should include a clear vision of the values within it, and those of the community outside. Those values include a respect for people and property; honesty and consideration for others; trust, fairness and politeness.

234

While there can be no attainment targets or performance indicators for these achievements, they are critically important in encouraging our children to grow up understanding what is right and wrong, and journeying into adulthood not just full of exuberance or individuality, but also appreciating the needs of others and their environment.[41]

While school sex education comes under the auspices of the Department for Education it is obvious that the targets identified in the *Health of the Nation* of reducing under-sixteens' pregnancies by 50% and gonorrhea rates by 20% will be impossible to meet without significantly improving provision. Yet at precisely the time that the Department of Health was looking to the Department for Education to move forward on sex education the Department for Education withdrew funding from Health Education Co-ordinators – key figures in the local co-ordination and support of sex and HIV/AIDS education. Meanwhile, the increasing devolvement of finances and managerial responsibility to schools under local management of schools removes from LEAs responsibility for and means to advise, support and monitor school sex education.[42]

A recent survey by the Association of County Councils into the future provision of local support in the area of health, drugs and sex education concludes that:

The action of central government in withdrawing funding from this particular area of activity directly contradicts the objectives set out in central government's key strategic document *The Health of the Nation* ... The action by the Department of Education in withdrawing this funding runs contrary to central government's pronounced aspirations to develop prevention for young people as one of its key themes and activities. It would appear that whilst asking local organisations to co-ordinate their activities there is significant lack of co-ordination within central government itself.[43]

The Department of Health may want to help schools provide effective sex education but it is not clear how far they will cross the Department for Education in order to enable this to

235

actually take place, or to what extent they are prepared to compromise the ethos and methodology of such interventions. It may be easier for the Departments of Health and Education to agree on abstention ('just say no') programmes rather than on interventions that aim to empower. Again, the net result of this conflict is that policy and resources are caught up around struggles over definition and control rather than in supporting teachers and improving provision.

Activism: Influencing the Agenda

In this chapter I have mapped the range of official discourses that define and constrain the nature of school sex education. These discourses are not static and their changing configuration both opens and closes windows of opportunity to influence the sex education debate. They can interact to reinforce, constrain and temper one another, giving rise to both unexpected and unholy alliances. The language of policy cannot be taken simply at face value but needs to be placed in political context and in relation to other competing official discourses. When understood in the context of the reorganisation of education, the moral authoritarianism of Thatcherite educational philosophy can be seen as a means to a specific political end (the destruction of the LEAs) and, to a certain extent, as tempered by the radical liberalism of 'parent power' and the pragmatism of the public health discourse. However the contemporary conjunction of public health pragmatism and religious moralism may prove to be a more constraining configuration. In the light of this shift I shall argue that the moral agenda should not be left to the domination of the religious right, but that progressive sexual politics should engage in this increasingly dominant discourse and challenge its framework of authoritarianism.

The focus on policy and the language of the public sphere in this essay may be somewhat misleading, in that it obscures the degree to which these official discourses are contested from within, as well as the ways private discourses of sexuality and sexual morality may have a far greater impact on young people's lives and awareness. It could be argued that the inclusion of HIV/AIDS issues in the British soap opera, *East Enders* and teenage pregnancy in the Australian-made *Home and Away*, has more cultural significance than the entire legislative framework for school sex education. Those with knowledge of schools will also know that the gap between official policy and actual school practice can be enormous. Nevertheless, I hope to have shown that public discourses are significant and that the political and policy pressures on school sex education over the last ten years have been constraining and have hindered curriculum developments and innovation.

Those innovations that have taken place in sexual health education have been mainly in the field of public health and community education. The advent of HIV/AIDS created a close relationship between public health and the voluntary sector, which has spearheaded the introduction of a number of progressive health education initiatives promoting client-centred approaches and empowerment strategies.[44] Innovations in this area have also been encouraged by the contribution of social research into sexual behaviour and HIV/AIDS. Such research serves to challenge the increasingly idealised public discourse of sexual moralism, and by bringing evidence of the rules and conduct of intimate relations into the public sphere encourages the 'personal to be made political'.[45] The identification of a gap between knowledge of sexual risks and actual behaviour has placed issues of power, control, masculinity, femininity and sexual identity tentatively on the public health agenda.[46]

The key to influencing policy-making within the discourse of public health has been effectiveness. Whether an initiative works (i.e. if it actually affects behaviour) has been the overriding imperative. Moral and religious sensibilities are seen as relevant where they are factors enhancing or blocking the communication of health education messages. These factors are seen as significant as aspects of individuals' identities rather than as ideologies to be promoted in themselves. Yet, clearly, this neutral pragmatism is equally open to progressive and reactionary influences. Despite this apparent meeting of interests, public health support for progressive tendencies is skin deep, a support born of pragmatism rather than principle.

Conversely, the ideological terrain of education is characterised by a concern with principle rather than pragmatism. Whether this be in the form of equal opportunities philosophies, 'parent power' or religious moralism, schools are institutions where the transmission of dominant social values is the primary aim. As the accompanying notes to the DES AIDS video comment, just because a sexual act is safe it 'does not mean it is morally acceptable or desirable'.[47] Ironically, the opportunity for activism in education may now lie in turning moral rhetoric into educational practice. Although the right controls the official moral framework for sex education, it has been unable to translate this hegemony of rhetoric into educational practice. Morals cannot simply be taught or imposed, 'morality' can only be made visible, modelled and enabled.

However uncomfortable progressive sexual politics may feel with the language of morality, it may be precisely this area which it is best equipped to address. The gap between knowledge and behaviour, between social and sexual identity, is also the arena of moral autonomy and empowerment. For sex education to be meaningful it needs to address and develop moral autonomy and to do this it needs to address power and interconnecting relationships of power.[48] Participatory and empowerment methodologies which creatively engage young people are coming to be recognised as having greater and more lasting impact than those which are morally prescriptive. Learner-centred methodologies such as role play and peer education, where young people define and address their own agendas around sexual health, are beginning to make an impact in education. And there is an increasing awareness that social and decision making skills can only be developed actively through participation, reflection and debate.

Yet there continues to be a gulf between the public agenda

of sex education as defined by 'gatekeepers' and policy makers and the needs and opinions of young people. Research into young people's attitudes and behaviour in relation to HIV/AIDS has uncovered widespread dissatisfaction with the approach and emphasis of school sex education,[49] and initiatives involving young people have found them to be forceful critics of policy makers in their own right.[50] The emergent discourse of children's rights in social policy potentially challenges the paternalistic character of the current sex education agenda.[51] For progressive sexual politics to make a meaningful contribution to contemporary school sex education, it is necessary to act strategically, to engage in the moral discourse, but also to challenge the authoritarianism that constructs sex education around the twin poles of 'just say yes' or 'just say no'. Rather than fall into a trap of fighting for the alternative, yet equally prescriptive, agenda, it would be more effective and more honest to champion an agenda which grows from an acknowledgement of the reality of young people's needs, centred on empowerment and skills development. A more appropriate slogan for such an approach might be 'just say *know*' – it could even be fun!

*

'So all the way from the fourth year we had all sex education ... two hours a week we used to have it ... it was more than adequate because it told you everything. Every type of contraceptive on the market, that was going to come onto the market, what had been on the market, what Cleopatra used. We were told everything, and our teacher was very good, she told us about her experiences. She told us all about orgasms and things like that ... There was two of them. One was I should say she was thirty, and the other was near enough retirement age. The younger one would talk about it freely and the older one would turn round and say "before I met Mrs. Barker I didn't even know what an orgasm was, and I thought crabs were things that walked sideways over the beach". It used to be dead informal, and we used to have discussions about mixed race marriages and things like that. I remember a discussion about abortion ... I did a role play with this lad and we had an almighty row because he said that abortions should not be allowed, even if the girl had been raped. I was stood there nearly in tears shouting at him. I could have killed him I was so annoyed ... We talked about homosexuality, we did loads, and it was really good. Because say a lad was sat there that was homosexual and we were just going by heterosexual relationships all the time, they would feel really alienated ... It was brilliant, we used to love it. If they were going to go through two subjects in a lesson, we always had a discussion at the end, so we only did one. It was dead good, they used to have loads of pamphlets and everything. We had a goody box, I remember the goody box, it had caps and condoms and coils and everything. And they used to have stuff on pieces of paper to show you what to do with them. You know, real ones, not just pictures, it was really good.'[52]

Notes

[1] See Nicky Thoroughgood, 'Sex Education as Social Control', *Critical Public Health* 3:3 (1992), pp43-50.
[2] *The Health of the Nation: A Strategy for Health in England* (London: HMSO, 1992).
[3] Department for Education, *Choice and Diversity: A New Framework for Schools* (London: HMSO, 1992).
[4] OFSTED, *A Handbook for the Inspection of Schools* (London: HMSO, 1992).
[5] Jeffrey Weeks, *Sexuality and Its Discontents: Meanings, Myths and Modern Sexualities* (London: Routledge and Kegan Paul, 1985), p4.
[6] Speeches delivered as part of the recent House of Lords debate on the inclusion of HIV/AIDS in the National Curriculum show how similar contemporary concerns around stability continue to dominate public discussion in this arena. Speaking of the DES booklet, 'HIV/AIDS: A Guide for the Education Service', Lord Pearson of Rannoch remarked: 'To ram some of the rest of that amoral booklet down the throats of even fourteen-year-olds, especially girls, would be a deeply immoral act ... I have here some material which I understand is widely used in schools. The thought of forcing that material down fourteen-year-old Muslim girls seems

to me to be asking for riots': *Hansard*, 11 June 1992, p1452.

[7] See, for example, Frank Mort, *Dangerous Sexualities: Medico-Moral Politics in England since 1830* (London: Routledge, 1987); Lucy Bland, ' "Guardians of the race" or "Vampires upon the nation's health"? Female Sexuality and Its Regulation in Early Twentieth-Century Britain', in Elizabeth Whitelegg, ed., *The Changing Experience of Women* (Oxford: Martin Robertson, 1982), pp373-88; and Weeks, *Sex, Politics and Society: The Regulation of Sexuality since 1800* (London: Longman, 1981).

[8] See Michael Schofield, *The Sexual Behaviour of Young People* (London: Longman, 1965); Christine Farrell in collaboration with Leonie Kellaher, *My Mother Said ...: The Way Young People Learned about Sex and Birth Control* (London: Routledge and Kegan Paul, 1978); and Isobel Allen, *Education in Sex and Personal Relationships*, PSI Research Report No.665, 1987.

[9] See Rachel Thomson and Sue J. Scott, *Learning about Sex: Young Women and the Social Construction of Sexual Identity* (London: The Tufnell Press, 1991); Barbara Hudson, 'Femininity and Adolescence', in Angela McRobbie and Mica Nava, eds, *Gender and Generation* (Basingstoke: Macmillan, 1984), pp31-53; and Michelle Fine, 'Sexuality, Schooling, and Adolescent Females: The Missing Discourse of Desire', *Harvard Educational Review* 58:1 (1988), pp29-53.

[10] See Barry Troyna, 'A Conceptual Overview of Strategies to Combat Racial Inequality in Education', in Troyna, ed., *Racial Inequality in Education* (London: Tavistock, 1987); Madeleine Arnot, ed., *Race and Gender: Equal Opportunities Policies in Education* (Oxford: Pergamon Press, 1985); and Haringey Council, *Equal Opportunities: The Lesbian and Gay Perspective* (1988).

[11] See Lorraine Trenchard and Hugh Warren, *Something to Tell You* (London: London Lesbian and Gay Teenage Group, 1984); and ILEA, *A Different Story*, Centre for Learning Resources, 275 Kennington Lane, London, SE11.

[12] See Helen Burchell and Val Millman, eds, *Changing Perspectives on Gender: New Initiatives in Secondary Schooling* (Milton Keynes: Open University Press, 1989); and Gaby Weiner, ed., *Just a Bunch of Girls: Feminist Approaches to Schooling* (Milton Keynes: Open University Press, 1985).

[13] See Farrell, *My Mother Said ...*, and Allen, *Education in Sex and Personal Relationships*.

[14] See Doggett in Allen, *ibid*.; and D. Reid, 'School Sex Education and the Causes of Unintended Pregnancy: A Review', *Health Education Journal*, 41:1 (1982), pp4-10.

[15] Sarah Franklin, Celia Lury, and Jackie Stacey, 'Feminism, Marxism, and Thatcherism', in Franklin et al, eds, *Off-Centre: Feminism and Cultural Studies* (London: HarperCollins, 1991), p37.

[16] See David Coulby and Leslie Bash, *Contradictions and Conflict: The 1988 Education Act in Action* (London: Cassell, 1991).

241

[17] Anne Marie Davies, Janet Holland and Rehana Minhas, *Equal Opportunities in the New ERA* (London: Tufnell Press, 1992); Jan Hardy and Chris Vieler-Porter, 'Race, Schooling and the 1988 Education Reform Act', in Dawn Gill, Barbara Mayor, and Maud Blair, eds, *Racism and Education: Structures and Strategies* (London: Sage, 1992), pp101-14.
[18] Roger Scruton et al, *Education and Indoctrination: An Attempt at Definition and a Review of Social and Political Implications* (Harrow: Education Research Centre, 1985).
[19] See Children's Legal Centre, *Section 28 and Sex Education: Children's Right to Know* (1989). Available from 20 Compton Terrace, London, N1.
[20] Stacey, 'Promoting Normality: Section 28 and the Regulation of Sexuality', in Franklin et al, eds, *Off-Centre*, pp284-304.
[21] Allen found that an overwhelming 96% of parents supported school sex education.
[22] Stacey, 'Promoting Normality', p296.
[23] See David Stears and Stephen Clift, *A Survey of AIDS Education in Secondary Schools* (Horsham: Avert, 1990); and Sex Education Forum, *An Enquiry into Sex Education* (London: National Children's Bureau, 1992).
[24] Gayle Rubin describes parallel examples of the surveillance of teachers in the United States: 'The more influence one has over the next generation the less latitude one is permitted in behaviour and opinion. The coercive power of the law ensures the transmission of conservative sexual values with these kinds of controls over parenting and teaching': 'Thinking Sex: Notes for a Radical Theory of the Politics of Sexuality', in Carole S. Vance, ed., *Pleasure and Danger: Exploring Female Sexuality* (London: Routledge and Kegan Paul, 1984), pp1-27.
[25] A survey of over 7000 16-18 year olds found that while 87% and 83% had learnt about puberty and pregnancy respectively at school, only 18% and 14% had learnt anything about homosexuality and lesbianism. When questioned on which subjects they felt their school had given them insufficient information, 8% and 11% mentioned puberty and pregnancy while 45% mentioned homosexuality: MORI, *Young Adults' Health and Lifestyle* (London: Health Education Authority, 1990).
[26] Philip Meredith, *Sex Education: Political Issues in Britain and Europe* (London: Routledge, 1989).
[27] DES, *Sex Education at School*, Circular No.11/87, 1987, p4.
[28] *Ibid.*, p5.
[29] *Ibid.*, p4.
[30] The imposition of a prescriptive framework in the area of sex education is mirrored by the imposition of a prescriptive model of 'cultural and national identity' in the curriculum in the form of the requirement of the 1986 Act for collective worship to be wholly or partly Christian.
[31] See Cindy Patton, 'What Science Knows: Formations of AIDS Knowledges', in Peter Aggleton, Peter Davies, and Graham Hart, eds, *AIDS: Individual, Cultural and Policy Dimensions* (Basingstoke: Falmer, 1990), pp1-17; and Peter Aggleton and Martin Norton, 'Pervert, Invert, and

Experts: The Cultural Production of an AIDS Research Paradigm', in Aggleton, Davies, and Hart, eds, *AIDS: Social Representations, Social Practices* (Basingstoke: Falmer, 1989), pp74-100.

[32] Sex education also appears in the National Curriculum as part of health education, a non-statutory cross-curricular theme – i.e. it is not tested and does not have to be taught by law. This curriculum encourages the use of participatory models of learning, and although information-based it also includes debate and discussion and positive messages about sex and social aspects of sexuality. Because of the non-statutory nature of cross-curricular themes, it is questionable whether it will be taught. National Curriculum Council, *Curriculum Guidance 5: Health Education* (York: NCC, 1990).

[33] Lord Stoddard of Swindon, *Hansard*, 11 June 1992, p1436.

[34] Baroness Blatch replying for the Government, *Hansard*, 11 June 1992, pp1460-61.

[35] Meredith, *Sex Education*, p2.

[36] This is particularly true in the area of sex education where equal opportunities in the area of gender increasingly being superseded by a requirement that sex and health messages be 'culturally appropriate': see Kaushika Amin, 'Values Conflicts in a Plural Society: The Case of Sex Education', *The Runnymede Bulletin*, 257 (1992), pp6-9; Yasmin Ali, 'Muslim Women and the Politics of Ethnicity and Culture in Northern England', in Gita Sahgal and Nira Yuval-Davis, eds, *Refusing Holy Orders: Women and Fundamentalism in Britain* (London: Virago, 1991), pp101-23; and Kaye Haw, 'Interactions of Gender and Race – A Problem for Teachers?' A Review of the Emerging Literature', *Educational Research*, 33:1 (1991), pp12-21.

[37] John Patten, 'There is a Choice: Good or Evil', *Spectator*, 11 April 1992, pp9-10.

[38] Baroness Phillips, *Hansard*, 11 June 1992, p1440.

[39] It is worth noting that *Choice and Diversity* selectively aims to promote students' spiritual and moral development, and fails to address the full entitlement to 'spiritual, moral, social and cultural development'.

[40] *Choice and Diversity*, p6.

[41] *Ibid.*, p7.

[42] See Sex Education Forum, *An Enquiry into Sex Education*.

[43] Association of County Councils, *Health Education Coordinators – LGDF Survey Results* (London: ACC, 1993).

[44] See Val Hamilton and Frankie Lynch, 'Educating Young People about HIV/AIDS', in Aggleton, ed., *Young People and HIV/AIDS: Papers from an ERSC Sponsored Seminar* (London: ESRC/University of London, 1992), pp31-35; Tim Rhodes and Richard Hartnoll, 'Reaching the Hard to Reach: Models of HIV Outreach Health Education', in Aggleton, Hart, and Davies, *AIDS: Responses, Interventions and Care* (Basingstoke: Falmer, 1991), pp233-48; MESMAC, *The MESMAC Guide to· Good Practice* (London: Health Education Authority, 1992).

[45] Simon Watney, 'AIDS: The Second Decade', in Aggleton, Hart, and

Davies, *AIDS: Responses, Interventions, and Care*, pp1-18.

[46] See Neil McKegney and Marina Barnard, *AIDS, Drugs, and Sexual Risks: Lives in the Balance* (Buckingham: Open University Press, 1992); Janet Holland, Caroline Ramazanoglu, Sue Scott, Sue Sharpe, and Rachel Thomson, 'Between Embarrassment and Trust: Young Women and the Diversity of Condom Use', in Aggleton, Hart, and Davies, eds, *AIDS: Responses, Interventions and Care*, pp127-48; Peter Wedderburn, Andrew Hunt, Ford Hickson, and Peter Davies, *The Sexual Lifestyle of Gay and Bisexual Men in England and Wales* (London: HMSO, 1992); and Danny Wight, 'Impediments to Safer Heterosexual Sex: A Review of Research with Young People', *AIDS Care*, 41:1 (1992), pp11-21.

[47] See Nick Baker, 'Facts versus Morals: Guidelines on Sex Education', *Times Educational Supplement*, 3747 (1988), pp18-19.

[48] See Holland, Ramazanoglu, Scott, and Sharpe, *Pressure, Resistance and Empowerment: Young Women and the Negotiation of Safe Sex* (London: Tufnell Press, 1991).

[49] See Thomson and Scott, *Learning about Sex*, and MORI, *Young Adults' Health and Lifestyle*.

[50] National AIDS Trust, *Living for Tomorrow: The National AIDS Trust Youth Initiative* (London: NAT, 1991).

[51] Article 13 of the United Nations Conventions of the Rights of the Child establishes children's right of access to education about health. See P. Newell, *The UN Convention and Children's Rights in the UK* (London: National Children's Bureau, 1991). The Children's Act (1989) also requires that young people are consulted and involved in decisions that affect their lives. There is growing concern that much of the recent education legislation is in contradiction to the ethos of the Children's Act.

[52] This is an example of what sex education can be. Young woman, aged 18, interviewed by the Women, Risk, and AIDS Project: Thomson and Scott, *Learning about Sex*, p15.

Postscript

In July an amendment passed through the House of Commons, without debate becoming Section 241 of the 1933 Education Act. The amendment was lobbied for by the Conservative Family Campaign, CARE and the Plymouth Brethren, and found sympathy with the acting Secretary of State for Education, Baroness Blatch. It secures an unfettered right for parents to withdraw pupils from sex education classes outside the National Curriculum, while also removing the study of HIV/AIDS, STDS and all 'non-biological' aspects of sex education from the National Curriculum for science. It further requires governors of secondary schools to provide sex education to all registered pupils leaving governors of primary and special schools to choose whether to provide sex education or not. The amendment threatens pupils' educational entitlement under the ERA (1988) and rights to information: contravening the European Convention on Human Rights and the UN Convention on the rights of the child. It also contradicts the ethos of the Children Act (1988) and the recognition that young people should be involved in decisions that affect their lives and futures. The passing of this amendment alongside recent remarks by John Patten (*Spectator*, October 1993) propounding the teaching of laws of nature in both religious education and science suggests that the influence of religious moralism on educational policy continues to rise relatively unchallenged.

The Politics of Law Reform: Lesbian and Gay Rights Struggles into the 1990s

DIDI HERMAN

In Britain today, there are increasing calls for lesbian and gay anti-discriminatory legislation. Many people also seek constitutional reform, including the enactment of a bill of rights, as the means by which to secure legal equality. Social movements, such as those fighting for lesbian and gay rights, are understandably demoralised by the possibility of parliamentary reform after thirteen years of Tory rule. Instead, rights activists look towards creating a mechanism where, once in place, future governments can be forced to address discrimination issues. The achievement of 'rights', whether statutory or constitutional, are for many lesbians and gay men a worthy and unproblematic goal.

Canada has had such a 'modern', constitutionally-entrenched rights document for over ten years now: the Canadian Charter of Rights and Freedoms (Charter). The Charter allows individuals (and companies) to challenge, in the courts, legislation passed by federal and provincial governments.[1] Individuals take their case to court, and judges rule on whether particular legal provisions are contrary to Charter rights (such as freedom of expression, association, and a specific right to equality in section 15 of the Charter). Should impugned legislation be found to contravene the Charter, governments may argue that the provision is nonetheless necessary (section 1); however, if the courts do not accept this argument, the offending law or clause can be altered or struck down.

In the late 1980s, lesbians and gay men began increasingly to make 'Charter challenges'; in other words, to litigate their exclusion from social benefits schemes, or to challenge discriminatory criminal law (for example, the age of consent), and so on. Claims were launched across a range of areas; initially, most failed.[2] Increasingly, however, courts and tribunals are finding in favour of lesbian and gay claimants. For instance, in the autumn of 1992 an administrative tribunal found in favour of a gay man who challenged the provincial law regulating his pension plan.[3] In its judgement, the adjudicators ordered the Ontario government to treat lesbian and gay partners as 'spouses' and to provide them with equal benefits to those received by heterosexual couples. In another recent case, an appeal court found that a federal anti-discrimination law was unconstitutional because it did not include a 'sexual orientation' ground; the court automatically amended the law to protect lesbians and gay men, and the federal government appears to have accepted this ruling.[4]

At the same time as launching Charter-challenges such as these, lesbian and gay rights movements have been very successful in lobbying for 'sexual orientation' amendments to provincial human rights codes (non-constitutional human rights legislation). By 1992, over half the Canadian provinces had made such amendments under which the majority of Canadian lesbians and gay men were given formal protection against discriminatory acts by landlords, employers, and service providers, in both the public and private sector. Canadian law and policy was increasingly acknowledging lesbians and gay men as a 'disadvantaged group', with many of the rights which follow from this sort of recognition.

The rights movement could well celebrate its successes.

Lesbians and gay men in other countries might look enviously at Canada's progress towards legal equality in the area of sexuality. For those still seeking the deregulation of gay sexuality, such as the repeal of anti-gay criminal laws, more 'positive' legislation, such as the inclusion of lesbian and gay identity within existing human rights legislation, might seem both a long way off, and an unequivocally desirable goal.

In this chapter, however, I suggest a more complicated analysis. Using both Canadian and American experience, I suggest that struggles for 'lesbian and gay rights' are both promising and problematic.[5] The acquisition of things called 'rights', or the use of rights language to articulate our demands, are not neutral solutions to the discrimination and oppression we face as lesbians and gay men, but constitute, rather, their own 'regulatory regime' (like criminal law, family law, or any other legal framework). In other words, the granting of human rights, whether they be for lesbians, gay men, or any one else, may cause or facilitate as many problems as they are intended to resolve, even when we 'win' our demands. That is not to say that I am against lesbian and gay rights campaigns – I am not – but more that I believe it is important to understand the complex, contradictory, and unpredictable implications of such struggles. I begin this essay by explaining the emergence of lesbian and gay legal equality demands, and continue by exploring several issues raised by lesbian and gay rights struggles.

Lesbian, Gay, 'Citizen'

One starting point to considering the relationship between lesbians, gay men, and rights reform is to explore why such reforms, and the organisations which fought for them, appeared on the political scene. One interpretation can be drawn from the work of Chantal Mouffe. Mouffe, in her analysis of social movements and democracy, argues that modern social antagonisms often result when 'new' subjects and identities emerge in a context where other discourses and practices continue to 'negate' them.[6] Her example is that of

Enlightenment discourse giving women the opportunity to reconstitute themselves as 'equal', this constitution being a 'contradictory interpellation' to that produced simultaneously by other, hierarchical or exclusionary discourses. According to Mouffe, the entrenchment of Enlightenment discourse, and its central value of 'equality', is at the heart of Western democratic subjectivities. Mouffe's analysis, in my view, provides helpful insights into understanding the emergence and development of a lesbian and gay 'rights consciousness'.

As various writers have argued, 'lesbian' and 'gay' identity, as opposed to same-sex sexual activity, is, historically, a relatively new phenomenon.[7] The claiming of such identities was contingent upon changes to the regime of sexual regulation, particularly the production of 'homo-' and 'hetero-' sexualities towards the end of the last century.[8] Gradually, these 'new subjects' formed the diverse strands of what came to be known as 'lesbian and gay movements'. Adapting Mouffe's analysis, lesbians and gay men can thus be viewed as newly emergent subjects confronted by contradictory discursive interpellations. For example, as asexual citizens they possessed formal equality; as homosexuals they were both denied official recognition/protection and subject to constant and changing medical 'diagnoses'; as 'lesbians and gay men' they created positive, affirming community structures and cultures. The development of lesbian and gay movements, therefore, followed from both the production of this distinctive identity, and its perceived exclusion (or inclusion as criminal or pathological) within dominant discourse.

Within capitalist democracies, legal 'equality' discourse is one of the foremost ways in which human subjecthood is recognised, or called into being. In more recent years, 'anti-discrimination' provision, or human rights laws, have become a significant means of ostensibly ensuring the principle of 'equal treatment'. If, as Mouffe argues, the value of equality is so intrinsically a part of Western consciousness (and this view is echoed by many others), it is not surprising that many lesbians and gay men, socialised in Canada and similar countries, demanded inclusion within and recognition by human (including constitutional) rights regimes, one of the primary forms of liberal equality.

From the perspective of many Canadian lesbians and gay men, human rights struggles were, therefore, not about rights per se, but about what rights were thought to signify – public/official recognition, social citizenship, and 'identification'. In this sense, the demand for 'lesbian and gay rights' is a struggle for membership in the 'human community', and perhaps also an expression of what bell hooks has called the 'postmodern' condition of 'yearning', the 'urge to voice of the marginalised'.[9]

The claim for rights, then, has always been a significant aspect to lesbian and gay social struggle.[10] Over time, a distinctive rights-oriented lesbian and gay movement emerged and became an important, indeed a predominant, movement for lesbian and gay liberation. Nevertheless, Mouffe and others appear to underplay the ways in which the extension of existing liberal categories to 'new' identities not only 'recognises', but regulates, contains, and constitutes them. The claiming of rights has posed significant dilemmas for lesbian and gay movements.

The 'Minority Rights Paradigm'

The model encouraged and produced by human rights-type struggles is one of a homogenous minority population. As applied to sexuality, the model represents society as having always contained a majority of heterosexuals, and minority of homosexuals. Often, this is made explicit through reliance on the concept of immutability – that sexual orientation is fixed genetically or in early childhood, and only waits to be discovered. It is suggested that there have always been and will always be those who sexually prefer their own sex. This preference, occurring without any conscious agency on the part of the individual, should not, liberal argument goes, be a basis for discrimination.[11] When liberals acknowledge that biological make-up may not be a determining factor, they tend to analogise sexual orientation with religious orientation – as a deep-seated, fundamental aspect of identity that cannot be changed except at great cost.

Liberal legalism, upon which human rights laws are premised, thus assumes a series of unassailable truths: society is pluralistic, there are majorities and minorities, true democracy necessitates the protection of minorities from the tyranny of majorities, and true minorities share characteristics that differentiate them from the majority 'norm'. The majority must exhibit qualities of tolerance, understanding, and compassion, ultimately evidenced by their willingness to extend legal protection to identified minorities. Even in periods when anti-discrimination laws are rolled back, as in the United States in the 1980s, and 'real' incidents of abuse escalate, this ideology continues to dominate. Even neoconservative politicians tend to pay it lip-service.[12]

However, the minority model is problematic when applied to any group of people; in relation to lesbians and gay men it seems particularly inappropriate. If, as many feminists and others contend, sexuality is socially constructed, and there is no necessary or 'natural' link between reproductive capacities, gender categories, and sexual desire, then representing lesbians and gay men as an immutable minority may restrict rather than broaden our understandings of sexuality. Lesbians and gay men are granted legitimacy, not on the basis that there might be something problematic with gender roles and sexual hierarchies, but on the basis that they constitute a fixed group of 'others' who need and deserve protection.[13] Human rights frameworks thus pull in 'new' identities thereby regulating them, and containing their challenge to dominant social relations.

Lesbian and gay legal rights struggles thus seem to contribute to the ideological hegemony of legal liberalism by confirming its categories of 'norm' and 'other' – majority and minority. There are also other, related, effects. The very goals of the rights campaigns mean that anti-discriminatory laws themselves remain unquestioned. They remain unquestioned not only as a legitimate way of addressing systemic

251

oppression, but also the mechanisms and procedures of this form of legislation cannot seriously be challenged within such a strategy.

Yet the experiences of classes of people previously included in such legislation – for example, under the grounds of 'sex' or 'race' – have not been positive. Particularly in the area of race discrimination, human rights laws have proved to be a somewhat ineffective weapon at best. In North America, the individual complaints (and perpetrator) model upon which such laws are often based, coupled with the regulatory commission's mandate to conciliate and effect a compromise, has not been perceived by human rights 'consumers' to have facilitated the eradication of racism. The experience of many who file complaints is one of massive delay, bureaucratic bungling, and poor results. These and other criticisms have been made of anti-discriminatory structures in Canada, the United States, and Britain.[14] And, as Kristen Bumiller has documented, many people who could file complaints, for a variety of reasons, do not.[15]

Bumiller argues, drawing on Foucault's analysis of power,[16] that anti-discriminatory provision is a 'disciplinary regime'. It functions as such by constructing a 'classification of identities' – categories of persons who are, in some way, 'lesser than' an unstated norm.[17] While Bumiller's analysis tends, as do many Foucauldian approaches, to reify an all-powerful discourse, she nevertheless provides an important insight into understanding human rights law. These legal regimes create fragmented identities, and people are forced to compartmentalise their complex subjectivities in order to 'make a claim'. Often, as Bumiller notes, the result is not to make a claim at all. Instead, individuals construct their 'problem' as trivial, view human rights law as ineffective anyway, and often get more satisfaction from 'sacrificing' themselves (by not complaining) than by 'losing control' through entanglement in bureaucratic procedures.[18] Ultimately, all of this serves to channel and diffuse social protest by reinforcing the 'victimisation' of the legislation's alleged beneficiaries.[19]

Another consequence of the minority rights strategy is that

it tends to entrench the liberal 'public/private' divide by locating the source of lesbian and gay oppression in the public spheres of employment, housing, and service provision addressed by most human rights laws. Judy Fudge has contended, in the context of women's rights, that too much attention paid to achieving inclusion within laws which reinforce the public/private divide may in fact further obscure 'private sphere' relations, a key site of women's oppression.[20] Feminists who critically analyse notions of political citizenship make a similar point.[21] I would extend this analysis and argue that, in the context of sexuality struggles, a focus on 'public sphere' discrimination may leave unsaid and therefore unaddressed one of the primary sites of the construction and enforcement of heterosexuality – home and family relations.[22]

A further drawback to the liberal minority paradigm is how it serves to obfuscate divisions within social movements, perhaps marginalising important political issues in the process. In many lesbian and gay rights campaigns, the heterosexual public is presented with a homogenous whole, a group of women and men self-defined as lesbian and gay, who suffer the same discrimination. There is no question, it is implied, that both lesbians and gay men deserve the same protections. Ironically, with the exception of rights organisations themselves, gay men and lesbians often prefer to work autonomously, finding differences more significant than similarities. Yet liberal equality discourse obfuscates any divisions within the 'minority', while rendering it nearly impossible for an individual to have their membership in one 'minority' related to their membership in another – each is seen to be discrete, and capable of individual resolution.[23] In the case of the so-called 'lesbian and gay minority', this has the effect of ensuring that peoples' experience as 'women', or 'black', or 'Jewish', and so on is submerged.

However, it may be worth here considering a point made by Judith Butler, writing in a somewhat different context.[24] She has observed, as have many others, that in public discourses, 'the lesbian' has been notably absent. While sex between men was certainly given an entirely negative

253

construction, at least male homosexuality was *present* in public debate, law, and other discourses. This, Butler argues, has offered to gay men a site from which to resist:

> To be prohibited explicitly is to occupy a discursive site from which something like a reverse-discourse can be articulated; to be implicitly proscribed is not even to qualify as an object of prohibition ... It is one thing to be erased by discourse, and yet another to be present in discourse as an abiding falsehood.[25]

Human rights laws, perhaps, offer to lesbians the opportunity to articulate a form of resistance. In debating our inclusion within this 'gender neutral' form of law, in contesting the paradigms of sexuality deployed to gain 'our rights', lesbians are perhaps able to participate in public sexuality debates as never before.[26]

Rights as Facilitative of Mobilisation and Communication

In the previous section, I considered how anti-discriminatory laws construct the 'lesbian and gay subject'. Here, I wish to explore the effects of lesbian and gay law reform activities upon movement mobilisation, and the public expression of lesbian and gay politics. I do this in relation to two specific Canadian examples: the successful struggle in 1986 for a 'sexual orientation' amendment to Ontario's *Human Rights Code* (known popularly as 'Bill 7'); and a gay couple's legal battle to be considered 'family' for the purposes of receiving employment benefits (the *Mossop* case).

In 1986, an amendment was introduced in the Ontario legislature to add a 'sexual orientation' ground to the province's human rights law. Although several politicians had attempted to do this in the past, they had not been successful. The amendment's introduction resulted in campaigns being organised hastily by social movement organisations on both sides of the debate – the Coalition For Gay Rights in Ontario (CGRO), on the one hand, and the Coalition For Family Values (CFV) on the other. Bill 7's travel through the legislature, and the desperate campaigning waged by both sides, largely through the media, became one of Ontario's key political events of the year. The amendment's eventual passage was celebrated by lesbians and gay men across the country. I would argue, however, that there are several different interpretations to make of this struggle.

During the events of Bill 7, despite the lesbian and gay rights movement winning their amendment campaign, it could be argued that the 'pro-family' movement mobilised more effectively than did the lesbian and gay. The Coalition For Family Values, which led the 'anti-' forces, was able to initiate a greater letter-writing and phone campaign, and succeeded in having the amendment discussed across a network of conservative churches. Furthermore, their statements were given ample publicity by politicians during debate, and by the media. The CFV's leader, the Rev. Hudson Hilsden, became a prominent spokesperson for the anti-amendment lobby. Indeed, of all social movement actors his individual role was most visible.

This was not the case for the 'pro' campaign. While lesbian and gay communities mobilised as well, it is difficult to argue that this occurred to the same extent. Perhaps this was due to the pro-campaign being rather top-heavy. On the one hand, the stability provided by the key gay rights organisation enabled it to effectively network with other, similar social movement bureaucracies. On the other hand, the broad, loose 'family values' coalition was better able to mobilise individuals and groups at a grassroots level.

Other effects were shared by the two movements. For example, each gained valuable experience, established provincial networks, and forged links between formal organisations and their constituencies. Both had some success in politicising previously inactive sympathisers. And each established ties with other social movements and organisations, although the key lesbian and gay rights organisation was, perhaps, more successful at linking with a wider range of interests, partly because it was, unlike the pro-family coalition, a single, formal entity with a defined set of goals and practices.

For lesbian and gay rights activists, and their constituency, the Bill 7 'victory' was, on one level, empowering and strengthening. However, losses often have the effect of retrenching social movements, and further provide a stark 'enemy' upon which 'losers' can focus future battles. Bill 7 was only one instance of a 'pro-family' gay rights intervention. In subsequent years there have been many more. 'Wins', on the other hand, can cause complacency, apathy, and the disintegration of coalitions that no longer have a clear purpose. With the important exception of AIDS activism, I would argue that Ontario's lesbian and gay communities have seldom been as collectively organised as with Bill 7.

I have thus far suggested areas in which conservative Christians (as represented by the Coalition for Family Values) may have either surpassed or equalled the achievements of the lesbian and gay movement, irrespective of the amendment's passage (much of this analysis might also apply to pro- and anti-choice struggles in the 1980s). I would argue that in only one area did gay rights activists establish a 'gain' that the CFV did not, and this was due to something quite unpredictable. During the Bill 7 campaign, important support for lesbian and gay equality was achieved both within the Liberal Party, and the left-of-centre New Democratic Party. The Coalition for Family Values, for its part, garnered substantial support from the Conservatives. However, the coming to power of a Liberal minority government shortly before Bill 7 signalled the end of over forty years of uninterrupted Tory reign in Ontario. Without these political shifts, Bill 7 might never have passed, and the inroads made into established parties by lesbian and gay organisations rendered of no consequence. Such events are unpredictable 'chaos' phenomena that send contained theories and strategies awry.

In terms of political communication, I would suggest that feminist and radical gay analyses of sexuality were not publicly expressed. Partly as a result of strategic decisions taken by gay rights activists, and partly due to the powerful exclusionary qualities of hegemonic liberal discourse, the only perspective publicly endorsing a 'sexual orientation' amendment was one embodied by a liberal politics – in other words, the minority rights paradigm. The struggle itself, then, did not become an occasion to convey oppositional analyses of sexuality.[27]

Was the *anti*-amendment campaign more 'successful' here, despite losing the short-term battle? To an extent, one might argue this was the case. As well as the factors already considered, 'pro-family' activists were quoted extensively in the press decrying the 'abnormality' of homosexuality. Yet at the same time, this was not unproblematic for them. While their words made it into print, this often occurred within a critical context which undermined their authority. The mainstream press, largely supportive of the amendment, often succeeded in representing anti-amendment campaigners as raving, religious fanatics. Thus, the illiberal pro-family contributions may have had little practical effect upon shifting the terms of debate.

Without engaging in too much repetition, I could construct a similar analysis for the *Mossop* case. Brian Mossop worked for the Canadian government as a translator. As a federal civil servant, his employment conditions were regulated by both a union agreement and the *Canadian Human Rights Act*, the federal human rights code. In the spring of 1985, the father of Mossop's partner died. Mossop attended the funeral and then applied to have his absence from work considered as 'Bereavement Leave' under the union agreement, specifically stating that his lover was male. The application was denied by the employer on the grounds that his relationship did not fall within the 'immediate family' category covered by the bereavement leave provision. Mossop, with the support of his union (the Canadian Union of Professional and Technical Employees), filed a grievance, which was rejected. He then laid a complaint under the *Canadian Human Rights Act*.

The crux of Mossop's argument was that the collective agreement contravened section 3(1) of the *Act* prohibiting discrimination based on 'family status'. The agreement provided bereavement leave for 'immediate family', including common-law couples of the 'opposite sex', and mothers and fathers-in-law. Mossop argued that this definition, and the resulting exclusion of same-sex families, constituted 'family status' discrimination. As there was no 'sexual orientation' ground in the federal human rights law, Mossop's case depended upon the acceptance of his relationship with his partner being defined as 'family'.

Mossop is of interest, not solely for the politics of its judgments thus far,[28] but also because, as with the Bill 7 struggle, the litigation itself has become a focus for social movement intervention. Aside from the two legal 'parties' – Mossop and the federal government – coalitions of lesbian, gay, feminist, disabled, and civil libertarian groups on the one hand (EGALE et al.), and conservative, evangelical Christian organisations on the other (REAL Women et al.), have seized on the case as a forum in which to do battle over sexuality.

In this instance, it was, arguably, the gay litigants and their supporters who fared significantly better than their Christian activist counterparts. Although both shared, in contrast to Bill 7, a *lack* of mass mobilisation and each, again, gained valuable experience, the coalition of progressive organisations intervening in the case (EGALE) arguably achieved a higher level of networking. Paradoxically, this was a direct result of federal funding. Critical scholars often argue that state funding of social movements often leads to co-optation and depoliticisation – this is no doubt true in many cases. However, the lawyer for the EGALE coalition suggests that the government funding of human rights challenges, led, instead, to greater communication and networking between social movements acting in legal coalitions – such as in *Mossop*.[29]

In terms of communicating a sexual politics, the gay litigants feel that they have been far more successful at this than their conservative Christian counterparts. In contrast to the Bill 7 episode, where the Coalition for Family Values had the only visible spokespeople on the public stage, legal cases such as *Mossop* have provided lesbians and gay men with opportunities to speak on behalf of their communities. However, this is not unproblematic. It may be that the lesbians and gay men the media select as newsworthy do not represent the diverse interests, identities, values, and politics of lesbian and gay communities. The fact that a lesbian's picture is on the front page of the *Toronto Star* says little about who she is politically, or whether lesbian communities appreciate her words.

I am suggesting, then, that while Bill 7 politicised and mobilised lesbian and gay communities, there was no concurrent effect of communicating a progressive sexual politics to them or any other group of people. And, while the *Mossop* litigation has provided a platform for individuals to speak out about sexuality, and organisational leaders to network, it has not acted as a catalyst for wider mobilisation.

Finally, it is important to remember that political mobilisation can occur at an individual level, and that individuals are what make up 'movements'. Take, for example, the experience of Karen Thompson, whose seven-year long battle for legal guardianship over Sharon Kowalski, her brian-injured partner, was a key symbol in the fight for lesbian and gay equality in the United States.[30] In writing about her experiences as a closeted lesbian in 'small-town America', Thompson explains how her life was irrevocably changed, and radicalised, through her attempts to have the courts recognise her, rather than Kowalski's parents, as the most suitable legal guardian. Towards the end of her largely autobiographical book, Thompson writes a symbolic letter to the hospitalised lover that she has not been allowed to visit for many years. In it, she expresses some of the effects her legal battles had upon her own political development.

> I want you to understand how fighting for our right to live our own lives and make our decisions has transformed me from the conservative, private person you knew into an activist and feminist. Activist and feminist: probably you know more than anybody how these words used to frighten me ...
>
> ... I still want to win this case for us, but in fighting for us, I have also begun to feel the pain of others who have also experienced oppression. And I have learned about the connections between different forms of prejudice and the people who profit from others misery. I have learned how people with power can

manipulate and twist 'facts' to blame those who are victims. I have experienced being called aggressive, crazy and vindictive when our rights were being violated and I sought to protect them ...

My commitment to you hasn't wavered, even though years have passed since I've seen you. If success means that you are free, than so far I have failed. But if success means that thousands of people have opened their minds or obtained legal protection as a result of our struggle, you and I have already made a difference in the world. ...[31]

Karen Thompson and Sharon Kowalski won their case in 1992, the court finally recognising their 'family of affinity'.[32]

My analysis suggests that, perhaps, we need to think more about the *process* of change, rather than simply achieving the goals of a particular campaign. Indeed, I would suggest that these processes be viewed as legitimate goals in their own right; that struggles for legal rights provide a forum in which to communicate a sexual politics – preferably a 'radical' one. In some cases, certainly not all, the struggle may be even more important than winning the demand (I have argued that the effects of wins are contradictory and unpredictable anyway). The *process* of engaging in debate, of fighting against opposing social movements, of communicating a radical politics, of conveying alternative visions, rather than simply reiterating the tenets of liberalism may be the key to achieving, through rights reform, more long-lasting social change.

Notes

I would like to thank Davina Cooper and Carl Stychin for their comments on an earlier draft.

[1] Canada has a federal system of government. There is a central government, based in Ottawa, and ten provincial governments.
[2] See, for example, *Andrews* v *Ont. (Min. of Health)* (1988), 49 D.L.R. (4th) 584; *Brown* v *B.C. (Min. of Health)* (1990), 42 B.C.L.R. (2d) 294.
[3] Leshner v *Ontario* [1992] [not yet reported].
[4] Haig v *Canada (Min. of Justice)* [1992] [not yet reported].

[5] The arguments and materials upon which much of this chapter are based are found in my doctoral thesis, *Rights of Passage: Struggles For Lesbian and Gay Legal Equality* (Toronto: University of Toronto Press, 1994). Elsewhere I have written on several aspects of lesbian and gay legal struggle not addressed in this paper, see 'Are We Family: Lesbian Rights and Women's Liberation', *Osgoode Hall Law Journal*, 28 (1990), p789; 'Sociologically Speaking: Law, Sexuality, and Social Change', *Journal of Human Justice*, 2 (1991), p57; 'Beyond the Rights Debate', *Social and Legal Studies*, 2 (1993), p5; and, with Davina Cooper, 'Getting the Family Right: Legislating Heterosexuality in Britain, 1986-1990', *Canadian Journal of Family Law* 10 (1991), p41.

[6] Chantal Mouffe, 'Hegemony and New Political Subjects: Toward a New Concept of Democracy', in Cary Nelson and Lawrence Grossberg, eds, *Marxism and the Interpretation of Culture* (Basingstoke: Macmillan, 1988), p94.

[7] The early work of Mary McIntosh paved the ground for many subsequent theoretical developments, see 'The Homosexual Role' in Kenneth Plummer, ed., *The Making of the Modern Homosexual* (London: Hutchinson, 1981), pp30-44. Michel Foucault is, perhaps, most often associated with articulating this 'social constructionist' perspective, see *The History of Sexuality: An Introduction*, trans. Robert Hurley (Harmondsworth: Penguin, 1976). Others developing this approach include: John D'Emilio, *Sexual Politics, Sexual Communities: The Making of a Homosexual Minority in the United States 1940-1970* (Chicago: University of Chicago Press, 1983); Lillian Faderman, *Odd Girls and Twilight Lovers: A History of Lesbian Life in Twentieth-Century America* (New York: Penguin, 1991); Gary Kinsman, *The Regulation of Desire: Sexuality in Canada* (Montreal: Black Rose Books, 1987); Jeffrey Weeks, *Coming Out: Homosexual Politics in Britain From the Nineteenth Century to the Present* (London: Quartet, 1977) and *Sex, Politics and Society: The Regulation of Sexuality since 1800* (London: Longman, 1981); and the collection edited by Plummer. See also, however, the debates in Edward Stein, ed., *Forms of Desire: Sexual Orientation and the Social Constructionist Controversy* (New York: Garland, 1990).

[8] See also Frank Mort, *Dangerous Sexualities: Medico-Moral Politics in England since 1830* (London: Routledge and Kegan Paul, 1987).

[9] bell hooks, *Yearning: Race, Gender, and Cultural Politics* (London: Turnaround, 1991), pp18-31.

[10] See Eric Marcus, *Making History: The Struggle For Gay and Lesbian Rights, 1945-1990* (New York: HarperCollins, 1992).

[11] For discussion of liberal psychology, see Celia Kitzinger, *The Social Construction of Lesbianism* (London: Sage, 1987).

[12] Witness George Bush's struggle around the 1990 Civil Rights Act in the United States – although clearly against the legislation's passage, he nevertheless felt compelled to defend its ideals.

[13] See also Carole S. Vance's discussion of the relationship between lesbian

and gay movements and notions of immutability, 'Social Constructionist Theory: Problems in the History of Sexuality' in Dennis Altman et al, eds, *Homosexuality, Which Homosexuality?* (London: GMP, 1989). The relevance or appropriateness of the concept 'minority' to lesbian and gay identity is an historical debate within the movement – see, for example, Jeffrey Weeks, *Sexuality and its Discontents: Meanings, Myths, and Modern Sexualities* (London: Routledge and Kegan Paul, 1985), pp95-201 and Kinsman, *The Regulation of Desire*, pp90-93 for different views. Here, I am focusing upon how human rights law encourages its adoption, despite this debate.

14 See, for example, Kimberley Crenshaw, 'Race, Reform and Retrenchment: Transformation and Legitimation in Antidiscrimination Law', *Harvard Law Review*, 101 (1988), p1331; Peter Fitzpatrick, 'Racism and the Innocence of Law', *Journal of Law and Society*, 14 (1987), p119; James Frideres and William Reeves, 'Research Note: The Ability to Implement Human Rights Legislation in Canada', *Canadian Review of Sociology and Anthropology, 26 (1989)*, p311; Alan Freeman, 'Antidiscrimination Law' in David Kairys, ed. *The Politics of Law: A Progressive Critique* (New York: Pantheon, 1982), p96.

15 Kristen Bumiller, *The Civil Rights Society: The Social Construction of Victims* (Baltimore: Johns Hopkins University Press, 1988).

16 See Michael Foucault in *Power/Knowledge: Selected Interviews and Other Writings, 1972-1977*, ed. Colin Gordon (New York: Pantheon, 1980).

17 Bumiller, above, pp61-69.

18 *Ibid.*, pp82-107.

19 *Ibid.*, pp49-51.

20 Judy Fudge, 'The Effect of Entrenching a Bill of Rights Upon Political Discourse: Feminist Demands and Sexual Violence in Canada', *International Journal of the Sociology of Law*, 17 (1989), p445.

21 See, for example, Carole Pateman, *The Disorder of Women* (Cambridge: Polity, 1989).

22 However, it is also possible to argue that any public discussion of homosexuality brings into question 'private choices'.

23 See Crenshaw, 'Race, Reform, and Retrenchment.'

24 Judith Butler, 'Imitation and Gender Insubordination' in Diana Fuss, ed., *Inside/Out: Lesbian Theories, Gay Theories* (New York: Routledge, 1991).

25 *Ibid.*, p20.

26 How and with what effects are other questions.

27 See also Peter Cichinno et al., 'Sex, Lies and Civil Rights: A Critical History of the Massachusetts Gay Civil Rights Bill' *Harvard Civil Rights – Civil Liberties Law Review* 26 (1991), p549.

28 I have discussed this elsewhere, see 'Sociologically Speaking' (1991).

29 Interview with Gwen Brodsky, December 1991.

30 Karen Thompson and Julie Andrzejewski, *Why Can't Sharon Kowalski Come Home?* (San Francisco: Spinsters/Aunt Lute, 1986).

[31] *Ibid.*, pp219-220.
[32] See 'Thompson and Kowalski Win', *Off Our Backs*, February 1992, p2.

Index

Index

HIV, 6-7, 27, 91, 103-04, 130, 155, 158, 166, 210, 226, 229-32, 235, 237, 239

Irigaray, Luce, 135

Jacques, Martin, 91
Jarman, Derek, 71, 81, 82
Jeffreys, Sheila, 4-5
Junor, Ann, 107

Kaplan, Cora, 48
Kitzinger, Celia, 36
Kofman, Sarah, 54
Kramer, Larry, 6
Kukathas, Chandran, 174
Kymlicka, Will, 173

Lacan, Jacques, 54, 57, 59-66
London Lesbian and Gay Centre, 123, 141
London Lesbian and Gay Switchboard, 141
London Lesbian and Gay Teenage Group, 222

McIntosh, Mary, 6, 12
McKerrow, Graham, 150
Marshall, John, 43-44
Mendus, Susan, 174
Mercer, Kobena, 31
Meredith, Philip, 231
Mitchell, Juliet, 48
Mouffe, Chantal, 248-50
Murray, Stephen O., 147

Nardi, Peter M., 147

Okin, Susan Moller, 181-82
Operation Spanner (*R v Brown and others*), 10, 166, 193, 199
O'Sullivan, Sue, 120
Outlook, 113
OutRage, 7, 10, 100, 116, 147, 161, 176

Paglia, Camille, 114
Paragraph 16, 10-11
Paul, Jay P., 127
Pettit, Philip, 174
Phelan, Shane, 186
The Pink Paper, 154
Plummer, Ken, 147
Power, Lisa, 119

Queen, Carol A., 132
Queer Nation, 1, 9-10, 100, 147

Radicalesbians, 4
Raz, Joseph, 173, 184-87
Reagon, Bernice Johnson, 162
Rechy, John, 4
Rich, Adrienne, 34-35
Rich, B. Ruby, 71, 80
Rubin, Gayle, 191-98
Ruehl, Sonja, 45

Schneider, Beth E., 145
Schuyf, Judith, 145
Section 28 (Clause 28 of the Local Government Act [1988]), 8, 25, 193, 224, 225
Sedgwick, Eve Kosofsky, 2, 105, 139
Sexual Offences Act (1967), 172-73, 175, 194
Sharp, Rachel, 107
Smith, Anna Marie, 10-11
Smith-Rosenberg, Carroll, 38-40
Smyth, Cherry, 9, 102-03
Spivak, Gayatri Chakravorty, 121
Stacey, Jackie, 225
Stonewall Inn, 3
Stonewall (campaigning group), 8, 116

Tapinc, Huseyin, 146
Trumbach, Randolph, 41, 43

Valverde, Mariana, 127
van de Pol, Lotte, 36
Vicinus, Martha, 36, 39

265

Index